Killing the SS

Also by Bill O'Reilly

Confronting the Presidents	*Legends and Lies: The Patriots*
Confronting Evil	*Legends and Lies: The Real West*
	Pinheads and Patriots
Killing Lincoln	*A Bold Fresh Piece of Humanity*
Killing Kennedy	*Culture Warrior*
Killing Jesus	*The O'Reilly Factor*
Killing Patton	*Who's Looking Out for You?*
Killing Reagan	*Keep It Pithy*
Killing the Rising Sun	*Those Who Trespass*
Killing England	*The No Spin Zone*
Killing Crazy Horse	*Hitler's Last Days*
Killing the Mob	*Lincoln's Last Days*
Killing the Killers	*The Day the World Went Nuclear*
Killing the Legends	*The Day the President Was Shot*
Killing the Witches	*Kennedy's Last Days*
	The Last Days of Jesus
The United States of Trump	*Give Please a Chance*
Old School	*Kids Are Americans Too*
Legends and Lies: The Civil War	*The O'Reilly Factor for Kids*

Killing the SS

The Hunt for the Worst War Criminals in History

Bill O'Reilly

and

Martin Dugard

ST. MARTIN'S GRIFFIN
NEW YORK

Published in the United States by St. Martin's Griffin, an imprint of
St. Martin's Publishing Group

EU Representative: Macmillan Publishers Ireland Ltd, 1st Floor,
The Liffey Trust Centre, 117–126 Sheriff Street Upper, Dublin 1, DO1 YC43

KILLING THE SS. Copyright © 2018 by Bill O'Reilly and Martin Dugard.
All rights reserved. Printed in the United States of America. For information, address
St. Martin's Publishing Group, 120 Broadway, New York, NY 10271.

www.stmartins.com

Designed by Meryl Sussman Levavi

The Library of Congress has cataloged the hardcover edition as follows:

Names: O'Reilly, Bill, author. | Dugard, Martin, author.
Title: Killing the SS : the hunt for the worst war criminals in history /
  Bill O'Reilly and Martin Dugard.
Description: First edition. | New York : Henry Holt and Company, 2018. |
  Includes index.
Identifiers: LCCN 2018017242 | ISBN 9781250165541 (hardcover)
Subjects: LCSH: Nazi hunters—History. | Nationalsozialistische Deutsche
  Arbeiter-Partei. Schutzstaffel—Officers. | World War, 1939–1945—Atrocities. |
  War criminals—Germany—History. | Fugitives from justice—Germany—
  History. | Israel. Mosad le-modi'in ove-tafòkidim meyuòhadim—History. |
  Harel, Isser, 1912–2003.
Classification: LCC D8O4.G4 O694 2018 | DDC 940.53/180922—dc23
LC record available at https://lccn.loc.gov/2018017242

ISBN 978-1-250-42096-1 (trade paperback)

The publisher of this book does not authorize the use or reproduction of any
part of this book in any manner for the purpose of training artificial intelligence
technologies or systems. The publisher of this book expressly reserves this
book from the Text and Data Mining exception in accordance with
Article 4(3) of the European Union Digital Single Market Directive 2019/790.

Our books may be purchased in bulk for specialty retail/wholesale,
literacy, corporate/premium, educational, and subscription box use.
Please contact MacmillanSpecialMarkets@macmillan.com.

First St. Martin's Griffin Edition: 2025

10 9 8 7 6 5 4 3 2 1

This book is dedicated to my son, Spencer, who likes history as much as his dad.

—BILL O'REILLY

Killing the SS

Legend

Physical features

～	Major roads
～	Minor roads
～	Railroads
～	Rivers
▨	Terrain
▨	Forest
▨	Wetland
⊙	City/town with urban area
★	Capital city
☠	Nazi concentration camp
←	Movement

Military features

🪖	Infantry
🛡	Armor

Prologue

―――❖―――

May 7, 1945
Reims, France
2:41 a.m.

The devil is being hunted.
 In a classroom of the École Professionelle technical school, Nazi chief of staff Gen. Alfred Jodl applies his signature to a sheet of foolscap, an oversize piece of paper, formally surrendering the German army after nearly six horrific years of fighting. Berlin has fallen. Nazi führer Adolf Hitler is dead from a self-inflicted gunshot to the head, his body then doused in gallons of gasoline and set ablaze by his personal bodyguard. Troops from the Allied powers of the United States, Great Britain, and the Soviet Union now swarm unopposed throughout Germany, quieting the few remaining pockets of resistance.

Despite the late hour, the walls of the schoolroom are lined with journalists and generals on hand to bear witness. Maps showing the progress of fighting in Europe cover the walls, their final update having taken place just one day ago. Newsreel cameras record the somber moment of Germany's defeat, the intense heat of their lights making the room stifling. American supreme commander, Gen.

Dwight Eisenhower, leader of the Allied forces in Europe, is present but does not participate in the formal signing. "Ike" prefers to let his chief of staff, Gen. Bedell Smith, act on his behalf.

"With this signature," Jodl announces in a noticeably emotional voice, "the German people and the German armed forces are for the better or worse delivered into the victor's hands."

⚡⚡

But the devil is not fully submitting, and neither are many of his disciples. They know their actions during the conflict will be considered war crimes. These men murdered and brutally tortured innocent human beings on a scale so large that the word *atrocities* does not even come close to describing the acts.

Thick dossiers on these "war criminals" have been compiled by American and British intelligence agencies. The special admonition IMMEDIATE ARREST has been stamped next to their names on this most wanted list. If caught and convicted, the punishment will be death.

Execution will be swift.

If they are caught.

⚡⚡

Nearly six hundred miles northwest of General Jodl's surrender, the most infamous Nazi murderer of World War II has no intention of delivering himself into the victor's hands. Instead, Reichsführer Heinrich Himmler is running for his life. The mass killer now hides in a small farmhouse with a handful of his most trusted aides, just outside the north German town of Satrup. Himmler and these men are all members of a Nazi paramilitary organization known in German as the Schutzstaffel.

The rest of the world calls these butchers by another name: the SS.

Schutzstaffel means "protection squadron," and for the first four years after its founding in 1925, watching over Nazi leader Adolf Hitler was its main priority. But when Hitler appointed Himmler as Reichsführer—supreme leader—of the SS in 1929, the twenty-eight-year-old former chicken farmer was not content to be a mere bodyguard. The SS soon began gathering intelligence about Hitler's enemies and, in its recruiting, demanding that all applicants demonstrate German "racial purity."

By 1933, when Adolf Hitler's National Socialist Party assumed power in Germany, the military was divided between the Wehrmacht—the traditional army, navy, and air force of the German state—and the SS, a paramilitary organization loyal to Hitler and the Nazi Party.

Hitler gave Heinrich Himmler and the SS sweeping powers to incarcerate all political opponents of the Third Reich, which came to include lawyers, homosexuals, gypsies, the mentally handicapped, Catholic priests, and the entire Jewish population. For the first time in modern history, anti-Semitism became governmental policy. Jews became foreigners in their own country, with a series of new laws rescinding their legal rights and forcing their removal from trade and industry. Virtually any man, woman, or child with the temerity to speak out against Adolf Hitler was in grave danger.

Heinrich Himmler controlled perceived enemies through a system of prisons known as concentration camps. These were administered by notoriously cruel divisions called SS-Totenkopfverbände—"Death's Head Units." All members of the SS, including the military arm that came to be known as the Waffen SS and concentration camp supervisors the SS-TV, wore the insignia of a skull on their caps. The Death's Head squad had the added distinction of wearing a special skull and crossbones badge on their right collar.

The emblem spread fear throughout all enemies of the Third Reich. Persecution of the Jews, in particular, rose to an unprecedented level once the war began in September 1939, with thousands forcibly deported from Germany, Austria, and Czechoslovakia. Even as the German army began waging war on Europe, the SS operated as a completely independent entity, exterminating Hitler's enemies and all those deemed racially impure. Beginning that same year, handicapped individuals throughout Germany were murdered

Heinrich Himmler, center, SS-Reichsführer

with poison gas at Himmler's command. In January 1942, that method of execution was also put into use against the Jewish population as part of Germany's "Final Solution" for complete genocide against that religion. Himmler prided himself on contriving brutal methods to transport, torture, and kill those deemed unworthy. He also destroyed their corpses.

"The conspiracy or common plan to exterminate the Jew was so methodically and thoroughly pursued that despite the German defeat and Nazi prostration, this Nazi aim largely has succeeded," American attorney Robert H. Jackson will declare at the opening of the 1945 Nuremberg Trials, where Nazi war criminals were prosecuted.

Only remnants of the European Jewish population remain in

Germany, in the countries which Germany occupied, and in those which were her satellites or collaborators. Of the 9,600,000 Jews who lived in Nazi-dominated Europe, 60 percent are authoritatively estimated to have perished. Five million seven hundred thousand Jews are missing from the countries in which they formerly lived, and over 4,500,000 cannot be accounted for by the normal death rate nor by immigration; nor are they included among displaced persons. History does not record a crime ever perpetrated against so many victims or one ever carried out with such calculated cruelty.

At the urging of Adolf Hitler, Heinrich Himmler planned and executed these murders.

The *Times* of London refers to him as "the most sinister man in Europe."

Others call Himmler the devil incarnate.

⚡⚡

Germany is in a state of chaos. The end of the war sees its major cities and ports reduced to rubble, due to Allied air and ground bombardments. Simple amenities like running water and electricity are often nonexistent. There is little food or livestock. Piles of trash and human excrement singe the nostrils, an aroma made worse by decomposing corpses still in need of disposal. Throughout Germany, the Americans and British try to care for the millions displaced by war, building refugee camps to house and feed those with no place to go.

An estimated twenty million people will fill the roads of Europe in the next six months, making the long march home before winter arrives. This is a familiar sight throughout the continent—for centuries, the end of war has meant vivid scenes of soldiers and former prisoners of war mingling on the roads as they return to their loved ones. World War II is the same, as German soldiers now mix with Polish and Russian prisoners of war—but it is also different. Because of the Nazi campaign designed to exterminate the entire Jewish race, the roads are also filled with recently released death camp residents, easily identified by their threadbare clothing and skeletal physiques.

For these DPs—displaced persons—as the Jews are known at war's end, the journey is harrowing, for they have no idea what awaits them. First the Germans, and now the Russian army approaching from the east, have stolen their homes and possessions. After months and years in captivity, some DPs hope to exact revenge. For this reason, these death camp survivors do not walk in an oblivious manner. Instead, they study their fellow travelers carefully, keeping a sharp eye on the German men and women whom they walk alongside, searching for the familiar face of a former prison guard in order to inflict immediate and brutal justice.*

⚡⚡

The breakdown of society actually helps members of the once-dreaded SS. They can hide among the refugees. But Heinrich Himmler is not an anonymous bureaucrat, thanks to newsreels and photographs, thus guaranteeing that if caught, he will be prosecuted for his crimes. Himmler is forty-four years old, with a wife, a mistress, and four children—two by each woman. He is a thin five foot nine, his chin is weak, and his teeth are too big for his mouth. Himmler's poor vision requires him to wear rimless glasses, and there is nothing in his physical appearance that suggests strength. But this middle-aged man is responsible for murdering millions.

Himmler shaves the graying whiskers of his mustache as he prepares for his escape. The wire-rimmed glasses, a signature accoutrement, are removed and replaced by a black eye patch. Himmler's lavishly decorated uniforms are discarded, replaced by the drab clothing of a military policeman named Sgt. Heinrich Hitzinger, who was murdered by the SS months ago for the crime of "defeatism."

Just in case things go very wrong, Himmler hides a vial of

---

* The Allies applied the term *displaced person* to any civilian who remained outside the boundary of their home nation at the end of the war. A *refugee* was a separate distinction, reserved for individuals who remained homeless within their own nation.

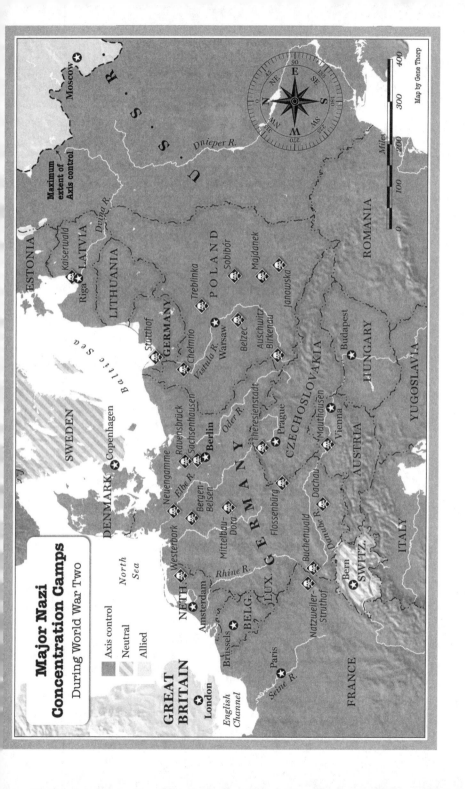

cyanide in his clothing. Biting down on the glass will send a lethal dose of poison into his system, killing him within fifteen minutes.

Himmler's SS fellow travelers also carry poison. They alter their appearances as well, removing insignia from their clothing and slipping new identity papers into their pockets as they prepare for life on the run. Among them are Josef ("Sepp") Kiermaier, Himmler's personal bodyguard; Dr. Rudolf Brandt, the Reichsführer's top assistant; SS surgeon Dr. Karl Gebhardt; SS-Colonel Werner Grothmann; and Maj. Heinz Macher. Otto Ohlendorf, an SS general major, chooses to travel separately.

Ohlendorf, in particular, is a monster, leader of mobile death squads known as the *Einsatzgruppen* that traveled alongside military units to exterminate civilian populations. When Germany invaded the Soviet Union in June 1941, the conquered territory was plundered of livestock, grain, and machinery in order to supply the German Reich. Soviet prisoners of war were not fed, leading some two million soldiers to starve to death. Simultaneously, troops under Ohlendorf's supervision rounded up the Jewish population en masse. Under his authority, more than ninety thousand people were killed either by gunshot or in mobile gas chambers.

The villains intend to travel due south to the Harz Mountains in central Germany, there to hide out, then perhaps flee farther south to the Alps or leave the country altogether. And this is not by accident. For more than a year, Heinrich Himmler has known the war in Europe could not be won. So he feverishly helped set up a "Fourth Reich" apparatus to ensure the future of a powerful postwar Germany. Adolf Hitler himself said that the Nazi empire was built to last a thousand years—Himmler and his SS are determined to see that pledge become a reality.

In years to come, some investigators will point to a clandestine meeting at the Maison Rouge Hotel in Strasbourg, France, on August 10, 1944 as the source of this hope. The top secret rendezvous was attended by leading German industrialists and bankers, among others.

But unbeknownst to the Nazi officials and German industrialists at the Strasbourg meeting, a French undercover military intelligence agent was among those in attendance. His report on what was being planned soon made its way to Cordell Hull, the U.S. secretary of state.

"German industry must realize that the war cannot be won," stated the document known as the Red House Report, "and that it must take steps in preparation for a postwar commercial campaign. Each industrialist must make contacts and alliances with foreign firms, but this must be done individually and without attracting any suspicion."

The report went on to state: "They must also prepare themselves to finance the Nazi Party which would be forced to go underground."

But perhaps the most audacious part of the plan was that German companies would begin operating abroad, all the while disguising their connection to Germany and the Nazis. In this way, they would continue conducting military espionage and systematically contributing to the eventual return of Germany's military might.

Those in attendance in Strasbourg were reminded, for example, that a patent for stainless steel was jointly held by Krupp and the American Chemical Foundation. Behemoths like U.S. Steel were beholden to Krupp for the use of this patent and therefore were a likely source of infiltration by Nazi spies.

"These offices are to be established in large cities where they can be most successfully hidden as well as in little villages near sources of hydroelectric power where they can pretend to be studying the development of water resources. The existence of these is to be known only by very few people in each industry and by chiefs of the Nazi Party. Each office will have a liaison agent with the Party," the report continued.

The final payoff would be financial, ensuring participation by the industrial concerns: "As soon as the Party becomes strong enough to re-establish its control over Germany the industrialists will be paid for their effort and cooperation by concessions and orders."

The meeting in Strasbourg has already paid off for the Nazis. More than $500 million has been transferred out of Germany to corporations in neutral nations like Spain, Switzerland, Portugal, and Argentina. In time, hundreds of companies will be anonymously purchased with these funds.*

Vital to the success of this plan is not just the smuggling of wealth out of Germany but the escape of influential Nazi leaders. This is what Heinrich Himmler is counting on.†

Whether Himmler and his minions will end up in the Alps or in some far-flung locale like South Africa or South America is now unknown. But escape is a very real possibility. They just need to move quickly. The journey will start in a fleet of four Mercedes automobiles. In time, that will become too conspicuous, but for now traveling by car is the fastest, most efficient method of transportation. But Himmler's acolytes make an enormous mistake: before departure they don the uniforms of the Secret Field Police, not knowing this group is high on the Allied watch list.

By May 12, five days after the German surrender, Himmler's caravan has traveled more than 120 careful miles. They have slept in fields and in train stations, like so many now roaming Europe. The Nazis' escape seems to be working.

At the North Sea port town of Brunsbüttel, Himmler's group confronts the first obstacle of their journey: the five-mile-wide estuary of the Elbe River. There is no way for the cars to ford the waters, so from this point forward the men must travel on foot. In the dark of night, Himmler pays a local fisherman 500 marks to row his group across the Elbe.

In the morning, Himmler and his men blend in with the mass

---

* This estimate is based on a 1946 U.S. Treasury Department report.

† There are some who believe that the escape of Nazis was assisted by a group known as ODESSA—Organisation der Ehemaligen SS-Angehörigen—comprised of former SS officers. The alleged organization is thought to be so secretive that there is still debate about the date of the group's founding and whether or not Himmler knew of its existence. Many even insist it did not exist at all, despite significant evidence to the contrary.

of soldiers clogging the roads. Himmler now wears civilian clothes under a blue leather motorcyclist's raincoat. He is not as strong as his fellow companions, so Major Macher and Colonel Grothmann slow their pace to match that of Himmler. They wear long green military overcoats and walk a few steps in front of him at all times, constantly looking back to ensure Himmler's safety. The days are a slow tedious march, followed by nights in the fields surrounded by hundreds of other men. There is little food and water, and no privacy at all, but at least Himmler is free.

By May 18, the column reaches the town of Bremervörde, west of Hamburg. There, British army troops of the Fifty-First Highland Division man a checkpoint on the bridge over the river Oste.

Not knowing if it is safe to cross, Heinrich Himmler and his men decide to stop and discuss how to proceed.

Himmler is nervous but does not even take the precaution of scouting the riverbank for a second crossing. If he had, he and his partners could have crossed the Oste without issue at a nearby ford, then continued their journey south.

This is yet another mistake by the Himmler group.

⚡⚡

Now, in order to assess the danger, the Reichsführer decides to send his bodyguard, Josef Kiermaier, to test the checkpoint. Weeks earlier, it was the ever-loyal Kiermaier who suggested that Himmler and his followers escape Germany by airplane. At the time, Berlin was not yet lost. A man such as Himmler had ample aircraft at his disposal. However, the Reichsführer, believing that he might make a separate peace with the Allies, did not take advantage of this escape option. It was his hope to split the Anglo-Soviet alliance. For the first time in the almost two decades in which he has served Adolf Hitler, Himmler conspired against the Führer.

"Our aim," traveling companion Otto Ohlendorf will recall of the plan of collusion with the Allies Himmler secretly concocted with other top Nazi leaders in April 1945, "was not to put up any resistance, but to let the Allies advance as far as the Elbe, having first concluded a tacit agreement that they'd halt there and thus to cover our rear for the continuation of the struggle against the East. These men, who were sober enough in all other respects, still believed that we had a sporting chance against the East."

Of course, the Himmler plan went nowhere.

Upon hearing of the duplicity, Adolf Hitler angrily removed Himmler from control of the SS, evicted him from the Nazi Party, and ordered his arrest—a command that was never carried out because of Hitler's suicide just days later.

But the time for escaping Germany by aircraft had long since passed. Himmler and his cronies remained in the north too long.

As late as May 9, Himmler still believed he could fight alongside the Allies to defeat the Soviet army advancing through Germany from the east. Even though the German army had already surrendered, the Reichsführer penned a letter to British field marshal Bernard Law Montgomery. Otto Ohlendorf edited the letter before Himmler handed it to an aide for delivery to Montgomery. Himmler delayed his escape and desperately awaited Montgomery's response. It never came.

Now, it is Sepp Kiermaier who pays the price for Himmler's delay. The bodyguard is detained by the British pending further investigation.

Heinrich Himmler, however, somehow erroneously believes his bodyguard has been allowed through the checkpoint to safety. Himmler and his traveling companions now approach the checkpoint in their field police uniforms. The blockade is manned by a group of former Russian prisoners of war, who promptly detain Himmler's suspicious-looking group and turn them over to the British.

Heinrich Himmler is in custody—but no one yet realizes it.

⚡⚡

Capt. Tom Selvester has spent his entire adult life in either the military or law enforcement. The young native of Edinburgh, Scotland, served seven years in the Scottish Black Watch infantry battalion, then left to become a plainclothes policeman on a Scottish police force, before returning to the Black Watch shortly before the war began, whereupon he was commissioned as a lieutenant. Selvester landed at Normandy on D-day and now commands the 031 Civilian Interrogation Camp outside the town of Lüneburg, Germany.

"One of the usual lorry loads of suspects came in last Wednesday," Selvester will later recount. "I did not pay much attention to the occupants."

But Heinrich Himmler, still in the guise of Sgt. Heinrich Hitzinger, has spotted Captain Selvester. He asks to meet with the British officer. The request is relayed to Selvester, who refuses the meeting. "I was busy," he will remember.

But Himmler persists, believing that his status as a Reichsführer would impress the Allied authorities, who would treat him with respect. He is also still hoping that Field Marshal Montgomery will contact him. The belief is delusional, but Himmler has been this way his whole life.

Hours pass. Finally, Selvester angrily agrees to meet with the prisoner wearing the eye patch. Himmler, along with Major Macher and Colonel Grothmann, are led into Selvester's office.

"The three men came in," Selvester will later remember, "the ill-looking shoddy Hitzinger—as he called himself—and his two powerfully-built adjutants."

Himmler waits until everyone is in the room. He then removes his eye patch and puts on his wire-framed glasses.

"I am Heinrich Himmler," he states proudly.

But the instant Himmler dons glasses, Selvester already knows who he is.

At 7:00 p.m. on the day of his capture, Himmler is placed under armed guard and then strip-searched. He protests when the vial of cyanide is discovered. "This is my medicine," says Himmler. "It cures stomach cramps."

The Reichsführer is then given a change of clothes. Against his protests, he is forced to don British battle dress, including shoes with no laces. Himmler is offered a light dinner of bread, cheese, and tea but barely touches the meal. He asks to bathe, a request that is granted.

To confirm the prisoner's true identity, Selvester requests that he provide a specimen of his signature. This is then checked against a known copy of Himmler's writing provided by the nearby British headquarters, confirming that Selvester is staring face-to-face at a notorious mass murderer. "There was nothing of the arrogant bullying Nazi about him—just an ordinary man in a leather motoring coat and looking shabby," stated the captain.

At 9:45 p.m., Col. Michael Murphy, Second British Army chief of intelligence, arrives to take personal responsibility for Himmler. An hour later, after being transferred to a second British facility, Himmler is strip-searched again. He takes off his clothes except for his socks and boots. The examining physician is Capt. C. J. Wells of the Royal Army Medical Corps. He methodically examines the area between Himmler's buttocks, along with the nostrils, ears, and areas between toes and fingers. Himmler is docile, even as he endures the humiliation of having his most private regions thoroughly examined by another man. Three military eyewitnesses look on.

Writing his report in the third person, Wells describes the proceeding: "Having searched the prisoner thoroughly he came to the mouth, where he noticed a small blue tit-like object sticking out of the lower sulcus of the left cheek."

Wells places his finger into Himmler's mouth to sweep out the curious article, only to have the Nazi bite down hard on his fingers. As Wells recoils, Himmler crushes the glass vial between his molars. The deadly aroma of prussic acid fills the small examination room. Wells, knowing this is another cyanide vial, grabs Himmler and shoves his head in a bowl of water, placed there for just such an instance to wash out the poison. He grabs Himmler's tongue to prevent him from swallowing any more poison, suffering repeated bites.

Maj. Norman Whitaker, one of the military observers, works with Wells to get Himmler under control. "There were terrible groans and grunts coming from the swine," Whitaker will later recall.

Himmler's body soon goes limp, but the fight to keep him alive continues for another fifteen minutes. Wells even risks his own life by attempting to resuscitate Himmler, but to no avail.

Heinrich Himmler is dead, soon to be consigned to an unmarked grave in a forest outside of Lüneburg.

This devil has received his due.

⚡⚡

Yet there are many Nazi war criminals actively evading justice. Postwar Germany has provided them with chaos and confusion as millions of people are in transition. Adolf Hitler and Heinrich Himmler are no more, but some of the Third Reich's most brutal murderers have slipped the Allied noose. In Berlin, Martin Bormann, Hitler's personal secretary, remained in the Führer's underground bunker for three days after Hitler shot himself. Then Bormann, the SS-Reichsleiter specifically selected by Hitler to assume control of the Nazi Party after the war, vanished.

To the east, a thirty-four-year-old physician named Dr. Josef Mengele is racing west, terrified of being captured by the advancing Soviet army. The SS-Hauptsturmführer, called the Angel of Death, performed horrific medical experiments on prisoners at the notorious Auschwitz death camp in Poland. Mengele oversaw the murder of thousands of innocent human beings and is well aware that he will hang if captured. He now seeks to blend in with the thousands of displaced persons clogging the roads of Germany.

In France, Klaus Barbie, the notorious "Butcher of Lyon" who not only tortured and killed thousands of French citizens but also ordered the deportation of children to the Auschwitz death camp, has successfully slipped away from the French partisans seeking his execution.

And in Austria, SS-Obersturmbannführer Adolf Eichmann, perhaps the most ruthless Nazi of all, and the man responsible for sending millions to their deaths, is hiding in plain sight. He has returned to his family in Linz as if the war had never happened.

These four men—Bormann, Mengele, Barbie, Eichmann—are

among the thousands of SS war criminals slipping quietly into the shadows. The Nazi postwar machine will help these war criminals gain passports, cross borders, and build new lives in sympathetic nations.

To counter that, a small band of men who will soon call themselves "Nazi hunters" are organizing teams of assassins and kidnappers.

The killing of the SS is about to begin.

1

December 26, 1945
Fort Dix, New Jersey
Morning

Benjamin Ferencz is finally out of the army. It is seven months almost to the day that the war ended, and almost as long since Heinrich Himmler killed himself. Discharge papers in hand, the scrappy twenty-five-year-old Harvard-educated attorney steps out into the pale midday light of this military demobilization center, eager to return home to New York City.

Though just five feet tall, Sergeant Ferencz served as an active duty enlisted man throughout the war. Ferencz survived the Normandy D-day landings, the Allied advance across France, and the Battle of the Bulge before the army began making use of his legal background. In 1945, he was reassigned from his artillery unit to the headquarters of Gen. George S. Patton's Third Army. A brand-new unit known as the War Crimes Section was being formed. Benny Ferencz was one of the first recruits.

Ferencz is known for being openly defiant of authority. "I am not *occasionally* insubordinate," Ferencz corrected an officer, who noted that description of his behavior in an official file. "I am *usually* insubordinate. I don't take orders that I know are stupid or illegal."

It was that independent streak, however, that allowed Ferencz to do a job few men would tackle. The New York native traveled by himself in a jeep with the German words "Immer Allein" (Always Alone) painted across the hood. His gruesome mission was to enter concentration camps immediately after their liberation and compile evidence of atrocities.

Benny Ferencz was born a Jew in the Transylvania region of Romania. If not for his parents' decision to immigrate to the United States just before his first birthday, Ferencz would most likely have been rounded up and sent to a death camp. In that respect, Benny Ferencz is lucky, for the United States would soon turn a blind eye to the growing German suppression of the Jewish population. Between 1933 and 1943, just 190,000 Jews were allowed to immigrate into America—a small fraction of the millions seeking asylum.

Ferencz has an active imagination, and as he drives alone through the hostile German countryside, he imagines himself to be a military version of the Lone Ranger.

In fact, the Brooklyn native is something far more daring: the world's first Nazi hunter.

⚡⚡

"They were all basically similar," Ferencz will later write of entering the death camps. "Dead bodies strewn across the camp grounds, piles of skin and bones, cadavers piled up like cordwood before the burning crematoria, helpless skeletons with diarrhea, dysentery, typhus, TB, pneumonia, and other ailments, retching in their louse-ridden bunks or on the ground with only their pathetic eyes pleading for help. Few had enough strength to muster a smile of gratitude. My mind would not accept what my eyes saw. It built a protective barrier to enable me to go on with my work in what seemed an incredible nightmare. I had peered into Hell."

Though Ferencz was not a trained investigator, his role required him to approach his job with the keen eye of a detective. His first stop at each camp was the *Schreibstube*—camp office—to pore over official files. The German penchant for detailed record keeping proved to be their undoing: the date and cause of death for each inmate was dutifully recorded. All too often the notation "auf den flucht erschosssen"—shot while attempting to escape—would appear next to a name.

"In English," Ferencz will write, "they would call it murder."

Thanks to the meticulous files, Ferencz learned when trains arrived in a camp, which country they came from, and how many prisoners were on board. At first, the job was intense but satisfying after three years of combat duty. However, over time, the gruesome work drained the young attorney.

"There is no doubt," Ferencz will later write, "that I was indelibly traumatized by my experiences as a war crimes investigator of Nazi extermination centers."

The camp at Ebensee has left the most haunting impression. Upon liberation, "some inmates caught one of the SS guards as he was trying to flee; judging by the violence of the assault, he may have been the camp commandant. First he was beaten mercilessly. Then the mob tied him to one of the metal trays used to slide bodies into the crematorium. There he was slowly roasted alive, taking him in and out of the oven several times.

"I watched it happen and did nothing," Ferencz will later write. "It was not my duty to stop it, even if I could have. And frankly, I was not inclined to try."

Ferencz's labors will make headlines on November 21, 1945, when the first Nazi war criminals are put on trial in Nuremberg, Germany. But that is none of his concern. All Benny Ferencz wants to do is go home. So the day after Christmas 1945, the war finally over and his discharge complete, Ferencz puts Nazi hunting behind him. He makes plans to marry Gertrude, his longtime sweetheart. What will happen after that, Benny Ferencz does not know. Like ten million other American soldiers just home from the war, he is out of a job and hoping to find work fast.

Of one thing, Ferencz is certain: he will never return to Germany as long as he lives.

He is wrong.

ᛋᛋ

On the same date of Heinrich Himmler's death, Gen. Otto Ohlendorf, former leader of the *Einsatzgruppen* mobile death squads, is detained by the Allies in the town of Lüneburg. Ohlendorf had separated from Himmler shortly before the Reichsführer's capture. It is the general's bad luck that he is captured by the British instead of Americans. The United States Office of Strategic Services (OSS) is not aggressively pursuing war crimes prosecutions. Instead, it is recruiting members of the Nazi Party to spy against the Soviet Union.

The American OSS station chief in Switzerland, the aristocratic Allen Dulles, is in fact actually subverting the work of Benny Ferencz and giving assistance to a number of leading Nazis. Incredibly, Klaus Barbie, the Butcher of Lyon, finds sanctuary with the OSS.

In March, at a time when Germany and America were still very much at war, another high-ranking SS official, Gen. Karl Wolff, made his way to Zurich, Switzerland—a neutral country. There he enjoyed a scotch with Dulles to discuss the early surrender of German forces in Italy. But Wolff also had a secondary goal of impressing upon Dulles that the Nazi SS general might be of assistance to the American spymaster once Germany finally surrendered.*

But Gen. Otto Ohlendorf, SS badge number 880, has no such connection to the OSS—and thus, no protection from the legal fury of Benny Ferencz.

Which will soon come with a vengeance.

---

* Throughout his career, Dulles was notoriously lenient toward individuals whose views and expertise assisted his agenda. General Wolff was one such individual. Though he was arrested after the war and served prison time for his role in the SS, Wolff allegedly went on to work for the CIA. He died in 1984 at the age of eighty-four.

2

October 1, 1946
Nuremberg, Germany
9:00 a.m.

The hangman awaits.

This morning begins the final day of what will go down in history as the Nuremberg Trials. The purpose of the proceedings is not only to prosecute the highest echelon of Nazi war criminals but also to reveal to the world once and for all the true extent of their depravities.

The Nazi defendants sit in the docket of the great courtroom at the Justizpalast—Palace of Justice. Behind them stands a row of white-helmeted American guards, hands clasped behind their backs. This security detail does not carry handguns, fearing that one of the accused might somehow gain possession of a weapon and open fire in the courtroom. Instead, each guard clutches a short billy club, prepared to maintain order if force is needed.

The chief prosecutor for the United States is Supreme Court Justice and former U.S. attorney general Robert H. Jackson. "The trial began on November 20, 1945, and occupied 216 days of trial time," Jackson will summarize in his report to American president Harry

S. Truman. "Thirty-three witnesses were called and examined for the prosecution. Sixty-one witnesses and nineteen defendants testified for the defense; 143 additional witnesses gave testimony by interrogatories for the defense. The proceedings were conducted and recorded in four languages—English, German, French, and Russian—and daily transcripts in the language of his choice was provided for prosecuting staff and all counsel for defendants. The English transcript of the proceedings covers over 17,000 pages. All proceedings were sound-reported in the original language used. In preparation for the trial over 100,000 captured German documents were screened or examined and about 10,000 were selected for intensive examination as having probable evidentiary value." More than twenty-five thousand captured still photographs were brought to Nuremberg, together with Hitler's personal photographer, who took most of them. More than eighteen hundred were selected and prepared for use as exhibits. The tribunal, in its judgment, states: "The case, therefore, against the defendants rests in large measure on documents of their own making."

The trial has been a phenomenon captivating the world. Four hundred spectators are on hand each day. Correspondents from more than three hundred media outlets from twenty-three countries chronicle the testimony.

The most anticipated testimony begins on March 13, 1946, when Hermann Göring is called to testify. He was arrested on May 9, 1945, by the U.S. Seventh Army's 636th Tank Destroyer Battalion. Wrongly believing that he could negotiate his freedom directly with Gen. Dwight Eisenhower, Göring turned himself over to American troops at the former SS headquarters at Fischhorn Castle in the mountains of Bavaria. As the most powerful Nazi figure to stand trial, his appearance is eagerly anticipated. The head of the German air force—the *Luftwaffe*—Göring has lived a full life. He grew up in a castle just thirty miles from where he now sits, the son of a cuckolded government official whose wife openly slept with the castle's owner. Young Hermann was sent to boarding school as a boy, then on to a military academy. He seemed destined for a career in the infantry, but Göring's sense of daring led him to the world of aviation. Initially passed over for a spot in flight school, Göring ended World War I as one of Germany's top fighter pilots, an ace credited with twenty-two aerial kills. By then, he had risen to become commander of Jagdgeschwader 1, nicknamed the "Flying Circus."*

But the arrogant Göring was deeply bitter about Germany's defeat, believing that Jews and a weak German government had betrayed the German people. Eventually, Göring witnessed a speech by a young former soldier who shared these views. Adolf Hitler was just thirty-three when Hermann Göring heard him speak in Munich in 1922. Göring believed so completely in the platform of Hitler's Nazi Party that he joined the next day. Hitler reciprocated by giving Göring command of the Sturmabteilung (SA), the fledgling paramilitary wing of the party. As Hitler's power grew, so did Göring's.

"I liked him," was Hitler's simple explanation for the series of promotions.

Between 1941 and 1945 Göring served as vice-chancellor of Germany, making him the second-most-powerful man in the country. In addition to being Reichsminister of the German air force, Göring was also in charge of forestry and economics. In 1940, shortly after the fall of France, Hitler named Göring Reichsmarschall des Grossdeutschen Reiches, or Reich Marshal of the Greater German Reich, the highest military rank in Nazi Germany. Over the years, the dashing young fighter pilot of World War I bloated into "der dicke Hermann"—Fat Hermann—in the words of many Germans. Göring ate and drank with abandon. He kept lions as pets, confiscated great works of art, and designed his

---

* The Flying Circus was previously commanded by Manfred von Richthofen, Germany's top fighter pilot in World War I. Richthofen, who was widely known as the Red Baron, was credited with eighty aerial victories before being killed in action on April 21, 1918.

Hermann Göring, former World War I flying ace and leader of Germany's Luftwaffe, shown here in 1938, nearly a decade before his death

own elaborate uniforms. He was the bon vivant to Hitler's ascetic, underestimated only by those who did not know of Göring's great intellect and lust for power.

⚡⚡

Göring does not disappoint on the stand. He alternately charms and philosophizes. It is a performance so full of bluster that it earns him the contempt of his fellow defendants.

Former Nazi armaments director Albert Speer will write: "Hermann Göring, the principal in the trial, grandiloquently took all responsibility, only to employ all his cunning and energy to deny that he bore any specific guilt. He had become a debauched parasite; in prison he regained his old self and displayed an alertness, intelligence, and quick-wittedness such as he had not shown since the early days of the Third Reich."

Nine days after taking the stand, Göring finally steps down. No other defendant will testify as long. "The only motive which guided me was my ardent love for my people, its happiness, its freedom, and its life. And for this I call on the Almighty and my German people to witness," he states in his closing remarks, rising to his feet just before delivering the statement.

When the verdicts are finally read on October 1, twelve of the defendants are sentenced to death, three are sentenced to life in prison, four are sentenced to jail terms of ten to twenty years, and three are acquitted.*

"I've never been cruel," Göring will confide to a court psychologist one morning. "I'll admit I've been hard. I do not deny that I haven't been bashful about shooting 1,000 men for reprisal, or hostages, or whatever you please. But cruel? Torturing women and children . . . that is so far removed from my nature."

"Maybe you think it is pathological of me, but I still cannot see how Hitler could have known about all those ugly details. Now that I know what I know, I wish I could just have Himmler here for ten minutes to ask what he was pulling off there."

By 10:30 p.m. on October 15, 1946, fourteen days after the verdict, Hermann Göring has already been served his final meal. The former Nazi leader sits alone in his cell here at the Palace of Justice. The prison gymnasium is just a short thirty-five-yard walk away from Göring. There, U.S. Army master sergeant John C. Woods oversees the gallows where Hermann Göring is scheduled to be hanged in less than three hours. Three black scaffolds now await the former Reichsminister and ten other Nazi leaders fated to die tonight. Each gallows is eight feet high and eight feet square, with thirteen steps leading to the platform. Ropes dangle from crossbeams supported by two posts.

---

* Radio personality Hans Fritzsche, industrialist Gustav Krupp, and banker Hjalmar Schacht were all acquitted. Fritzsche was found not guilty, Krupp was excused for medical reasons, and Schacht had actually been held in a German concentration camp for a period of time. This was seen as proof of his innocence.

Sergeant Woods has no expertise as a hangman—indeed, he fabricated a prewar history as an executioner in order to get the job. He is an unkempt alcoholic with yellow teeth and chronic bad breath. But the heavyset thirty-five-year-old Kansas native and his assistant, military policeman Joseph Malta, will soon adjust thick hemp nooses around the necks of Göring and the other convicted Nazi war criminals. Woods will then release the trapdoor, commencing their final drop to death. In the case of a normal hanging, the victim's neck would snap at the bottom of the drop and death would occur almost instantly. But Woods's inhumane methods leave the neck unbroken and the victim slowly strangling to death, a process that can take more than ten minutes.

Hermann Göring has no intention of taking that plunge. He has already requested that he be shot by firing squad, believing this a more suitable ending for the head of the German air force—the *Luftwaffe*. But that request was denied two days ago.

Once widely lampooned for his obese figure, the former president of the Reichstag has lost sixty pounds since surrendering to the Allies on May 7, 1945. The time in prison has also seen Göring kick his longtime morphine addiction. Ironically, Hermann Göring is the healthiest he's been in decades.

Meanwhile, Col. Burton C. Andrus, the American officer serving as security commandant, is marching across the prison yard to death row. He will once again read the official sentence of death that was conferred on Göring two weeks ago. Once that is done, Göring's hands will be shackled and he will be led to the gallows.

However, as was the case with Heinrich Himmler, Hermann Göring's death will come at the time and place of his own choosing—and that time is now. An American guard stands outside his cell, ordered to watch Göring's every move. The security detail's shift is just two hours long in order to preclude boredom. So Göring knows to be cautious with his movements.

The significant weight loss has shrunk his torso, leaving great folds of loose skin hanging off his frame. In time, some investigators will believe that the Reichsmarschall hid a cyanide capsule under his skin. In fact, Göring refused to take a shower for more than two weeks before his pending execution.

The cyanide was given to Göring by nineteen-year-old American private Herbert Lee Stivers, a prison guard in love with a young German girl. The girl, who gave her name as Mona, convinced Private Stivers to secretly deliver three pens to Göring inside his cell. A subsequent investigation revealed that two men, never identified, gave the pens directly to Stivers, saying they contained medicine for Göring. It was not until 2005, nearly sixty years after Göring's death, that Stivers admitted to passing the poison into the war criminal's cell. He delayed his admission of guilt due to fear of punishment.

⚡⚡

Hermann Göring places the cyanide capsule between his teeth. He bites down hard, shattering the glass vial. Hydrogen cyanide, also known as prussic acid, spills onto his tongue and eases down his throat, filling the cell with its almond-like smell.

Göring dies almost instantly. He is fifty-three years old.

⚡⚡

Among the condemned at the Nuremberg Trials, only Gen. Ernst Kaltenbrunner is a member of the SS. The others are publishers, industrialists, politicians, ambassadors, and soldiers. It is as if the many crimes of Nazi Germany are being laid upon the men in charge rather than soldiers who cold-bloodedly carry them out.

And while SS-General Kaltenbrunner will be executed shortly after midnight on October 16, 1946, thousands of other SS officers and soldiers are getting *away* with murder.* In fact, Adolf Eichmann,

---

* Obergruppenführer Ernst Kaltenbrunner was Austrian by birth and rose to become one of the most feared men in the SS. He was distinguished by his towering six-foot-four-inch height, dueling scar, and ferocious temper. Kaltenbrunner was among those most instrumental in implementing Adolf Hitler's "Final Solution" on the Jewish population.

the "master" of killing Jews, was actually in custody at the end of the war, although the Allies had no idea of his true identity. Eichmann has since escaped from an American POW camp in Bavaria. He has gone to ground completely, his location soon to become one of the world's great mysteries.

And Adolf Eichmann will not be seen again for a very long time.

3

December 24, 1946
Rome, Italy
9:00 p.m.

Benny Ferencz is back in Europe.

With the Nuremberg Trials at an end, Ferencz and his bride, Gertrude, are finally taking a honeymoon. The couple steps in from the cold of the Via Vittorio Veneto, eager to spend a few hours resting in their room at the Excelsior Hotel. Though Jewish, they are intent on hearing Pope Pius XII say Midnight Mass at the Vatican before their return to Ferencz's work in Berlin. The focus of war crimes prosecutions is shifting away from soldiers to civilians, in particular the industrialists who violated international law. Ferencz works for Brigadier Gen. Telford Taylor, who has been ordered by the Pentagon to put together prosecution teams and gather evidence for twelve more trials.

"My job, as organizer and Chief of the Berlin Branch," Ferencz will later write, "was to scour the official German records in the Nazi capital to supplement evidence previously assembled in Paris and Frankfurt."

So it goes, day after day, Ferencz and a team of researchers examine financial documents for signs of grand-scale fiscal impropriety. It is vital work but also quite functional. With the war over and the Nuremberg Trials resulting in convictions and executions, it seems as if the need to place any more military men on trial has passed.

So far Benny and Gertrude's honeymoon has been a memorable tour of Germany, Switzerland, and Italy. Outside Milan, the couple visits the gas station where Italian dictator Benito Mussolini and his mistress were hanged by an angry mob. But in Rome, the vacation takes a negative turn, as there are no rooms available at the Excelsior.

"We landed in a fleabag hotel with a solitary light bulb hanging over the bed," Ferencz will write. "Since we were exhausted by the ordeal, and it was only 10 PM, we decided to rest before heading for the holy midnight celebration. We did not shut off the light and we kept our clothes on since there was no heat. Soon, I was awakened by my wife's anguished cry, 'It's 2:00 AM. Oh, my God!' That was as close as we came to prayer that night. We had missed the midnight mass. There was nothing left to do but go to sleep and blame it on Divine providence."

Benny Ferencz will never hear Pope Pius XII celebrate Mass. But this is not the last time the Nazi hunter will cross paths with His Holiness.

New Year's Eve finds the Ferencz family back in Berlin. 1947 is about to dawn—it will be a year Benny Ferencz will never forget.

⚡⚡

It is the spring of 1947, one year since Benny Ferencz was "persuaded" by the United States government to return to Germany. Ferencz's research into Nazi industrial crimes continues. Yet there are other war criminals who also command his attention: men like Otto Ohlendorf, who has been in custody for two years, are only months away from going free, and Ferencz cannot let that happen.

The breakthrough that abruptly shifts his investigation away from industrialists comes from a set of reports hidden in a remote annex near Berlin's Tempelhof Airport. Top Secret Gestapo files describe the daily operations of the *Einsatzgruppen*—the mobile killing unit in which Gen. Otto Ohlendorf commands group D. The SS, the Gestapo, and the Sicherheitsdienst (SD) have been designated as criminal organizations in the Nuremberg Trials, akin to a highly organized version of the Italian Mafia. The tales outlining their actions are atrocious, and it is clear they were pursuing very defined goals to further Nazi ambitions. But it is all too clear that these groups also committed slaughter for the sake of slaughter.

"On a little adding machine, I added up the numbers murdered," Ferencz will write. "When I passed the figure of one million, I stopped adding. That was quite enough for me. I grabbed the next plane down to Nuremberg."

But Ferencz's boss, Brigadier Gen. Telford Taylor, is of little help. He has been granted an appropriation for precisely twelve additional trials. He has neither the manpower nor the funding for any more.

"In desperation," Ferencz will write, "I told him that if no one else was available I could do the job myself. And so I became chief prosecutor in what was certain to be the biggest murder trial in history. I was twenty-seven years old and it was my first case."

Ferencz will continue: "I was not nervous . . . I didn't murder anyone. They did. And I would prove it."

But *murder* is too kind a word for what these men have done.

Ferencz plans to use another term, newly coined by a Polish American lawyer named Raphael Lemkin to describe the Nazi extermination of the Jews: *genocide*.*

ᛋᛋ

Ferencz doesn't waste any time. Just five months elapse from the discovery of the *Einsatzgruppen* files and the first day in court. The

---

* First used in Lemkin's 1944 book, *Axis Rule in Occupied Europe*, the term comprises the Greek word *genos* (race) plus the word form *-cide* (killer). The literal term refers to the killing of a tribe. The German term for such murders is *Völkermord*.

The indomitable Benjamin Ferencz, chief prosecutor at the Einsatzgruppen *trial at Nuremberg*

"Subsequent Nuremberg Trials," as they will unofficially one day be known, are about to begin.

The date is September 29, 1947. The weather is cloudy, temperatures hovering between cool and frigid. Court adjourns in Nuremberg's Palace of Justice, two years after the war ended. Of the thousands of *Einsatzgruppen* he could have put on trial, Benny Ferencz has narrowed the list to just twenty-four officers—he chooses that number because there are just twenty-four chairs in the docket. Each of these men has participated in Adolf Hitler's "Final Solution to the Jewish Question" by personally coordinating and murdering Jews.

Ferencz could have put many an enlisted man on trial, for they were traditionally the heavy-fisted bruisers who actually did the torturing and killing. But Ferencz's history as a combat sergeant tells him that the officers gave orders. So it is the officers who will pay the price.

A special elevator carries the accused from their prison cells beneath the courtroom. Ferencz will long remember how ordinary they look as they file into their chairs—not at all what he expected from a man such as Otto Rasch, whose *Einsatz* unit massacred exactly

33,771 Jews over a two-day period outside Kiev, Russia. However, it will be no surprise at all when these same defendants, Rasch included, respond with a simple reply to the charges against them: "Not guilty."

Three black-robed American judges stand ready to hear the evidence. The defense counsel—all former members of the Nazi Party—have prepared voluminous evidence on their clients' behalf, ready to refute any and all eyewitness testimony.

But while the defense attorneys for the SS will present a staggering 136 days of argument on behalf of their clients, Ferencz will not call a single witness. He doesn't need to—he has damning documents showing precisely how many died, where the murders took place, and exactly who did the killing.

Throughout the proceedings, one defendant appears to be the most self-righteous of all. Gen. Otto Ohlendorf slouches in his chair, hands clasped across his midsection, face tense, looking for all the world like a man ready to pass sentence—rather than receive one.

⚡⚡

"One of the more interesting and repulsive arguments in defense of genocide was put forth by the lead defendant, SS General Otto Ohlendorf," Benny Ferencz will write. "He was a fairly handsome man, father of five children, and had earned a degree in economics. He was distinguished by the fact that Einsatzgruppe D, the unit under his command, reported they had killed 90,000 Jews. Of course, he denied any culpability."

Ferencz finds himself in a hard place. His cross-examination of Ohlendorf would have been a masterpiece. But Ferencz wanted to win more than he wanted to impress people. In fact, he didn't care if he never tried a case again.*

"I decided to assign the (lead) role to James Heath, whose mature stately manner and Southern drawl might make a better impression on the Germans—and avoid any taint of Jewish vengeance. Jim

---

* He didn't. The "biggest murder trial of the century," as it was known in the Associated Press, would be Ferencz's one and only trial.

knew he was on the verge of being fired for his incapacitating alcoholism. It would be his last chance and we went over the questions and answers carefully."

⚡⚡

In a classic courtroom Q and A, James Heath destroys the SS killer:

> OHLENDORF: The Jews were collected at one place; and from there they were later transported to the place of execution, which was, as a rule, an antitank ditch or a natural excavation. The executions were carried out in a military manner, by firing squads under command.
>
> PROSECUTOR: In what way were they transported to the place of execution?
>
> OHLENDORF: They were transported to the place of execution in trucks, always only as many as could be executed immediately. In this way it was attempted to keep the span of time from the moment in which the victims knew what was about to happen to them until the time of their actual execution as short as possible.
>
> PROSECUTOR: Was that your idea?
>
> OHLENDORF: Yes.
>
> PROSECUTOR: And after they were shot what was done with the bodies?
>
> OHLENDORF: The bodies were buried in the antitank ditch or excavation.
>
> PROSECUTOR: What determination, if any, was made as to whether the persons were actually dead?
>
> OHLENDORF: The unit leaders or the firing-squad commanders had orders to see to this and, if need be, finish them off themselves.
>
> PROSECUTOR: And who would do that?
>
> OHLENDORF: Either the unit leader himself or somebody designated by him.

PROSECUTOR: In what positions were the victims shot?
OHLENDORF: Standing or kneeling.

⚡⚡

PROSECUTOR NIKTCHENKO: In your testimony you said that the Einsatz group had the object of annihilating the Jews and the commissars, is that correct?
OHLENDORF: Yes.
PROSECUTOR: And in what category did you consider the children? For what reasons were the children massacred?
OHLENDORF: The order was that the Jewish population should be totally exterminated.
PROSECUTOR: Including the children?
OHLENDORF: Yes.

⚡⚡

Benny Ferencz listens to the responses, baffled by Ohlendorf's arrogance. "He told his men never to use infants for target practice nor smash their heads against a tree. He ordered his men to allow the mother to hold her infant to her breast and to aim for her heart. That would avoid screaming and would allow the shooter to kill both mother and infant with one bullet. It saved ammunition.

"Ohlendorf said he refused to use the gas vans that were assigned to his companies. He found that when the mobile killing vehicles arrived at their destination, where they were supposed to dump their asphyxiated human cargo into a waiting ditch, some of the captives were still alive and had to be unloaded by hand. His troops had to dig out the vomit and excrement—and that was very hard on his men."

Most unforgettable among Ohlendorf's offensive comments was that each murder was an act of self-defense.

⚡⚡

The sentences are read on April 10, 1948. The courtroom is almost empty as the defendants are brought in one by one to hear their fate.

Otto Ohlendorf appears, flanked by two large African American military policemen gripping white batons in front of them. Ohlendorf does not speak English, so he slips on a pair of translation headphones.

"Defendant Otto Ohlendorf, on the counts of the indictment on which you have been convicted, the Tribunal sentences you to death by hanging."

Ohlendorf says nothing, betrays no emotion. He slips off the headphones and is returned to his cell.

⚡⚡

Four years later, Benny Ferencz is still in Germany. Ferencz served throughout the Second World War as an enlisted man, rising to the rank of sergeant. He was granted the rank of colonel when he returned to Germany to investigate war crimes. Because of his ongoing legal duties, he and his wife, Gertrude, won't return to America for another six years. Of the twenty-two defendants in his one and only trial, fourteen received death sentences. The others were sentenced to prison terms. All of those convicted were members of the SS.

Of the fourteen sentenced to be hanged by the neck until dead, only four will actually feel the noose. The others will be released in 1958, their crimes in the past, allowed to walk the streets as free men.*

One of the four who will hang is Gen. Otto Ohlendorf.

Just after midnight on June 7, 1951, the SS-Gruppenführer walks to the gallows at Landsberg Prison—the same penitentiary where Adolf Hitler dictated *Mein Kampf* a quarter century ago. Pope Pius XII himself has made an appeal on Ohlendorf's behalf, requesting that his sentence be commuted. The petition was denied by Gen.

---

* Those who weren't executed were spared for lack of evidence, demonstration of remorse, or having openly opposed the crimes for which they were charged.

Lucius D. Clay, commander of American forces in occupied Germany.*

The last meal of fried chicken, potatoes, green peas, and carrots has been cooked thirty miles away in Augsburg to prevent anyone from slipping poison into the food. Ohlendorf was always lean in his SS uniform but has gained weight on the high-calorie prison diet. That won't matter in just a few minutes. Wearing the uniform of black pants, black shirt, leather belt, and sandals in which his body will be hanged, Ohlendorf walks to the gallows. His wrists are tied behind his back.

There is only one rope. With multiple men to be hanged, Ohlendorf must wait his turn. He hears the sickening thud of SS-Standartenführer Paul Blobel's body dropping through the trap. Once Blobel is declared dead, the body is pulled back up and the rope untangled from around his neck. Blobel's corpse is placed in a coffin and the lid is immediately nailed shut.

SS-Brigadeführer Erich Naumann is next.

Then, near half past the hour, Otto Ohlendorf walks up the gallows steps. His ankles are bound so that he will not kick wildly once the trapdoor is sprung. A U.S. military chaplain says a prayer. The black hood is fitted over Ohlendorf's head.

Death comes almost instantly. Otto Ohlendorf, a man who encouraged his soldiers to save ammunition by shooting babies nestling against their mother's breast, is spared this inhumanity. The rope is just long enough that he dies quickly.

---

* Some postwar Catholic leaders in Germany believed Ohlendorf was not guilty because he was following orders. In addition, a West German law (*Grundgesetz*) passed in 1949 forbade capital punishment. The Nuremberg death sentences were not originally open to appeal, but this was reversed by General Clay's replacement, American high commissioner John McCloy. On January 30, 1951, bowing to pressure from the Church, media, and German politicians, McCloy reduced the sentences of twenty-one men convicted to die in the *Einsatzgruppen* and the Dachau war crimes trials. They were instead sentenced to lifetime prison terms. However, by the mid-1950s, the West German government no longer viewed these men as war criminals but as political prisoners. All were subsequently released.

"The Jews in America will suffer for this," Ohlendorf warns Ferencz shortly before his death.

ᛋᛋ

But the work started by Benny Ferencz is not finished.

"I had 3,000 *Einsatzgruppen* members who every day went out and shot as many Jews as they could and Gypsies as well. I tried twenty-two, I convicted twenty-two, thirteen were sentenced to death, four of them were actually executed, the rest of them got out after a few years.

"The other 3,000—nothing ever happened to them. Every day they had committed mass murder."*

But it is difficult to hide forever. And soon, with Benny Ferencz wrapping up his work, a new generation of Nazi hunters will emerge.

For the SS villains on the run, these men will become a scourge.

---

* There were originally twenty-four defendants in the *Einsatzgruppen* trial. However, only twenty-two were tried. Defendant Otto Rasch was removed from the trial for medical reasons and died soon after. Defendant Emil Haussmann committed suicide in his cell before the initial arraignment.

4

April 18, 1949
The Alps
5:45 a.m.

A quarter moon is just setting as "Fritz Hollmann" finishes his early morning preparations. A thirty-eight-year-old man, he is dressed in the boots and simple clothing of a Bavarian farmworker, a job that he has held since the war's end. Hollmann, or "Andreas," as he is calling himself during this clandestine journey, arrived at the Austrian side of the Brenner Pass just yesterday—Easter Sunday.

The traveler is glad to leave Germany and Austria behind. Since the end of the war, both nations have been occupied by the conquering armies of the United States, Britain, France, and the Soviet Union. But Italy, with its Mediterranean seaports, returned to self-rule years ago. This makes it the safest and quickest way to flee Europe.

Hollmann spent last night at a small inn owned by Nazi sympathizer and former SS soldier Jakob Strickner. The two men rose hours ago, then took to the narrow mountain paths in darkness to avoid Italian border guards. Thanking Strickner profusely, Hollmann then walks into Italy undetected.

Fritz Hollmann is a scientist at heart, a man who revels in documenting life's small details. In his journal, he makes note of the quarter moon and the yellow primroses just now beginning to bloom as spring comes to the Tyrol region. He travels alone, having left his wife, Irene, behind in Günzburg, the south German city in which he was born and raised. If anyone asks, Hollmann's final destination is unknown, though right now that is not important.

All that matters is not getting caught.

Due to investigators like Benny Ferencz, Germany has become unsafe for anyone with a Nazi past. And as Fritz Hollmann well knows, his real identity is extremely high on the list of wanted Nazi war criminals, infamous enough to have been discussed during testimony at the Nuremberg Trials. Hollmann considered his wartime medical experiments on twins, children, and dwarfs to be groundbreaking. Allied prosecutors do not share this point of view. To them, Hollmann committed abominable crimes against humanity, such as when, in 1943, he ordered hundreds of children under the age of five thrown alive into a fire pit to burn to death. Those who attempted to climb out were hurled back into the flames by armed guards. At the time he gave those orders, Hollmann's rationale was that the gas chambers were an ineffective means of murdering such young children.

So while he has been able to hide out since the war's end, Hollmann has long known that it is just a matter of time until he is arrested and hanged—if he stays in Germany.

The fugitive hops a train and arrives in Sterzing, Italy, shortly thereafter. He leaves the train and walks a half mile to the Goldenes Kreuz Inn.* Despite the early hour, an Italian contact who goes by the code name Nino is waiting for him.

"Rosemary," says Hollmann, stating the password.

Nino hands over an official identity card. The document expired in 1945 but clearly states that it was issued in the nearby town of Brixen. This serves as proof that Hollmann spent the war as a German citizen living in Italy.

---

* The inn is still operating in the town of Sterzing.

But the truth is, Hollmann served as an officer in the SS, working as a doctor in the death camps. His medical experiments were mostly performed on children. He was fond of whistling cheerfully as he worked. Like Heinrich Himmler, he was detained by the Allies immediately after the war. But rather than resorting to attention-getting behavior, Hollmann remained calm. He gave military police his real name, convincing his American captors that he was a simple private in the German army. All members of the SS had their blood type tattooed under their left armpit. But as a medical professional, Hollmann had successfully argued that it was unnecessary. So when the Americans made a physical examination of Hollmann and found no tattoo, they believed his story and let him go.

Nino introduces Hollmann to a German who calls himself "Erwin." In actuality, Erwin is Hans Sedlmeier, manager of a farm machinery company run by Hollmann's father. Erwin brings greetings from home, along with much-needed cash to fund Hollmann's escape.

In the weeks that follow, Fritz Hollmann travels across northern Italy to the port city of Genoa. A chain of people and havens now allow Hollmann to travel undetected. In Genoa, a man named "Kurt" instructs him to visit the Swiss consulate. There, the International Red Cross issues him identity papers. The date is now May 16, 1949. These travel documents, known officially as "10.100s," will serve as Hollman's passport.*

"Fritz Hollmann" can now legally travel anywhere in the world.

※

The name for the path Hollmann follows to freedom is a "ratline." There are several in place, with some going through Genoa and others through Spain. Their specific purpose is to smuggle influential Nazis out of Europe. A variety of unlikely organizations are assisting in this process, among them the Swiss government, the Red Cross, and even

---

* In 2011, researchers will discover that more than 120,000 of these papers were handed out by the Red Cross. Overwhelmed by the millions of applicants, the Red Cross often had no way to discern the difference between genuine refugees and former SS men.

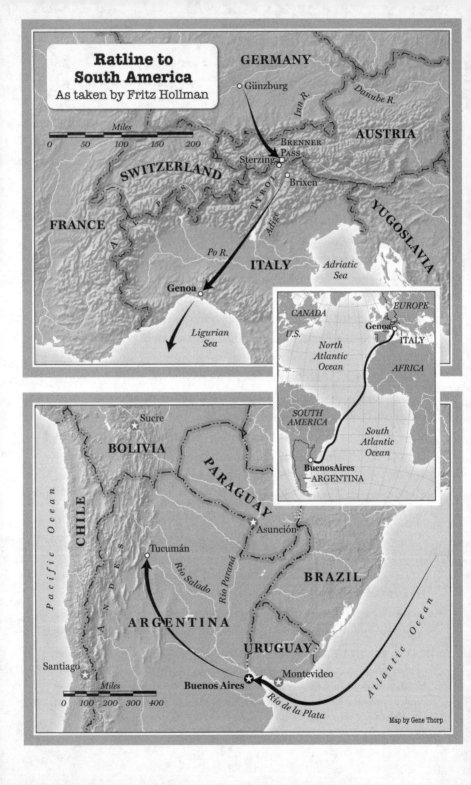

the Vatican. Pope Pius XII first compromised with Adolf Hitler and the Nazi Party in 1933, when he negotiated the Reichskonkordat, guaranteeing the rights of Catholics in Germany to practice their religion. There were many at the time who believed that Cardinal Eugenio Pacelli—later renamed Pius XII upon ascending to the papacy in 1939—legitimized the Nazi Party through this document. The pope said nothing when German troops rounded up Jewish citizens of Rome in October 1943. Hitler reciprocated by allowing the Vatican to function throughout the war without German occupation.

Like many in Europe, Pius XII is deeply threatened by the Soviet-led rise of atheistic communism. He is also concerned by the decline of the Church throughout Europe and aspires to see the faith once again on the rise. This is why he appeals for the clemency of a convicted Catholic like Otto Ohlendorf and assists Nazis who might join the fight against global communism.

"The Vatican of course is the largest single organization involved in the illegal movement of emigrants," reads a secret May 1947 report from the U.S. embassy in Rome to the State Department in Washington. "The Vatican further justifies its participation by its desire to infiltrate, not only European countries, but Latin American countries as well, with people of all political beliefs as long as they are anti-Communist and pro–Catholic Church."

Stopping the Communist threat is also the focus of the new U.S. Central Intelligence Agency as well as the U.S. Army's Counterintelligence Corps (CIC). These organizations now consider the Soviets to be the primary enemy and assist former Nazis in their escape from prosecution in exchange for spying and intelligence information. Klaus Barbie, who will one day be synonymous with Nazi war crimes in France, is among those aided by the Americans.

Barbie's acts of brutality are infamous, but the most inhuman occurred on April 6, 1944. In a carefully orchestrated roundup mission, three German trucks traveled fifty miles from Lyon to the village of Izieu. The trucks stopped at the farmhouse owned by a naturalized French woman named Sabina Zlatin, who was born in Poland. Barbie had received information that Zlatin had been smuggling

Jewish children over the border into nearby Switzerland. There were reports that she was harboring even more young Jews. Indeed La Maison d'Izieu was a secret home for Jewish orphans and refugees.

It was breakfast time as the trucks came to a halt. Hot chocolate was being prepared in the kitchen when soldiers under Barbie's command surrounded the farmhouse. The children had been hiding for a year without incident, but now soldiers grabbed them and hurled them into the back of the vehicles "like sacks of potatoes," in the words of a villager who witnessed the raid. Some children were as young as four. The oldest was seventeen. Their cries and screams echoed up the valley in the still dawn air.

Some of the children were lucky, having seen the approaching trucks—they ran away. But forty-four of them were caught. These innocents, along with seven adults running this small orphanage, were arrested. Under the orders of Klaus Barbie, all of the prisoners were loaded onto a train the next morning and shipped to Auschwitz to be gassed. Sabine Zlatin was not arrested, but her husband was. Miron Zlatin was shipped to the Tallinn death camp in Estonia, where he was executed by firing squad.

Barbie could not have been more pleased. He returned to his office in Lyon after the raid and typed up his mission report. He mistakenly underestimated the number of children taken captive.

"This morning the Jewish children's home 'Children's Colony' in Izieu-Ain was liquidated. Altogether forty-one children aged three to thirteen were arrested. Furthermore, it was possible to arrest the whole Jewish staff consisting of ten persons, including five women. Cash or other valuables could not be seized."

Almost every one of the individuals taken prisoner at La Maison d'Izieu on April 6, 1944, was murdered in a death camp. Just one lived to tell the story. Her name was Léa Feldblum, one of the adult administrators. And she would remember these children forever. "I loved them very much. The tiniest ones cried. The others sang . . . they burned all of them."

⚡⚡

Now, the same Klaus Barbie who took glee in murdering innocent children, is employed—and protected—by the U.S. government. He makes no attempt to conceal his true identity, much to the amazement of his coworkers.

"This guy killed, on one occasion I know of, two hundred Frenchmen himself, hung 'em up by the thumbs in the basement of his headquarters," one CIC agent will later recall of his eight months working with Barbie.

"I reported to headquarters: 'You know you're working with a real war criminal?' The answer comes back: 'Yes, we know all about it. But he's still valuable.'"

⚡⚡

In 1947 alone, an estimated eight thousand members of the SS safely travel to Canada and the United States utilizing false documents.*

But Fritz Hollmann has chosen not to go through Allied channels.

His Italian contact, "Kurt," has booked passage for him on the ship *North King*, due to sail for Argentina on May 25. Hollmann's escape from the Nazi hunters now seems inevitable.

But after more than a month of flawless execution, Hollmann's journey hits a snag. Kurt has bribed an Italian official and instructed him to stamp Hollmann's exit visa. But this bureaucrat has chosen to take the day off. Thinking quickly, Hollmann slides a 20,000-lira note into his documents and steps forward to get his stamp from an official unaware of this skullduggery.†

Hollmann's attempted bribe immediately lands him in prison. Days pass, with the impending departure of *North King* looming closer and closer. If Hollmann misses the ship, the next departure won't be for two long months. Once again, it is Kurt who comes to

---

* This figure was unearthed by researchers in 2011. It is based upon the International Committee of the Red Cross's own internal archives.

† One American dollar was equal to 625 Italian lira in 1949, making the bribe equivalent to $32. Adjusted for inflation, this would be $320 in modern currency.

the rescue, using his connections within the Genoa police department to free Hollmann. Kurt's reputation precedes him, for the once-haughty *polizia municipale* now treat Hollmann with astounding deference as they release him. Italy has been flooded with hundreds of thousands of refugees since the war's end. Distinguishing among prisoners of war, wanted war criminals, and refugees has become nearly impossible for the police. Unable to determine Hollmann's true identity, the *polizia* ask if he is a Jew—a remark the former SS officer chooses to ignore.*

On May 25, as *North King* leaves her berth and sails into the Mediterranean Sea en route to Argentina, Fritz Hollmann stands at the rail. He is surrounded by hundreds of refugees, almost all of them Italian—or at least pretending to be—escaping chaotic postwar Europe for a new life. As the hours pass, the Italian coastline slowly slips from view and with it the threat of Hollmann's prosecution for his Nazi past.

"Waves," he will write of the sea that now provides his escape. "All is waves."

On June 22, 1949, four weeks after setting sail, Hollmann steps onto Argentine soil at Buenos Aires, a free man. There, he presents his passport and other travel documents to immigration officials. The Red Cross papers give Hollmann a new identity: Helmut Gregor. It states that he was born in Italy and makes his living as a mechanic.

In fact, Argentina's newest citizen is actually the notorious Dr. Josef Mengele, the butcher who spent the war practicing his own twisted version of medicine at the Auschwitz death camp.

There, he was given the one true name that will follow him the rest of his life: the Angel of Death.

---

* Italian contacts working with the Nazi underground routinely paid lucrative bribes to the local authorities.

5

August 22, 1951
Buenos Aires, Argentina
5:00 p.m.

More than one million Argentineans roar their approval as President Juan Perón steps onto the narrow balcony looming over the boulevard known as Avenida 9 de Julio. It is a Wednesday, but many in this working-class crowd have taken a day off to secure a place in the throng. Tall and physically powerful, with neatly groomed black hair and the regal posture of a former general, Perón projects the very image of political authority. However, El Presidente is a corrupt man leading an equally immoral government, and for that he is unloved by many in the crowd below.

The same cannot be said of his wife.

For it is not Juan Perón these Argentineans have come to see. They have endured a long winter day on their feet to hear the words of Maria Eva Duarte de Perón—or, as she prefers to be known—"Evita."

Yet the regal lady is nowhere to be seen.

José Espejo, leader of Argentina's largest trade union, the General

Evita Perón, shown here with her husband, Argentine president Juan Perón, in 1950

Confederation of Labor of the Argentine Republic, follows President Perón onto the balcony. The CGT, as the labor organization is more commonly called, has spent lavishly on this political rally, erecting the stage and hanging enormous sixty-foot-tall banners bearing the images of Juan Perón and Evita. This is to be the evening in which the union formally endorses the fifty-four-year-old Perón's reelection. His efforts to eradicate poverty and support labor have made him popular with the powerful CGT, giving him a huge advantage in the election.

But as Espejo begins his opening remarks, the chanting crowd drowns him out.

"Evita!" they cry. "Evita!"

Espejo anticipated this moment. He calmly speaks into the microphone, explaining to the mob that Eva Perón has chosen not to attend the rally.

The people don't seem to hear him. "Evita! Evita!" they cry.

Feigning indignation, Espejo leaves the stage. The boisterous chanting only grows louder. It is all President Juan Perón can do to remain stoic, his face creased in a benign smile as he awaits the hysteria that is soon to come.

At last, Evita Perón steps onto the balcony. Avenida 9 de Julio becomes a scene of bedlam. Evita is five foot five with golden hair. The former actress and radio star rose from a poor childhood to a life of wealth and power. Her heavily chronicled Rainbow Tour of Europe in 1947 saw her feted by dictators and the pope alike.* She has graced the cover of *Time* magazine, cementing her worldwide celebrity. But it is Evita's connection with the Argentinean people that makes her so special. She loves them, and they love her in return, giving her a unique political strength El Presidente will never know.

Evita moves quickly to the microphone at the center of the stage. Juan Perón stands to her left. Instead of the elaborate hairdos for which she is well known, Evita's hair this night is pulled back in a tight bun. Unlike the designer couture and Cartier jewels that so often grace her lithe figure, she wears a simple tailored suit. Evita is thinner than normal today, just beginning to show signs of the fatal illness now ravaging her body.

The crowd grows still. Evita is second to no man when it comes to public speaking. Her message tonight is aimed at the working poor. The words pour forth in a powerful narrative, reminding the masses of her loyalty to the people and her disdain for the wealthy. She pounds her fist and makes dramatic hand gestures, speaking loudly in curt, declarative sentences. It is no coincidence that Evita's

---

* In 1947, Spanish military dictator Francisco Franco invited Juan Perón to visit Spain. Franco was one of the few remaining Fascist leaders in Europe. Thinking the move to be politically dangerous, particularly with the United States, Perón instead sent Evita. To make it seem as if the visit wasn't focused solely on Spain, Evita Perón branded the journey a "goodwill" tour, also paying her respects to other European leaders, including Pope Pius XII and Charles de Gaulle. King George VI of Great Britain refused to meet with Evita because of Argentina's association with Hitler.

speaking style is very similar to those of Adolf Hitler and Benito Mussolini, for both she and her husband patterned their rise to power after those Fascist leaders.

Comrade is a favorite word of Evita's, and she uses it several times to reinforce her bond with the left-leaning crowd.

"Comrades, it is said throughout the world that I'm a selfish and ambitious woman. You know very well that this isn't the case. But you also know that everything I did, it was never so I could have any political position in my country. I never want any worker of my country to lack arguments when those people full of resentment, those mediocre people who never understand me and do not believe everything I do, I do for the lowest motives."

Evita Perón knows the people want her to run for vice president. But whether or not Evita chooses to seek that office is tonight's great secret. "We shall wait here for her decision," labor leader Espejo announces as Evita concludes her speech and leaves the stage. "We shall not move until she gives us a reply in accordance with the desires of the people."

And so the crowd waits noisily, chanting their hopes that Evita will announce her candidacy.

Darkness falls, and still the people linger, clamoring for her to step forth and confirm their wishes. They believe in her and see their beloved Evita as a woman they can trust.

However, Evita Perón is keeping two great secrets tonight.

The first is that she is dying. The First Lady is already experiencing fainting spells and severe internal bleeding. Evita refuses to see a doctor and has no idea what her illness might be, but as her weight drops and she continues to lose great amounts of blood, something is clearly wrong. In fact, cervical cancer is now racing quickly through her body. Tonight's speech will be among the last Evita will ever give.

The second secret is Juan and Eva Perón's deep ties to the Nazi Party. During Perón's previous career as a military attaché, he toured Germany just as the Second World War began. In the process, he developed a disturbing respect for the efficient manner in which the Nazis waged war. He also shares their anti-Semitic views and actively works to prevent Jewish migration to Argentina. Perón's personal secretary and intelligence chief, Rodolfo "Rudi" Freude, is a Nazi sympathizer whose father funneled German money into Perón's first presidential election campaign in 1946. While the majority of the world saw the Nuremberg Trials as the moment when evil finally got its due, Perón considers the tribunals "a disgrace, and an unfortunate lesson for the future of humanity."*

Perhaps the most shocking part of Juan Perón's worldview is that he has designed a secret program to convince millions of European refugees to resettle in Argentina. Immigrants with a scientific background and a history working with armament were preferred—so much so that Perón paid their airfare. In all, forty thousand immigrants with a German heritage are allowed to enter Argentina during Perón's reign. It is a program designed to advance Argentina's standing on the world stage by bolstering their industry and military. But a significant, though less well known, aspect of Perón's agenda is to help Nazi war criminals escape justice. The Argentine president has gone so far as to recruit a group of former SS soldiers to comb Europe for hidden war criminals, find them wherever they might be, and bring them to Argentina.

Juan and Eva Perón's "rescue teams" are spreading their tentacles throughout Europe, opening up new escape routes through Switzerland, Belgium, and even Sweden and Denmark. They are successfully bringing not just German war criminals in from the

---

* Juan Perón spent the first two years of World War II in Italy as a military observer, where he gained great respect for Benito Mussolini and Adolf Hitler. In 1941, Perón returned to Argentina, which remained neutral throughout most of the war, despite Allied pressure to declare war on Germany. Argentina's reluctance to do so was based on a large German immigrant population and an admiration of Germany's military history, which predated the First World War. It wasn't until March 27, 1945, that Argentina gave in to these demands, mostly out of fear of postwar economic isolation. At the time, Juan Perón was serving as Argentina's minister of war. He was first elected president by a popular vote in 1946.

cold, but also hundreds of French and Belgian collaborators who committed atrocities on behalf of the SS. All are given safe haven and immunity from extradition upon their arrival in Argentina.

Each of these killers believes himself untouchable once he steps off the boat in Buenos Aires.

As the night falls over Avenida 9 de Julio, the people of Buenos Aires make torches by lighting rolled-up newspapers—all the better to see and hear their beloved Evita. In less than two months she will be too weak to stand without assistance and will then undergo a lobotomy in a misguided attempt to manage her pain.* It will be Juan Perón himself who will order the procedure. As Evita's cervical cancer progresses, her public appearances become erratic—sometimes she says inappropriate things, threatening her husband's hold on power. The lobotomy will help her manage the tortures of cancer, but it will also numb her passion and silence her fiery speaking voice once and for all. She will never run for the vice presidency.

But the people of Argentina cannot possibly imagine that right now. In Evita's rise from poverty to power, they see their own lives, believing she is the face of their ascendant nation. So great is Evita's aura that she will soon become the one and only person in Argentinean history to be given the official title Spiritual Leader of the Nation.

Nor does the crowd realize that hundreds of Nazi war criminals are now part of their nation. And while Juan Perón may be offering his government's full protection to these callous murderers, the people who are hunting them will not relent in their determination to track them down.

---

* A lobotomy is a procedure that severs the neural connections between the prefrontal cortex and the rest of the brain. The prefrontal cortex is a powerful organizational center, responsible for planning, personality, and creativity. It is located just behind the forehead. The procedure is performed by inserting a slender probe into the eye socket, breaking through the thin bone behind the eye, and twirling the probe to slice through the prefrontal cortex. The procedure is then repeated on the other eye socket. In all, a lobotomy takes less than ten minutes.

ᛋᛋ

It is January 3, 1946, when Dieter Wisliceny testifies at the Nuremberg Trials. The pudgy SS-Hauptsturmführer from East Prussia worked hard to eradicate the Jewish population of Hungary, Slovakia, and Greece during the war. Even though the thirty-four-year-old SS henchman committed mass murder on a grand scale, he does not take responsibility for his many executions. Instead, he shifts blame to those who gave the orders. The SS motto—"Meine Ehre heist Treue" (My Honor Is Loyalty)—that Wisliceny once held dear is now forgotten as he desperately tries to save his skin. The only loyalty he knows now is to himself.

Under oath, Wisliceny tells the Nuremberg tribunal about the man who gave him the orders to destroy Jews. The individual is bowlegged and walks slightly bent forward. His handshake is soft and limp, his forehead is high, and his hair is dark blond. For purposes of dental verification, Wisliceny swears that the individual in question has two gold bridges and many fillings. Wisliceny knows this because they went to the same dentist.

This man, Wisliceny states for the record, is the true architect of the Holocaust, an officer who zealously pursued the extermination of the entire Jewish race. Wisliceny also testifies that this officer enjoyed the process of capturing, transporting, and executing Jews so completely that he once flippantly stated that having the deaths of "five million people on his conscience" gave him "extraordinary satisfaction."

Meanwhile, just thirty miles east, the SS officer of whom Wisliceny speaks is being held inside an American prisoner of war camp. The mass murderer once described as "a block of ice" for his emotionless demeanor has changed his name and gone undetected during seven months of captivity.

Adolf Eichmann is five foot nine, a man so thoroughly ordinary in appearance that it seems ludicrous he might be a killer—no bulging muscles, no sadistic gleam in his eye. Just a simple man approaching middle age. He has a receding hairline, a bemused smile, and claims to have served as an Untersturmführer—second lieutenant—in the SS during the war. The Americans have no reason to disbelieve him.

But the safety and anonymity of the man called Otto Eckmann, as the SS killer now calls himself, disappears the moment Wisliceny addresses the court.

Eichmann instantly becomes a wanted man. Alarmed by Wisliceny's testimony, and not knowing he is already in American captivity, the United States Army's war crimes section begins an intense manhunt, scouring all of Germany for this bureaucrat who happily murdered millions.

It is a moment Eichmann has anticipated for years. Even at the height of SS success, he rarely allowed himself to be photographed. Not only do the Nazi hunters not know where Eichmann might be, they also have little idea what he looks like.

Two days later, alerted by a clandestine SS network that his life is in danger, Eichmann escapes from the American POW camp at Oberdachstetten. He is just two months shy of his fortieth birthday and still has a long life ahead of him—if he can evade the Nazi hunters.*

In truth, Eichmann did not personally murder a single human being. "I never killed a Jew," he will one day explain. "I've never killed anybody. And I never ordered anybody to kill a Jew, or ordered anybody to kill a non-Jew. No. Never."

Eichmann's role was actually far more insidious.

So-called concentration camps had been established in 1933 as a means of removing anti-Nazi individuals from the general population. As the war began, a system of more than one thousand ghettos was also established as a means to segregate the Jewish population. Families were forcibly relocated to these cramped, squalid communities, where they could be closely monitored. The

---

* Many American POW camps became porous after the end of the war, and many of those being held simply walked out the front gate.

Adolf Eichmann, shown here in 1942

first ghetto was built in the central Polish city of Piotrków Trybunalski in October 1939. None were created in Germany, but ghettos soon spread throughout Poland, and eventually the Soviet Union as the German army conquered more and more territory. The largest ghetto, in Warsaw, saw more than four hundred thousand Jews jammed together within 1.2 square miles of the city. Understandably, they became hotbeds of sedition.*

In July of 1941, the SS began systematically murdering the Jews within the newly captured regions of the Soviet Union. But the

---

* The term *ghetto* is Italian, given to the Jewish quarter of Venice in the sixteenth century. City officials compelled the Venetian Jews to reside solely within that confined area.

mobile death squads that gassed and shot a million people were deemed inefficient. Thus, on January 20, 1942, in the Berlin suburb of Wannsee, a conference of top Nazi Party officials gathered to coordinate official policy about the extermination of German and European Jews. This new phase of the "Final Solution" would remain in the hands of the SS. Instead of slow death through slave labor, this new phase would see the establishment of death camps whose sole function was extermination. Jews would be rounded up from the ghettos, jammed into cattle cars, and taken by train to these new killing grounds. Upon their arrival they would be gassed, shot, or worked to death as slave labor.

Adolf Eichmann became the acknowledged "master" of these deportations, in the words of Heinrich Himmler. Eichmann likened the rounding up of Jews to catching fish, and he took delight in combing through France and Belgium in search of men, women, and children to load onto his death trains. "When I reached the conclusion that it was necessary to do to the Jews what we did, I worked with the fanaticism a man can expect from himself. No doubt they considered me the right man in the right place," he proudly stated.

"My interest here was only in the number of transport trains I had to provide. Whether they were bank directors or mental cases, the people who were loaded on these trains meant nothing to me."

In 1944, recognizing that the Jewish population of Hungary was still intact, Himmler gave an order to "send down the master in person." The approximately eight hundred thousand Hungarian Jews were the largest remaining Jewish community within the German occupation. As the Third Reich's "Expert for the Jewish Question," Eichmann reveled in the task, requiring just a few weeks to round up more than five hundred thousand men, women, and children for deportation to death camps. Most were gassed immediately. Just one in four survived the war.

Describing Eichmann, Auschwitz camp commander Rudolf Höss will marvel: "[He] was completely obsessed with his mission and also convinced that this extermination action was necessary in order to preserve the German people . . . if he could succeed in destroying the biological basis of Jewry in the East by complete extermination, then Jewry as a whole could never recover from that blow."

But because the SS officer never pulled a trigger, or turned on the gas, Eichmann comforts himself with the thought that he had never killed a single person.

Incredibly, his loving wife, Vera, to whom he is routinely unfaithful, insists that her husband spent the war as nothing more than a pencil-pushing bureaucrat.

⚡⚡

After escaping the POW camp, Adolf Eichmann makes his way to northern Germany, where he takes a job cutting down trees near Bremen. The SS officer who once enjoyed an opulent lifestyle leases a primitive hut in the forest, where he lives alone, reading newspapers and books about his "exploits." He takes extreme precautions to remain hidden, still refusing to have his picture taken. His wife and three young sons live hundreds of miles south in Linz, Austria, but Eichmann stays away for fear of being arrested. To ensure that his deception is complete, Eichmann makes no contact with his wife whatsoever, allowing his family to believe he is dead.

For four long years, Eichmann waits, hoping his pursuers will give up the chase. He hides in plain sight, unwilling to leave Germany, sure that the passage of time will make the Nazi hunters grow frustrated and quit. When the lumber company closes, he takes a job raising chickens. Very often he sells the eggs on the black market, particularly to the Jews of the nearby town of Belsen, former site of one of his death camps. Eichmann remains a steadfast Nazi, firm in his belief that murdering the Jews was right and just. "I'm no anti-Semite," he will explain. "I was just politically opposed to the Jews because they were stealing the breath of life from us."

Above all, Eichmann never retreats from his sworn SS oath: "I vow to you, Adolf Hitler, as Führer and chancellor of the German Reich, loyalty and bravery. I vow to you and to the leaders that you set for me, absolute allegiance until death. So help me God."

But Eichmann underestimates his pursuers. If anything, they are just as dogmatic as he is. Instead of abandoning the hunt, they become more daring: one Nazi hunter, a swashbuckling Polish Jew named Manus Diamant, locates a photograph of Eichmann by going to the extreme measure of seducing one of his former mistresses.*

To Eichmann's great frustration, the German public grows more rather than less curious about his whereabouts. In a nation now occupied and controlled by four of Germany's former enemies, Eichmann becomes a symbol of defiance. "In the press, on the radio, and in books my name was being constantly mentioned," he will lament of this unwanted celebrity.†

By early 1950, Adolf Eichmann's travel documents are about to expire. He must act.

Through SS networks still in place throughout Germany, he makes contact with Juan Perón's Nazi rescue teams. Another group known as Die Spinne,‡ said to be led by legendary Nazi commando Otto Skorzeny, assists Eichmann in his final preparations for escape. By June 1950, Eichmann is following the same ratline across northern Italy utilized by Josef Mengele a year earlier. When he arrives in Genoa, the willing alliance of the Red Cross, the Swiss govern-

---

* Diamant pretended to be a former Dutch SS official in order to win the trust of forty-year-old Maria Mösenbacher and eventually secure the photograph. During the war, Diamant lived for a time in the Warsaw ghetto before being sent to Auschwitz.

† The press got onto the story of the Nazi fugitive when American authorities announced he had escaped from the POW camp. Myths about him getting killed by partisans in Austria and escaping to the Middle East became widespread.

‡ Die Spinne (The Spider) was allegedly founded by Otto Skorzeny, a German commando during World War II. There is conjecture whether it was a branch of ODESSA or its own entity. Another founding member was Reinhard Gehlen, a former Nazi intelligence officer who later worked for the CIA and West Germany. Evidence suggests Die Spinne operated out of Fascist Spain in the decade after the war, then relocated to South America in the 1980s.

ment, and members of the Catholic Church provides the falsified documents and official passport that Eichmann needs. Just like Mengele, he receives a new name: Ricardo Klement.

⚡⚡

On June 17, 1950, Adolf Eichmann boards the SS *Giovanna C*, bound from Genoa to Argentina. He does not call attention to himself by traveling in the relative opulence of first class but instead settles for a cramped third-class berth below the waterline. He wears a black hat and bow tie with his suit. In Eichmann's coat pocket is a small vial of German soil. But he is ready to leave. "I felt like a hunted deer that has finally managed to shake off his pursuer," Eichmann will write about the moment the *Giovanna* cleared the harbor. "I was overcome by a wave of the sense of freedom."

Four weeks later, on July 14, 1950, the freighter chugs up the broad Rio de la Plata estuary and waits for the morning sun to allow docking in Buenos Aires.

Eichmann is ecstatic. At long last, he is free to reveal his true identity.

"I knew that in this 'promised land' of South America," he will later recount, "I had a few good friends, to whom I could openly, freely and proudly say that I am Adolf Eichmann, former SS-Obersturmbannführer!"

Eichmann immediately begins to set up his new life. Within a month, he is employed in the northern Argentine city of Tucumán. Though he has no background in construction, his SS connections allow him to land a position with a company called CAPRI, known throughout the SS community for hiring German-speaking men who are less than fluent in the Argentinean national language of Spanish.

Four months later, Eichmann utilizes the ratlines once more, sending a coded message to his wife admitting that he is alive: "the uncle of your children, whom everybody presumed dead, is alive and well—Ricardo Klement." Almost two more years pass before Eichmann also sends enough money to allow Vera and their three sons to book passage to Argentina. Posing as "Uncle Ricardo," he greets the SS *Salto* as it docks in Buenos Aires.

The date is July 28, 1952, just two days after the death of Evita Perón. Argentina is in mourning, with flags at half-mast and all government offices just reopened after a short grieving period. Thousands of Argentineans still line up every day to view her body as it lies in state.

But none of that matters to the Eichmann family. Finally, seven long years after the end of World War II, Adolf Eichmann, his wife, and their three sons are together again. "The reunion," he will later remember, "was indescribable."

Eichmann must remain careful about hiding his identity, if only so that the Nazi hunters will continue to believe that he is alive and well in Europe. Even as he stands on the dock, he watches closely for signs of suspicious behavior by those around him. But as time passes, Adolf Eichmann lowers his guard. He becomes bitter that he makes so little money. But otherwise, his past slips further into the distance. Eichmann is making friends within the Argentine Nazi community, among them Josef Mengele, who has prospered in Buenos Aires and offers free medical advice that Eichmann routinely ignores. Eichmann reads the pro-Nazi monthly *Der Weg*, drinks his beer at the ABC *Biergarten*,* and enjoys weekends of hunting and womanizing. This is not the Fatherland, but the German community in Argentina is large and welcoming. The Eichmann family has at last resumed a normal life.

Argentina is truly his "promised land."

But Adolf Eichmann is deluding himself.

Throughout all the years this coldhearted killer deported Jews to the death camps, he never imagined how many would survive the war. These men and women are now building new lives—many of them in a new country.

---

* The ABC Restaurant and Bar, as it is formally known, first opened in 1929. Its specialty is German food and beer. Located at the corner of San Martin and Lavalle Streets in downtown Buenos Aires, the ABC is still open for business.

The state of Israel, the true Promised Land to the Jews of Europe, now beckons. Its citizens learned well the lessons of the Holocaust. When attacked, they no longer turn the other cheek.

Instead, the Israelis believe in a practice known as the law of retaliation. As it says in the Torah: "Show no pity—life for life, eye for eye, tooth for tooth, hand for hand, foot for foot."*

Or, as Adolf Eichmann will soon learn: cold-blooded revenge.

---

* The Torah is the five books of Moses (Genesis, Exodus, Leviticus, Numbers, and Deuteronomy), part of the Tanach (comprised of the Torah, Prophets, and Writings). It mentions the "eye for an eye" punishment in the books of Exodus and Deuteronomy. These were likely authored by Moses between 1446 and 1406 BC. However, the "eye for an eye" punishment was used three hundred years earlier by the Babylonian king Hammurabi, who codified a series of laws and punishments. In legal terms, this law of retaliation is known as *lex talionis* and today refers more often to settling financial disputes rather than physical issues.

6

SEPTEMBER 19, 1957
FRANKFURT, GERMANY
8:00 P.M.

Fritz Bauer comes straight to the point: "Eichmann has been traced."
 The fifty-four-year-old German attorney is meeting secretly with Dr. Felix Shinnar, Israel's top diplomat in Germany. The two men were originally supposed to get together in the heart of Frankfurt, but Bauer is well known for his outspoken desire to see all Nazi war criminals brought to justice. Fearing he might be recognized, and knowing the explosiveness of this revelation, Bauer insisted they drive to a small inn outside of town to ensure total privacy.
 "Adolf Eichmann?" Shinnar asks skeptically. There have been countless Eichmann sightings but not a single confirmation since his escape from the American POW camp in 1946.
 "Yes," Bauer replies with confidence. He has tufts of white hair on his head, and his suit bears the faint aroma of the small cigars he smokes throughout the day. "Adolf Eichmann. He is in Argentina."

Fritz Bauer, the relentless crusader who played a vital role in bringing Adolf Eichmann to justice

It has been more than a decade since the war's end. Nazi hunters continue searching for Eichmann, but with every passing year it seems more unlikely that he will ever be found.

In that time, the nation of Israel has been born. After the great suffering endured during the war, the Jewish people built their own homeland. The location is the same place where Moses led the Jews on their journey out of slavery in Egypt more than three thousand years ago. The Jews believe this sanctuary was pledged to them by God—the "Promised Land." Since the time of Moses, Jews have been driven from their "sanctuary" time and again by the other great kingdoms of the Middle East.

Time and again they have returned.

Those same enemies still surround them, most notably the Arab powers intent on crushing Israel by aligning themselves with the Soviet Union. But after the horrors of Nazi Germany, the Jewish people will bear any burden and fight any war to be free.

A key engine of Jewish survival is the Mossad: Israel's intelligence agency.* Surprisingly, up to now, they have shown little interest in capturing Adolf Eichmann—or any other Nazi. As new emigrants from Eastern Europe flood into Israel, the Mossad's greater concern is investigating these newcomers to make sure they are not spies for the Soviet Union.

But now, Fritz Bauer hopes to alter that policy.

He is no stranger to challenge. In 1930, at the age of twenty-seven, the Jewish Bauer became the youngest judge in Germany. The Nazi rise to power in 1933 saw Bauer arrested and sent to a concentration camp for nine months. He was released only after signing a pledge of loyalty to the party.†

Knowing that he would never be safe in this new Germany, Bauer fled to Denmark. From there he moved to Sweden, where he lived out the war. Since returning to the German bench in 1949, Bauer has kept a low profile. He does not talk about his religion, knowing that many people in Germany still revile the Jews. Nor does he reveal that he is gay, because Nazi-era statutes against homosexuality are still enforced.

Jewish, gay, and anti-Nazi—there can be no greater pariah in West Germany than Fritz Bauer. He regularly receives death threats and is shunned by his peers. Yet the prosecutor risks his welfare each day in his fervent desire to prosecute Nazi war criminals.

Bauer has already issued an official warrant for Eichmann's

---

* *Mossad*, which means "institute" in Hebrew, is shorthand for the Institute for Intelligence and Special Operations.

† Bauer was a leading member of the Social Democratic Party and was working to organize a strike against the Nazis when he was taken prisoner and sent to the Heuberg concentration camp.

arrest. But he knows that the decree will never be enforced. It was a ceremonial gesture, designed to remind Germans that the hunt for Nazi war criminals is far from over.

Immediately after the war, a group of Jewish partisans known as the Nokmim traveled throughout Germany and Austria hunting down former members of the SS. Also known as the Avengers, this band of mercenaries paid by the government of Great Britain made northern Italy their home base.* The Avengers would sometimes appear at a suspect's home late at night. Other times, they grabbed men off the street, shoving them into cars. Their message was simple: the SS wasn't safe anywhere.

The Avengers never turned their captives over for a trial. They became executioners. Death was swift once the SS tattoo under the left armpit was confirmed. Some Avengers took war criminals into the forest and shot them in the head. Others were strangled—the use of bare hands was preferred to piano wire because it was cleaner. Sometimes the SS captives were forced to hang themselves in order to make the death look like a suicide.

The Avengers disbanded more than a decade ago. But even as Bauer and Shinnar meet here outside Frankfurt, small bands of Jewish mercenaries in Europe, South America, North America, and Egypt are still tracking down and murdering the SS.

But Fritz Bauer is a man of the law, opposed to vigilante killing. Ideally, Adolf Eichmann should be taken alive and made to stand trial.

Using the Israeli military is out of the question. Their intervention would constitute an act of war. Also, Bauer knows that America will not help. In 1953, the Central Intelligence Agency pronounced: "We are not in the business of hunting war criminals."

---

* Great Britain did not know they were funding the Avengers. In 1944, the British controlled Palestine, the land that would become Israel. Many Jewish residents of this region joined the British army and fought as a unit known as the Jewish Brigade. They were not disbanded until long after the war, allowing some of these soldiers to conduct anti-Nazi exercises in Europe under the guise of carrying out normal operations.

So that leaves only the Mossad. While Dr. Shinnar's official capacity is diplomatic, Bauer has no doubt that this conversation will soon make its way to the spy bureau in Israel. What will happen after that, Bauer does not know, but he is desperate and out of options.*

"I'll be perfectly frank with you," he tells Shinnar, anticipating the diplomat's question about why Bauer chose to give him this news instead of telling the German police. "I don't know if we can altogether rely on the German judiciary here, let alone the German embassy staff in Buenos Aires. That is why I was so interested in talking to you. I see no other way but to turn to you."

This is an understatement. The West German government is rife with former Nazis. The national security adviser, for example, is Hans Globke, who helped write the Nazi race laws that sought to destroy the Jews.†

"You are known to be efficient people," Bauer tells Felix Shinnar, "and nobody could be more interested than you in the capture of Eichmann. Obviously, I wish to maintain contact with you in

---

* Israel declared itself an independent nation on May 14, 1948. The Mossad was formed on December 13, 1949.

† The race laws were enacted in 1935, forbidding marriage, sex, and a number of other relationships between Germans and Jews. Penalties included fines and prison with hard labor. Globke personally helped write the Enabling Act of 1933, which helped Adolf Hitler rise to power, and the Reich Citizenship Law, revoking the right of Jews to be German citizens. After the war, the forty-seven-year-old Globke testified for both the prosecution and defense at the Nuremberg Trials. Due to the fact that he had been denied membership in the Nazi Party because of his Catholic faith, he was not charged with any crimes. Globke quietly became a powerful figure in postwar Germany, using personal relationships formed during his many years in the Nazi regime to become a behind-the-scenes force in the German chancellery. In 1951, Globke pushed through legislation that provided benefits, pensions, and even back pay to civil servants who served in the Nazi regime. Noted author John le Carré wrote of the law's passage: "civil servants of the Hitler regime . . . would henceforth receive full restitution of such pay, back-pay, and pension rights as they would have enjoyed if the Second World War hadn't taken place, or if Germany had won it." As Globke gained power and became familiar with secrets about German intelligence operations, the CIA and German government actively sought to suppress public knowledge of his past.

connection with this matter, but only provided that strict secrecy is kept."

Shinnar understands the subtext. If Bauer had brought this information to German police, someone would likely tip off Eichmann, sending him deeper into hiding. So Bauer has reached out to the Israelis, even though it is an act of treason in Germany to pass information to the representative of a foreign government.

"Thank you from the bottom of my heart," Dr. Shinnar replies. "Israel will never forget what you have done."

⚡⚡

It is spring in Argentina, as seasons in the Southern Hemisphere are the opposite of those in the north. And it is love that is finally flushing Adolf Eichmann from hiding. His twenty-year-old son Nicholas—known alternately as Klaus or Nick—has adapted well to life in Buenos Aires. While his father still pretends to be Ricardo Klement, his four sons keep the family surname. The tall, blue-eyed Nicholas is fond of riding horses and hunting pumas. He frequently spouts anti-Semitic rhetoric, so it will one day surprise him to learn that the pretty German immigrant, with whom he has fallen in love, is half-Jewish.

The fourteen-year-old brunette's name is Sylvia Hermann. Her father, Lothar Hermann, is a Socialist. The Nazis murdered his parents and he himself was imprisoned in the Dachau concentration camp outside of Munich, Germany, in 1935 for his political leanings. The severe beatings he endured at the hands of the Gestapo left him blind. Now fifty-six, Hermann immigrated to Argentina in 1938, shortly after the horrific night of rioting and destruction known throughout Germany as *Kristallnacht*, the Night of the Broken Glass. This pogrom took the National Socialist Party's persecution of the Jews to a new magnitude in an attempt to force mass emigration. Though the two have never met, Adolf Eichmann was stationed at Dachau shortly before Hermann's imprisonment.

Sylvia is taken with Nick Eichmann, yet she is not allowed to visit his home or even know the address. But Nicholas often comes calling, making himself comfortable in the Hermann household. While there, he speaks in German, claiming that his father served as an officer in the Wehrmacht, and openly laments that the Nazis did not complete their extermination of the Jews.

Lothar Hermann listens to the vitriol—yet says nothing.

Hermann wears the dark glasses of a blind man and tends to dress in a natty suit and tie. He is a handsome man with the unassuming air of someone who has learned to keep his opinions to himself. But inside he seethes about his family's treatment in Germany and chafes at Nick Eichmann's offensive ranting. Lothar longs to "even the score with the Nazi war criminals who caused me and my family so much agony and suffering."

At first it seems bewildering to Lothar Hermann that the young man in front of him is the son of the notorious Adolf Eichmann. Legends abound about the massive amounts of wealth the Nazi higher-ups smuggled out of Germany after the war, yet the Eichmanns, like the Hermanns, live in the lower-middle-class Olivos neighborhood of Buenos Aires. Houses are simple and in some places squalid. The odds of a once-powerful man like Eichmann living in such a run-down part of town are unlikely.

Sylvia Hermann and Nick Eichmann begin dating in December 1956, and the relationship is still blossoming a few months later when Lothar Hermann decides to move his family away from Olivos. In a radical change, Hermann relocates from the cosmopolitan Buenos Aires to the ramshackle village of Coronel Suárez, hundreds of miles southwest in the grasslands of Central Argentina. A single dirt road lined by small wooden shacks runs through the distant town.

But Coronel Suárez is safe, free from the pro-Nazi elements so common to Buenos Aires. In fact, it is home to a prominent German-Jewish community. While Hermann makes plans to open a new law practice, Sylvia and Nick correspond by mail. Young Eichmann still refuses to give her his home address, asking Sylvia to post her love letters to him through a mutual friend.

In April 1957, four months after falling for Nick Eichmann,

Sylvia comes across a newspaper article detailing a war crimes trial in Frankfurt, Germany. The prosecuting attorney is Fritz Bauer. *Argentinisches Tageblatt*, the anti-Nazi German-language daily, specifically reports that one prominent Nazi has escaped prosecution. His name, the newspaper notes, is Adolf Eichmann.

In an instant, Sylvia is convinced that Nick Eichmann is the son of this killer. She is conflicted, for her feelings for Nick are still strong, but she shares the revelation with her father, knowing he will take action. She is correct.

Lothar has never seen Adolf Eichmann and does not even know where he lives, but the former concentration camp inmate's desire for revenge is strong.

So Hermann makes the bold move of writing to the famous anti-Nazi jurist Fritz Bauer in Frankfurt.

The letter contains the explosive revelation—Adolf Eichmann is alive in Argentina.

There are few people with whom Fritz Bauer can share the news. "As soon as I leave the confines of my office," he once confided to a friend, "I am on enemy territory."

But in Lothar Hermann, Fritz Bauer has a true ally—a man willing to take enormous risks to capture Adolf Eichmann.

The three-hundred-mile train ride from Coronel Suárez to Buenos Aires lasts ten hours. Sylvia Hermann, wearing a blue dress, sits with her father. They depart the train at the stately Retiro Station, located right next to the port where Adolf Eichmann first arrived in Argentina almost a decade ago. Their goal for the long journey is simple: pinpoint the SS killer's home address.

Father and daughter then travel by commuter bus to their old neighborhood ten miles north. But when it comes time to step off and begin the journey on foot, Sylvia Hermann must travel alone. To appear at the house of her old boyfriend with her blind Jewish father in tow would be too conspicuous.

Sylvia and Lothar agree on a rendezvous location, then the now fifteen-year-old boldly marches off by herself to find one of the world's most notorious killers. No one knows exactly where she is going, not even her father.

Sylvia's plan is simple, at best: walk the streets of Olivos until she finds Nick Eichmann. She will then ask him where he lives.

By chance, Sylvia runs into an old friend who knows Nick's address.

Summoning up her nerve, the teenager walks alone down Chacabuco Street to number 4261. Her story is simple: she is a girlfriend of Nick's who has moved away but returned for a brief visit. Her heart pounds as she steps through the front gate and knocks on the door.

Nick's mother answers. She has given birth to a fourth child since leaving Germany and has gained considerable weight.

"Is this the home of the Eichmann family?" asks Sylvia.

Vera Eichmann is pleasant, if guarded.

Much to Sylvia's surprise, a man roughly sixty years old steps to the plump woman's side. He wears glasses and walks slightly stooped. His appearance matches the photograph of Eichmann.

Sylvia introduces herself as a friend of their son. "Is Nick at home?" Sylvia says nervously.

"Pleased to meet you, young lady," the gentleman answers in German. He bows slightly at the waist, in an Old World display of manners.

To Sylvia's surprise, she is invited to come inside for coffee and cake. Nick has stepped out, but Sylvia is welcome to stay and wait for him.

Vera holds the door open. Sylvia has come too far to lose her courage now. She steps into the home. Dieter Eichmann, Nick's younger brother, sits in the small room.

"He left an hour ago," Dieter informs Sylvia. Though Nick's mother does not refer to Dieter by name, he appears to be in his late teens, as the German prosecutor's dossier suggested.

So far, there is nothing at all sinister about the Eichmann family. Their warmhearted courtesy toward a complete stranger is unexpected, but Sylvia does not relax her guard.

Impulsively, Sylvia asks, "Are you Mr. Eichmann?"

The elderly man does not answer.

"Are you Nick's father?" Sylvia presses the matter. Her tone is polite and deferential, as would be expected from a teenager addressing the head of a household.

But the man is upset nonetheless. "No," he replies sharply. Sylvia will remember his tone as "unpleasant and strident."

A long and uncomfortable silence fills the room as the man prepares his answer.

"I'm his uncle," he finally declares.

Sylvia backs off. The conversation descends into small talk as everyone awaits Nick's return home. No one seems to suspect that Sylvia has an ulterior motive. As her father would later point out, the Hermanns were accepted as "German in every way" in the Olivos area. Sylvia does not do anything to dissuade the Eichmanns from this assumption.

Coffee is served. Time passes. The man claiming to be Nick's uncle is no longer angry with Sylvia. When she professes that she would like to one day study foreign languages, he even admits to learning a little French during his wartime service.

Suddenly, Nick bursts through the door. The sight of Sylvia fills him with rage. It is as if they never had any feelings for each other. "Who gave you my address?" he demands.

"Did I do something wrong?" she replies, adding that mutual friends had shown her the way.

It is the uncle who defuses the scene, telling Nick that he has no problems with Sylvia's presence. But she has had enough. There is every reason to believe that she is in the room with Adolf Eichmann himself. That is the purpose for her visit and nothing more can be gained.

As the middle-aged uncle sees Sylvia to the door, Nick steps forward. In an unguarded moment, he makes a slip.

"Thank you, Father," he states. "I will see Sylvia to the bus."

The family says a warm good-bye, but Nick is tense as he walks Sylvia back to the bus station. He has been forbidden to bring home guests and he is unsure if there will be any punishment upon his return.

Sylvia's thoughts are of a different nature. She no longer has any feelings for Nick. His display of anger terrifies her and she is wary of further outbursts. But it is vital she ask him one simple question before they say their good-byes.

"Why do you call your uncle 'Father'?" Sylvia asks.

※

As expected, it doesn't take long for Dr. Felix Shinnar to pass Fritz Bauer's information about Eichmann to his superior in Israel's Ministry of Foreign Affairs. They in turn contact the director of the Mossad.

That man is Isser Harel. Russian by birth, he is small in stature and his large ears are his most distinguishing personal feature. Harel is Byelorussian by birth. He immigrated to Palestine at the age of sixteen, traveling by ship from Genoa, carrying a pistol concealed in a loaf of bread for protection. He is married, with two children, and enjoys reading detective novels in his spare time. His work is top secret, as is his profession: Harel's neighbors have no idea that he is one of the most powerful men in Israel.

Under normal circumstances, the director would put little credence in yet another suspicious Eichmann sighting. "We had never succeeded in verifying any of the so-called reliable evidence of people who claimed to have seen him," Harel will later write. But even though Fritz Bauer refuses to reveal the name of his source, something about the prosecutor's claim rings true: "Instinct told me this was no rumor plucked out of thin air."

Israel's legislature, known as the Knesset, passed a law in 1950 ordering the prosecution of Nazi war criminals and their collaborators. Yet Harel has just one man on his staff focused on arresting these murderers. Rather than add to his burden, Harel sets out to educate himself, ordering every available file on Eichmann delivered to his desk. One of his habits is to catalog information on small cards. When the files are in his possession, Harel spends an entire night making his notes. "In my mind's eyes," Harel will write, "an image took shape, the image of an archfiend whose vicious crimes were unprecedented in the annals of humanity, a man on whose shoulders rested the direct responsibility for the butchery of millions."

Harel became Mossad director in 1952. Since that time, attitudes about Nazi war criminals have shifted. In Germany, there is currently talk of commuting the sentences of those convicted at the Nuremberg Trials. Part of the problem is with the Jews themselves—few Holocaust survivors wish to discuss those horrible years. Their silence only adds to the belief that the past should be forgotten.

"People were tired of atrocity stories," he will later reflect. "Their one desire was to dismiss those unspeakable happenings from their minds; they maintained that, in any event, there was no punishment on earth to fit the perpetration of outrages of such magnitude, and they were reconciled to the violation of law and the perversion of justice."

Only one war crimes trial has been conducted in Israel. Ironically, it focused on a Jewish-Hungarian journalist accused of collaborating with Adolf Eichmann. The residue of that inquiry is still fresh in Harel's memory. Rudolf Kastner, as the individual was known, was convicted of helping the Nazis, but that conviction was overturned. Then, just six months ago, Kastner was assassinated in Tel Aviv by a three-man hit squad associated with the radical militia group dedicated to avenging the Holocaust. Sadly, Kastner was not entirely innocent of all collaboration charges, but this was necessary to brazenly negotiate the freedom of more than sixteen hundred Hungarian Jews with Adolf Eichmann. These men, women, and children were smuggled out of the country in June 1944, arriving safely in Switzerland after a long and perilous journey.

Kastner's trial and subsequent assassination reveals the deep divide in Israel concerning war crimes. Those he had smuggled out of Hungary were among the wealthiest Jews in the country, willing to pay the Nazis dearly in exchange for their lives. Indeed, the price for a space inside the thirty-five railway cars that would become known as the "Kastner train" was a fortune in gold, diamonds, and cash. Poor Jews, lacking such resources, were instead sent to the death camps. Rather than seeing Kastner as heroic, one prosecutor stated that he "sold his soul to the devil" in negotiating with Eichmann. The fact that Kastner and his family secured spots on the train to Switzerland reinforced the view that he was nothing more than a selfish collaborator.*

The guilty verdict in Kastner's trial was so contentious that it brought down the Israeli government. Rather than Jews working together to arrest Nazi war criminals, the Jewish people are fighting against one another, arguing over what constitutes a good and a bad Jew.

But Harel will not allow justice to be perverted any longer. Vetting incoming refugees may be a more functional use of Mossad's resources, but bringing "the head butcher" to justice is the morally proper thing to do—despite what public opinion might believe.

Thus, with Fritz Bauer's intelligence in hand, Isser Harel adds a new priority to the Mossad mandate.

"I resolved that if Eichmann were alive, come hell or high water, he'd be caught."

---

* The "Kastner train" is one of World War II's most bizarre happenings. The thirty-five cattle cars loaded with more than a thousand of Budapest's wealthiest Jews (and 388 people from Rudolf Kastner's hometown of Kolozsvár) rolled out of the city on June 30, 1944. Rather than heading straight to Switzerland, the train was routed hundreds of miles north to the Bergen-Belsen concentration camp because Adolf Eichmann wanted to review passengers' statuses. There, in an example of the privileged treatment that would see Kastner placed on trial, the passengers were held in a special section of the facility, where they enjoyed poetry readings and intellectual discussion. By mid-August, the first of the group were loaded onto trains and taken into Switzerland. The final passengers would not leave the camp until December 1944. A total of 1,670 individuals made it safely into Switzerland, where they occupied luxury hotels until the end of the war.

7

October 11, 1959
Tel Aviv, Israel
Dawn

The news could not be more devastating.

As the sun rises over this beachfront Mediterranean city, Mossad director Isser Harel stares at the morning headlines. *Yedioth Ahronoth* and *Maariv*, Israel's largest daily newspapers, are both claiming that Adolf Eichmann has been found. According to German Nazi hunter Erwin Schule, attorney general of the city of Ludwigsburg in the south German state of Baden-Württemberg, Eichmann has been spotted, alive and well. But he is not in Argentina, as Fritz Bauer has insisted. Instead, the murderer is in Kuwait, working as an oil company engineer.

The Mossad headquarters are in a section of Tel Aviv known as Sarona, first settled by Germans in 1871. The buildings were used as a military base during World War II, with a network of underground tunnels connecting the stone houses. Now, the complex is known as the Kirya, the provisional capital of Israel, housing the Israel Defense Forces and other government buildings. There is no sign advertising that this red-roofed building is the home of Israeli intelligence. It looks like any other modest structure. Harel's office is not elaborate, decorated with just a desk, phone, conference table, and small safe. But the future of Israel is as dependent upon the handful of men and women working in this stone building as it is upon the nearby military base.

Harel is unsure whether the rumors about Eichmann are true. Though his team of spies has not yet pinpointed the Nazi's exact location, he strongly believes Eichmann to be somewhere in Argentina—not Kuwait. Harel clings to two pieces of evidence that support this theory: the first is that Sylvia Hermann definitely knows a young man by the name of Nick Eichmann, whose age and physical description match those of Adolf Eichmann's oldest son. She claims to have visited his home in Buenos Aires, where she believes she has seen the war criminal face-to-face.

The second indicator is that Vera Eichmann and her three sons abruptly departed their home in Austria in 1952. Clearly on the run and trying to hide her tracks, Vera and the boys made their way to Argentina. This should be enough evidence for Isser Harel to launch a major undercover investigation into Adolf Eichmann's whereabouts.

The truth, however, is that Isser Harel no longer knows what to believe about Eichmann's location.

The killer's trail has gone stone-cold.

ᛋᛋ

Years later, when the Israeli government lifts the vow of secrecy and allows him to tell his story in full, Isser Harel will write of his unrelenting zeal in chasing down Adolf Eichmann. But that is an exaggeration. Lacking the finances and manpower to investigate Fritz Bauer's initial tip in 1957, Harel waits four months before sending a man to investigate 4261 Chacabuco Street, Eichmann's purported home in the Buenos Aires suburbs.

Upon tracking down the address, Mossad agent Emanuel Talmor is stunned that the residence is not a palatial mansion but instead a two-story apartment building.

As a way of proving his theory about Eichmann's location correct, the German prosecutor reluctantly reveals to Isser Harel and the Mossad the name of his undercover source: Lothar Hermann.

Two months later, in March 1958, Israeli agents once again attempt to locate Eichmann at the Chacabuco address. They do not see any physical sign of the SS killer and arrive at the same conclusion as Agent Tamor: a powerful Nazi like Eichmann would never reside in a run-down apartment.

However, the two men—one Mossad, the other a policeman working in Argentina as a member of Interpol—take the investigation one step further by making contact with Lothar Hermann. Both men are astounded that he cannot see, and are equally impressed by the concentration camp survivor's willingness to take great personal risks, at his own expense, to locate Adolf Eichmann. If Hermann's name ever became known to the Nazi factions residing undercover in Argentina, the blind man's life would be in danger.

Yet Hermann has made a crucial mistake that undermines his theory about Eichmann's whereabouts. Up until this point in the investigation, Hermann has shown himself to be a very capable detective. With Sylvia's assistance, he has done a thorough search of property records in the provincial capital at La Plata. He has learned that the home on 4261 Chacabuco Street is divided into two apartments. The owner is an Austrian named Francisco Schmidt who had come to Argentina after the war. Hermann had heard a rumor that Schmidt actually arrived by submarine, which would have made him a very high-ranking individual.

The property was purchased on August 14, 1947. Each apartment has its own electricity meter. One electric bill is sent to a tenant named Dagoto. The other is sent to the name Klement.

This is where Hermann blunders. Based on Francisco Schmidt's alleged Austrian heritage, Hermann deduces that he is in fact Adolf Eichmann. But one look at Schmidt's identity card would reveal that he looks nothing at all like Adolf Eichmann.

Rather than investigate whether or not the individuals living under the names Klement or Dagoto bear a likeness to Eichmann, and not being able to see these individuals himself, the blind man chooses to ignore his daughter's first-person encounter with the man whom Nick Eichmann called "Father." In an enormous lapse of logic, Lothar Hermann assures Israeli investigators that Francisco Schmidt is Adolf Eichmann. The two names on the electric meters are false, he claims, meant to conceal Eichmann's identity. Hermann explains the discrepancy by explaining what he believes to be true: that the SS murderer has undergone enormous amounts of plastic surgery to change his appearance.

"Francisco Schmidt," Lothar Hermann assures the Israelis, "is the man we want."

But Lothar Hermann has made the same elemental mistake committed by Israeli investigators: he assumes Eichmann to be wealthy. The stories about the Kastner train are well known, as is the great wealth paid to Eichmann in exchange for letting Jews escape Hungary. It never crosses Hermann's mind that Eichmann would be the tenant, not the owner.

When the Mossad follows up, they discover that Francisco Schmidt does not reside on Chacabuco Street. When the Israelis locate Schmidt, they see no evidence of a wife and sons the same ages as Eichmann's.

"These findings damaged Hermann's trustworthiness irretrievably," Isser Harel will write.

So in March 1958, less than a year after his first meeting with Fritz Bauer, Harel dropped the case, citing lack of progress. By August of that year, Israeli agents were told to cease all contact with Lothar Hermann.

"The Mossad file on Eichmann was deposited in the archives," one fellow Mossad agent will remember bitterly. "Even Bauer's attempts to have the case reopened did not help."

Now the news about Adolf Eichmann being in Kuwait nineteen months after the case was closed troubles Harel deeply. It is sure to get picked up by the wire services, where it will quickly flash around the world. Wherever he might be, Eichmann himself may read the dispatches and go deeper into hiding. The Mossad might never again come so close to finding him. On the other hand, if Eichmann believes investigators are looking for him in Kuwait instead of Argentina, he may adopt a false sense of security. After careful deliberation, Isser Harel decides that this morning's headline is actually good news.

The greater problem is Eichmann's notoriety. He is more than just another Nazi on the run. The fact that he makes headlines after more than a dozen years in hiding is proof. Adolf Eichmann is a symbol of Nazi bloodlust, abhorrent to peace-loving people everywhere but an inspiration to those who practice a manifesto of racism and hatred. The Israeli government and the media have begun to demand Eichmann's capture, if only to stem a global rise in pro-Nazi sympathy.

In Germany, throughout the late 1950s, radical groups trying to revive the Nazi movement are spreading hatred against the Jews. The swastika, the emblem of Nazi power that was banned after the war, is once again on display. Former SS soldiers in large numbers are escaping Nazi hunters by joining the French Foreign Legion to wage war in Indochina.*

Isser Harel puts down his paper and sips his coffee. In order to counter the Fascists, Mossad needs to strike a crushing blow. But finding Eichmann appears to be an impossibility. It would take extraordinary new evidence to convince Harel to reopen the case.

Of course, Adolf Eichmann is not the only Nazi on the run. Mossad would do well to find the location of the heinous Dr. Josef Mengele, who is also rumored to be living in Argentina.

---

* The French Foreign Legion is comprised of individuals from other nations who willingly take up arms in defense of France and its territories. Germans have long outnumbered other nationalities as members. This was particularly true between 1945 and 1950, when it is said that the Legion recruited ex-SS soldiers straight out of POW camps and into their ranks. The focus of French fighting in the 1950s was in their colony of Indochina—later to be known as Vietnam. The French lost this war, with the Battle of Diem Bien Phu, now seen as one of history's most stunning examples of a smaller nation defeating their colonial master. The French ranks were filled with German noncommissioned officers at that time.

There also may be a third notorious Nazi in Argentina. As recently as a year ago, Adolf Hitler's personal secretary, Martin Bormann, was allegedly spotted in Bariloche, a Nazi haven on the shores of Lago Nahuel Huapi in the Andes Mountains. The brutal Bormann was Adolf Hitler's handpicked successor to lead the Nazi Party's resurgence after the war. British intelligence agents will soon file a report stating that Bormann has successfully fled to the Argentine city of Posadas, having arrived by submarine on July 29, 1945. Between 1945 and 1952 the British spy agency MI5 was overwhelmed with reports of Bormann sightings around the world, largely from agents trying to make names for themselves. "He has been seen riding the Loch Ness monster," one British agent finally joked in exasperation, recognizing that Mengele would be the world's next big news story. Sir Percy Sillitoe, director general of the security service, put little credence in the Bormann reports and they eventually came to an end.

Isser Harel knows that capturing Eichmann, Mengele, or Bormann would be an enormous triumph.

Capturing all three, however, would be even better.

But first, Harel must find them.

⚡⚡

It is May 1, 1945. Berlin is lost. No German is safe. The Soviet army terrorizes the city, raping and looting as they battle their way toward the ultimate prize: the Reichstag. Capturing the vaunted seat of Nazi power and Adolf Hitler himself will avenge Germany's invasion of Russia five years ago. The streets are nothing but rubble; full of corpses and waste. Dead German soldiers hang by their necks from street corner lampposts, executed by fanatical Nazis for retreating. The Berlin skyline is a haze of smoke and fire, the thud of artillery fire never ending.

Inside Adolf Hitler's underground bunker, the party is coming to an end. Ever since the Führer committed suicide two days ago, the soldiers, secretaries, and other bunker staff have danced and drunk champagne, knowing these might be their final days. The paranoia that preceded Hitler's death has now been replaced by cold fear about what comes next. The Russians will not go easy on the Führer's personal staff. Whether they will be murdered or imprisoned in a Soviet gulag, no one knows. Each man and woman longs to escape—flee the bunker and run for their lives. But that is not a possibility, for such behavior might be deemed a betrayal. The penalty could be a gunshot to the head by the SS or Gestapo who remain on duty.

Only Martin Bormann remains calm. The bunker now belongs to him. The forty-four-year-old bureaucrat has been loyal to Adolf Hitler for more than a dozen years, serving as his personal secretary and right-hand man. Bormann holds the title of SS-Reichsleiter.

Nothing Hitler accomplished during the war has taken place without Bormann's knowledge. He has been married for sixteen years to the former Gerda Buch, who has given him ten children. But Bormann rarely sees his family—his loyalty has been to Hitler alone. The Brown Eminence, as Bormann is known, was the Führer's confidant, financial adviser, and babysitter, enduring his leader's moods and whims with patience and cunning, always searching for ways to increase his own personal power.*

Bormann is a short, heavyset man with a fondness for cruel revenge. It was Bormann who suffered a perceived snub by famed tank general Erwin Rommel in the early days of World War II, then repaid the insult five years later by persuading the Führer to order Rommel's execution after a failed plot to kill Hitler.†

Bormann is also a realist, foreseeing the fall of the Reich as long

---

* The color of Bormann's Nazi Party uniform was brown. The term *Brown Eminence* is a derivation of the French term *éminence grise* ("gray eminence"), which referred to the seventeenth-century French cardinal Richelieu's power-wielding assistant, François Leclerc du Tremblay, a friar fond of dressing in an unbleached woolen tunic.

† Rommel was given a choice between the disgrace of a public hanging or privately committing suicide by biting down on a cyanide capsule. He chose suicide and was rewarded with a lavish state funeral.

as two years ago. With Hitler's blessing, he began making plans for Germany's postwar resurrection. In August 1944 he allegedly coordinated a gathering of German industrialists in Strasbourg to facilitate the movement of corporate capital to other countries, where it could be sheltered until after the war. Because of Bormann, 750 new companies have been established around the world to hide Nazi assets.

Argentina is home to ninety-eight of these hidden corporations. Additionally, Bormann has overseen the shipment of diamonds, gold, and blue-chip stock certificates into the South American country. In an outrageous and still unproven act of deception, Bormann allegedly concocted Operation Tierra Del Fuego to ship this wealth to Buenos Aires by submarine. Bormann has also spent hours meticulously planning his eventual escape route from Berlin to Argentina, where he envisions a new life of power and luxury. He will be the new Führer, a head of state whose nation has just fallen. "Bury everything," Adolf Hitler warned Bormann, anticipating his own death. "You will need it to return to power."

Bormann just needs to get out of the bunker alive.

The air is stale and suffocating as Martin Bormann assembles the bunker staff to explain their escape. They will form into small groups, then travel by tunnel to the underground train station at Wilhelmsplatz. There, they will follow the subway tracks to another station at Friederichstrasse. Each group will leave the second subway station and climb to ground level. There they will walk the city streets, avoiding the Soviet tanks taking up position along the banks of the river Spree. They will then cross the Weidendammer Bridge. Finally, the group will disperse and assimilate into the local population. After that, each man and woman is on his or her own.

Bormann's group moves out shortly before midnight. He personally witnessed the last will and testament of Adolf Hitler, which gave him control of the Nazi Party after the Führer's death.* This effectively makes Bormann Germany's head of state.

---

* Hitler's last will and testament is now held in a secure vault at the U.S. National Archives in College Park, Maryland.

The bunker staff has been underground night and day for weeks, so it is wrenching to arise and see their city in flames. After the tunnel escape, Bormann travels along the road known as Invalidenstrasse, heading toward the Stettiner Bahnhof, the main railway station.

All around him, Russian soldiers prowl the streets, shooting both German soldiers and civilians on sight.

A Russian antitank barrier blocks the road. Bormann and the rest of his group, which includes Hitler's pilot, driver, and surgeon, wait for a small detachment of German panzers to move forward and lay siege to the obstacle. Bormann takes cover behind the first panzer, using it as a shield as it rolls powerfully toward the Russian blockade. Concentrated firepower destroys the barrier, but in the same instant a round from an antitank bazooka known as a *Panzerfaust* strikes the German tank. The massive explosion hurls Bormann through the air, slamming him hard into the ground. Others in the group are also injured, causing confusion to spread throughout their ranks.

At this moment, in the dark of night, amid the chaos of Berlin's fall, surrounded on all sides by the enemy, Martin Bormann vanishes. Artur Axmann, the thirty-two-year-old leader of the Hitler Youth movement, swears that he sees Bormann lying dead on the ground. Others in the group will state that they could not get close enough to where Bormann fell to confirm whether the Brown Eminence is alive or dead—they never see his body. Yet another member of the Waffen SS will tell of meeting Bormann later that night at a German field hospital in Königs Wursterhausen, twelve miles outside Berlin. The young sergeant will recognize Bormann, who is suffering from an injured foot, thanks to the explosion. The two men, along with Dr. Ludwig Stumpfegger—Hitler's surgeon—join forces and plan to travel to a safe house belonging to the sergeant's dead uncle. Another officer overhears their conversation. So it is that the four men travel to the address at Fontanestre 9, Berlin Dahlem, and let themselves into the unoccupied residence. Outside, Russian forces patrol the streets.

"We stayed inside for the next three days. None of us dared to go outside," the unnamed Waffen SS soldier will recount in interviews in 1971 and 1977. "After the third day, Reichsleiter Bormann, the officer who was his companion, and the third officer decided to leave. The third officer went one way. Bormann and his friend headed northwest into Mecklenburg, to a place where they said other clothing, some gold, and various currencies had been secreted for this escape."

The Soviet Union will also conduct their own two-year investigation. KGB major L. Besymenski will report to his superiors that Bormann made a "successful escape to South America." And American journalist Paul Manning, who covered the war for CBS News with legendary broadcaster Edward R. Murrow, will also conduct a thorough search for Martin Bormann.

"After countless interviews and laborious research in German and American archives for revealing documents of World War II, I knew that the Bormann saga of flight [money] and his escape to South America was really true," Manning will conclude in a book he wrote about Martin Bormann.

"It had been covered up by an unparalleled manipulation of public opinion and the media. The closer I got to the truth, the more quiet attention I received from the forces surrounding and protecting Martin Bormann, and also from those who had a direct interest in halting my investigation. I was the object of diligent observation by squads of Gestapo agents dispatched from South America by General [Heinrich] 'Gestapo' Mueller, who directs all security matters for Martin Bormann, Nazi in exile, and his organization, the most remarkable business group anywhere in the secret world of today."

Manning adds: "Martin Bormann was last seen for sure in a tank crossing the Weidendamm Bridge in Berlin, on the night of May 1, 1945. Then, for most of the world, he vanished."

Paul Manning subsequently went to his grave believing Martin Bormann escaped from Germany in the final days of the war. Shortly after the publication of his book *Martin Bormann: Nazi in Exile* in 1981, Manning's publisher will have both his legs broken in a savage attack. More horrifying, the author's son, Gerry, will be brutally murdered. On February 18, 1993, in the hallway of his second-floor apartment on Twenty-First Street in New York, the thirty-nine-year-old aspiring artist is shot dead during a robbery.

Paul Manning believed that both of these attacks were attempts to make him halt further investigation into Martin Bormann's location.*

In 1945 one thing was certain: the Brown Eminence disappeared.

⚡⚡

Three years later, on June 16, 1948, American president Harry S. Truman is drawn into the Bormann intrigue. It is an election year. Truman, who assumed the presidency following the death of Franklin Delano Roosevelt just weeks before the end of World War II, is one of the most unpopular presidents in American history. Yet he has chosen to run for a full term.

Truman loves traveling by train, and on this Wednesday he is returning from California in the presidential railcar known as the *Ferdinand Magellan*. Armor-plated, air-conditioned, and outfitted with bulletproof glass windows three inches thick, *Magellan* is considered by Truman to be the world's finest method of travel.

Unlike FDR, whose many physical maladies made high-speed rail journeys uncomfortable, Truman enjoys clickety-clacking across America at eighty miles an hour. As the president makes his way back to Washington, the *Magellan* will often stop at some city or small burg, whereupon Harry Truman will stand on the rear platform and make a speech to the waiting crowds. In all, he will travel almost ten thousand miles and deliver seventy-three speeches in eighteen states on this journey alone. In the fall, when his campaign

---

* Despite the fact that his son died twelve years after the publication of his Bormann book, Paul Manning thoroughly believed that the murder was revenge. He subsequently stopped researching a follow-up book titled "The Search for Martin Bormann," which was never published. Paul Manning died of natural causes in 1995.

becomes all-consuming, he will make the cross-country journey again—this time traveling thirty-one thousand miles and delivering more than two hundred speeches.

The affairs of the world are ever present, as he deals with policy matters great and small while making his way across Kansas—stopping at Dodge City, Hutchinson, Newton, and Emporia within the span of five hours. For example, Israel has just declared itself an independent nation, and Truman is making plans to announce diplomatic ties with the new country upon his return to Washington.

Then there is another matter, one that the president initially attempted to deflect. Even as Truman travels across America, Robert H. Jackson, the lead prosecutor at the Nuremberg Trials, is writing to the president, imploring him to intensify the search for Martin Bormann. The Nazi bureaucrat was tried and convicted in absentia at Nuremberg. Jackson would very much like to see justice served. Eyewitnesses state that Bormann is living in Argentina under the alias Don Fritz. He allegedly entered that country a few months earlier disguised as a Jesuit priest.

Justice Jackson, a member of the United States Supreme Court, first learned of this one month ago. He presented his findings to Truman, only to have the president refuse to pursue the matter. But Jackson is persistent. To buttress his case, he has taken the unusual step of sharing the Bormann evidence with Federal Bureau of Investigation director J. Edgar Hoover.

"My suggestion," Jackson writes to Truman on this overcast June day, "is that the FBI be authorized to pursue thoroughly discreet inquiries of a preliminary nature in South America.

"First, it is possible Bormann is there.

"Second, even if he is not, publicity might be given to the fact that this information was laid before United States officials, who did nothing and therefore are charged to be, in effect, protecting him.

"I have submitted this summary to Mr. Hoover and am authorized to say that it meets with his approval. You may inform him of your wishes directly or through me, as you prefer."

Harry Truman gets the message.

When the president arrives in Washington on Friday, June 18, his face is flushed from sunburn, because of many hours outdoors giving speeches. But rather than take the weekend off, he works Saturday and Sunday.

It is Monday morning, June 21, when Harry Truman is presented with Justice Jackson's letter. The wording appears friendly and official, but Truman knows a warning when he sees it. The slightest murmur that he is soft on a notorious Nazi war criminal could affect the election. The fact of the matter is that hundreds of SS officials are now in the United States, with some even working for the CIA. This is a truth that must never be revealed.

On September 3, 1946, President Truman had signed a top-secret order permitting German scientists into America to help develop the nation's new rocket program. Known as Operation Paperclip, this presidential decision would allow more than one thousand former Nazis and Nazi collaborators to work in the United States.

If word leaks about America's apathetic stance on Nazi war criminals, it would not just derail the Truman presidency but would also create the unthinkable situation of giving the Soviet Union the high moral ground on this very emotional matter.

Thus, President Harry Truman authorizes the FBI to hunt for Martin Bormann.

8

December 24, 1959
Cologne, Germany
Dawn

Nazi terror is back!
Bright red paint drips down the Gothic brownstone exterior of the Roonstrasse Synagogue. A monument to those who lost their lives in the Holocaust is also defaced. It has been just two months since the Jewish place of worship was reopened to the public, twenty years after it was burned to the ground by rampaging fanatics of the Third Reich. A swastika the color of blood and the hateful words *Juden Raus*—"Jews out"—now defames the stately structure. Cologne police are already looking for the suspects, but the damage is done. This city that has been home to Jews longer than any place in Germany is once again rife with mistrust. It is a horrifying reminder that Adolf Hitler's pledge to "exterminate" the Jewish race and "root it out, branch by branch," is still followed by some German citizens.

The problem of anti-Semitism is not unique to Germany. It has existed since the ancient days of the Greeks and Romans, was nurtured during the early times of the Christian Church, and has been a continuous presence throughout Europe for the past several centuries. Even in the United States, there is a growing prejudice against the Jews. This powerful hatred has ethnic, religious, and economic roots. Among some people there is great resentment over what many perceive to be Jewish control of the financial world.

During his rise to power, Hitler stoked these suspicions, blaming Germany's World War I loss on Jewish financial treachery. All of that seemed to have diminished with Germany's defeat in the Second World War. Those Jews who chose not to immigrate to Israel resumed their lives in Germany. Synagogues have been rebuilt, and Jewish families no longer live in fear. But as the sun rises over the nearby Rhine River on this crisp winter morning, wounds have been reopened.

The older Jews of Cologne are wary. They recall that horrible night before the war, when the Roonstrasse Synagogue was defiled for the first time. It was the evening of November 9, 1938. In a wave of unprecedented destruction and terror that went well into the next morning, Hitler and his associates put the German Jews on notice.

Coincidentally, November 9 is the fifteenth anniversary of Hitler's famous "Beer Hall Putsch," in which the Nazis staged a failed takeover of the Bavarian government.* Hitler was subsequently convicted of treason and sentenced to five years in Landsberg Prison, where he famously wrote his manifesto, *Mein Kampf*.

Kristallnacht: Jewish homes, businesses, and places of worship throughout Germany were destroyed. Many, such as the Roonstrasse Synagogue, one of six Jewish holy places in Cologne, were burned to the ground. Hundreds of Jews died, while an estimated thirty thousand more were taken into custody—eventually sent to concentration camps. The German police did nothing as torch-bearing SS mobs sought anything Jewish to burn and shattered shop windows. When arrests were finally made, it was not the SS or those doing

---

* The name comes from the Bürgerbräukeller, a beer hall in central Munich from which Hitler tried to stage his revolution.

the destruction who were taken into custody but rather Jews who tried to fight back.

Most calamities begin with a minor incident, this the Jews of Cologne know all too well. What started as Adolf Hitler blaming Jewish politicians for the loss of World War I spread into the vandalism of *Kristallnacht*, then later became the unrestrained brutality of the Nazi death camps. Innocent children even became the subject of vile medical experiments conducted by Nazi doctors. As one seventeen-count indictment against a Nazi physician specified, the doctor was charged with "killing numerous people with phenol, benzene, and/or air injections; killing numerous prisoners in the gas chambers; killing one fourteen-year-old girl by splitting her head with a dagger . . . injecting dye into the eyes of women and children, which killed them, and ordering that a number of prisoners be shot because they would not write to their loved ones saying they were being well treated."

Despite that gruesome document, filed against one Dr. Josef Mengele, some Germans *still* refuse to condemn anti-Semitic behavior. Behind the curtain, known Nazis are being aided and abetted.

The notorious Mengele is one of them.

⚡⚡

As the people of Cologne wake up to the vandalism of the Roonstrasse Synagogue, 250 miles south in Bavaria, citizens of the small farm town of Günzburg remain silent about a Nazi sighting in their midst.

The Bavarian hamlet was once accustomed to the presence of the SS—so much so that the United States made it the subject of special postwar scrutiny. The local Nazi Party *Kreiswirtschaftsberater*—economic adviser—was arrested and interrogated twice. The elderly gentleman was a World War I veteran whose farm equipment company had benefited greatly through his membership in the National Socialist Party. More than a thousand residents of Günzburg worked in his factories, building threshing machines and manure spreaders. The local titan was known to be a cold, hardworking man whose

Josef Mengele, the infamous Angel of Death, shown here in a passport photo from 1956

wife was equally distant and industrious. Together, they raised three boys, though one has died since the war ended—and another has vanished.

The Americans care little about the German businessman, but they would very much like to talk with his missing son, Josef—the same Josef Mengele who was called the Angel of Death at Auschwitz. But Mengele was spirited out of Germany a decade ago. At first his father swore his son was missing in action. Later, he lied that Josef was dead. Eventually the American investigators got tired of looking.

Had they investigated further, U.S. authorities might have found that Karl Mengele knew that his fugitive son was living in South America. The elder Mengele not only funded his son's escape to exile but has financed Josef's life since then. His devotion is so unwavering that the widow of Karl's deceased younger son was actually sent by the father to Argentina to marry Josef. Martha Mengele and her son from that first marriage, Karl-Heinz, arrived in Buenos Aires in 1956.

But now that arrangement has been fractured. Martha and the boy remain in Buenos Aires while Josef has fled to Paraguay, the poorest country in South America. The reason he left his family was a gut belief that Nazi hunters were closing in—in that, Josef Mengele was correct.

At the same time Isser Harel and the Mossad were tracking Adolf Eichmann closely, they were also zeroing in on Mengele. But he eluded them. And now his new hiding place is unknown to anyone but his family.

Physically, Mengele is almost unchanged. He is approaching fifty, but his hair is still dark brown with few signs of going gray. The gap-toothed smile that even some Auschwitz prisoners amazingly called "charming" still comes easily, although it is now hidden beneath a bushy mustache. He still whistles to himself. Mengele's hobbies, if they can be described as such, are reading medical books and acting as a physician whenever he can. Indeed, Argentinean authorities arrested him a year ago for performing illegal abortions and otherwise practicing medicine without a license. Until the arrest, Mengele had believed himself completely safe in Argentina. His wife had openly taken his last name, and Mengele had begun telling friends his true identity. But even though the charges against Mengele were quickly dropped for lack of evidence, the arrest troubled him deeply. Weary lines now form around his brown eyes as he finds himself unable to sleep at night. Friends note that he is easily agitated and often nods off during the day.

Under normal conditions, an individual must live in Paraguay at least five years to be granted citizenship, but because of a pro-Nazi government and perhaps hefty bribes, Josef Mengele has become a Paraguayan national in just six months. His passport number is 293,348. "Jose" Mengele, as his identity card now calls him, even lives in a heavily anti-Semitic German-speaking region of southeastern Paraguay known as Nuevo Germania—New Germany. The vegetation is tropical: palm trees, jungle, and dirt roads. The homes, however, are Southern German to the core, designed to look and feel just like the Fatherland. Swastikas sometimes decorate local restaurants, and framed photographs of Adolf Hitler are occasionally seen.

The year 1959 has been uncomfortable for the Angel of Death. On June 5, just one month after his hasty flight from Argentina, West German authorities issued a worldwide warrant for Mengele's arrest.

But that did not prevent Paraguay from granting Mengele a passport and citizenship. When West German agents proceeded to the capital city of Asunción with orders to review all files on Josef Mengele, the Paraguayan authorities sanitized the paperwork, rendering the investigation useless.

Then on November 17, 1959, Karl Mengele died in Günzburg. He was seventy-five. His death came after the best year in the history of his business, for the success of their new Doppel-Trumpf manure spreader has allowed the company to double its size to two thousand employees. It was rumored that West Germany's secret police would be incognito at the funeral, in the hopes that Josef Mengele might try to slip into the crowd to pay his respects to his father. Just a few years ago, in 1956, the Angel of Death did actually travel to Switzerland for a family skiing vacation. He was never stopped or questioned, and returned to South America without incident. The vacation would be one of the few times that his son Rolf, from his first marriage that ended in divorce, had the chance to speak with his father in person.

But West German agents do not attend the graveside service. If they had, they would have seen a massive floral wreath that Josef Mengele sent anonymously, with the words "Greetings from Afar" across the ribbon.

Authorities might also have noticed something ominous at the funeral. A bearded stranger stands on the outskirts of the cemetery wearing sunglasses. This is odd, as the first days of the Bavarian winter, when the light is pale, have descended. Nobody thinks to approach the stranger to ask his business, or why he would intrude upon a private family burial. However, his appearance is a poorly kept secret in town. Students at the local Catholic girls' school know him to be the man who has been secretly lodging there for about a week.

That evening, the bearded stranger disappears.

For years to come, when the people of Günzburg are asked about whether Josef Mengele attended his father's funeral, they will adopt a tight-lipped code of secrecy.

Incredibly, some of these folk will wonder why the world cannot show forgiveness to the brutal Mengele.*

⚡⚡

In Cologne, where the Roonstrasse Synagogue has been cleansed of the hateful markings, there have been arrests. Two youths swearing allegiance to a neo-Nazi Party are imprisoned. Their actions have an unlikely inspiration: the word *Kristallnacht* is uttered again and again by the local people who remember that night all too well. Within days, copycat crimes in New York, Vienna, London, and even South Africa will demonstrate that Nazi fanaticism has been reborn. For a solid month, well into January 1960, Jewish sites worldwide are desecrated.

⚡⚡

In Jerusalem, Isser Harel and the Mossad seethe. "The worldwide scope of these paintings of swastikas and vilifications aroused grave anxiety," Harel will write.

But rather than just wringing his hands, Harel plans to do something about the Nazi revival.

And soon.

---

* Opinion is divided over whether Josef Mengele attended his father's burial. Many say there is no photographic evidence to support this claim. However, Petra Kelly, a German politician who attended the Catholic girls' school in Günzburg at the time of the funeral, claimed in 1985 that several of the nuns in residence told her that Mengele spent four to five days hiding in the local convent. Nazi hunter Simon Wiesenthal has made a similar claim.

9

March 3, 1960
Buenos Aires, Argentina
Morning

The Mossad is on the move.

Agent Zvi Aharoni landed at Buenos Aires's Ezeiza Airport two days ago, traveling on a diplomatic passport. Aharoni is a loner skilled in espionage. He is not a formal member of the Israeli spy agency but has been borrowed from Shin Bet, Israel's version of the FBI. Aharoni's primary strength is interrogation: there is no man better qualified to question a high-level suspect in order to secure conviction in a court of law.

Aharoni travels under the name Rodan, taking the cover from his old wartime friend Bobby Rodan, with whom he served in Italy. The anti-Semitic violence that began in Germany has also spread to Argentina. Aharoni poses as an employee of the Israeli Ministry of Foreign Affairs, allegedly traveling to South America to investigate this global rise of anti-Jewish fervor. He utilizes the Israeli embassy on tranquil Arroyo Street as his home base of operations.

In fact, Aharoni is in Argentina to identify once and for all the location of Adolf Eichmann. If the Nazi is alive, the Mossad plans to kidnap Eichmann and smuggle him to Israel. Despite his considerable skills in extracting the truth from men who would prefer to keep silent, Zvi Aharoni believes it would be easier to kill Eichmann and make it look like an accident. But no less than Israeli prime minister David Ben-Gurion has decreed that Eichmann must stand trial for his war crimes in Jerusalem. The global rise in anti-Semitism demands that Nazi atrocities be publicly exposed, so that such horror can never happen again.

But first, of course, Eichmann must be located.

Agent Aharoni flew out of Jerusalem on February 26. He made stops in several South American countries along the way to give credence to his cover story. He traveled light, just a suitcase and a sealed diplomatic pouch containing a thick dossier on Adolf Eichmann, which includes his SS personnel file and physical measurements. Aharoni has committed the documents and old photographs to memory.

On the evening of March 1, he finally landed in Buenos Aires. The late summer heat was intense, even so late in the day. After depositing the Eichmann dossier in a safe at the Israeli embassy, he checked into his hotel and went to his room. Sylvia Hermann, the only eyewitness so far to Eichmann's location, has moved to America to attend college. However, that does not matter to Aharoni. He prefers to go it alone and has made no attempt to contact Lothar Hermann or his beautiful daughter.

At his hotel, Aharoni pored through the local phone books, looking for the name "Klement."

He found two listings.

Now, two days later, using a newly purchased street map, Aharoni drives his rented Fiat down the tree-lined dirt streets of the Olivos neighborhood. At first, he passes by large villas, but those are soon replaced by crumbling apartment buildings. He is searching for 4261 Chacabuco Street, an apartment, and the suspected home of Eichmann.

Aharoni is almost forty. He made his name by interrogating captured Nazis for the British during the war. He is a thin man known for being stubborn, honest, and logical. His feelings about Eichmann are very clear—the Nazi was responsible for the deaths of many relatives and friends, and if not for a series of fortunate events, Aharoni himself might have been one of Eichmann's victims.

Parking the Fiat five hundred yards from the apartment on Chacabuco Street, Zvi Aharoni wonders to himself if finding this wanted mass murderer can really be so simple as looking up a name and address in the phone book.

⚡⚡

It has been three months since Israeli intelligence reluctantly reopened the Eichmann file. Fritz Bauer returned to Israel in December 1959 with new evidence from a second source, a high-ranking former SS officer who requested that his name not be revealed, who claimed that Adolf Eichmann traveled to Argentina under the name Ricardo Klement.

Bauer's contact assured him that Eichmann is living in Buenos Aires under this name. A check of the records showed that Lothar Hermann previously stated that "Klement" was the name on one of the electricity meters at 4261 Chacabuco Street.

Bauer did not hand this information directly to the Mossad, as he felt Isser Harel had mishandled the investigation. Instead, he flew to Jerusalem and arranged a meeting with Israeli attorney general Haim Cohen. Bauer didn't choose Cohen at random. The balding, middle-aged jurist is considered a founder of Israeli law, and even the "conscience of this country," in the words of one prominent Israeli judge.

This matter of conscience is what drives Fritz Bauer. He is still haunted by the memory of signing the loyalty oath to Nazi Germany that allowed him to be freed from a concentration camp before the war.* Bauer is also well aware that he is living a double life, married to a Danish woman since 1943 but secretly pursuing male lovers. The only blemish on Bauer's otherwise pristine legal reputation is a prewar arrest for soliciting gay prostitutes in Denmark—a fact he struggles to keep hidden from his German legal counterparts.†

Perhaps Bauer's biggest personal contradiction is that he pretends not to be Jewish. Fearing that his fellow German prosecutors will think him a man whose zeal for tracking Nazis would lead to witch hunts, he keeps his religion a secret.

Yet as a Jew living in Germany, he is deeply unsettled by the rising national desire to pretend the Holocaust never happened. Death camps are not mentioned in school textbooks, and incredibly, the actions of Adolf Hitler and the Nazis are sometimes taught as heroic. A neo-Nazi group known as the German Reich Party is growing in power. Even now, in West Germany, there is talk of reducing the statute of limitations for murder to twenty years. This means that in just five years Adolf Eichmann and every other Nazi war criminal will be shielded from paying for their crimes.

An apathetic Isser Harel reluctantly attended the meeting with Bauer and Attorney General Cohen. The drive from Tel Aviv to Jerusalem is long and he resented having to make the journey for an investigation gone cold. He considered the invitation to be a courtesy, but he soon learned that this was not the case.

Fritz Bauer's true intentions were to humiliate the Mossad leader. After presenting the new intelligence about Eichmann, Bauer

---

* The document that allowed Bauer to be released from the Heuberg concentration camp read, "We unconditionally support the Fatherland in the German fight for honor and peace." One of Bauer's fellow inmates and a good friend, Kurt Schumacher, refused to sign. He would not be released from German custody until the end of the war in 1945, making him one of the longest-serving prisoners of the Third Reich. Fritz Bauer openly marveled at this display of "incredible belief and courage."

† Paragraph 175, the article of German law prohibiting intimate relations between men, was first passed in 1871. Homosexual acts were subject to criminal prosecution. It was not until 1994 that this law was repealed.

taunted Harel's incompetence. "This is simply unbelievable!" Bauer yelled. "Here we have the name Klement: Two completely independent sources, who are strangers to each other, mention this name. Any second-class policeman would be able to follow such a lead! Just go and ask the nearest butcher or greengrocer and you will learn all there is to know about him!"

There was a fourth man at the meeting—Zvi Aharoni. The spy was there by order of Attorney General Cohen, who has made use of his specialized services on numerous occasions for cases involving espionage and high treason. The two men have enormous respect for each other and maintain a friendship outside their work.

The same cannot be said of Aharoni and Isser Harel. They drove up from Tel Aviv together but spoke little. Aharoni was insulted that he was not told about the Eichmann case before. He'd been in Buenos Aires on top-secret business just a few months ago and could have easily detoured to the house on Chacabuco Street to see if Hermann's story was true.

After hearing Bauer's outburst, Aharoni collected his revenge.

"I want Zvi to go to Buenos Aires and check out this story once and for all," demanded Attorney General Cohen. "We can't play around with this any longer."

Isser Harel does not take orders from Haim Cohen. But the consequences of not following through on the investigation could be enormously embarrassing. The payoff, on the other hand, could be world changing.

Isser Harel had no choice: the Mossad leader reopened the Eichmann case.

ᛋᛋ

The boy was born in Germany and given the name Hermann Aronheim in 1921. His father had fought for the Fatherland in the trenches of World War I, but when the Nazis came to power Heinrich Aronheim's years of service did not matter because he was a Jew. No longer allowed to practice law or otherwise pursue his chosen career as a result of growing Nazi oppression, he moved his family to Berlin in the hopes of being less conspicuous in the big city. Heinrich was wrong. With every passing year, life became more horrendous for German Jews. Simple pleasantries like eating in a café or attending the theater were banned. The books of Jewish writers were burned in great bonfires, and Jewish musicians were forbidden from performing the works of Bach and Brahms.

In 1937 Heinrich died of cancer. His widow, Eugenie, took charge. She wisely arranged for the family to immigrate to Palestine. It was a year before the proper documents could be arranged, but in late October 1938, just a few short weeks before *Kristallnacht*, she and her two young sons began the journey to Palestine by boarding the train in Berlin.*

"At the station we met some of our relatives," Hermann Aronheim will later remember. He was just seventeen when the time came to flee Germany.

"They had come to say a tearful good-bye. We were well aware that centuries of Jewish life and Jewish culture in Germany were coming to an end. But obviously no one could conjure up a detailed picture of the approaching 'Endlösung' (Final Solution), even in his wildest fantasies. The fact was, that we were never again to see any of our relatives. They all died in the Holocaust."

The journey by train and ship to Palestine was grueling, but upon stepping ashore in Tel Aviv—at the time, the world's only Jewish city—Aronheim and his family felt instantly at home.

"We had reached the land of our dreams—our Holy Land," he will later write. "Everything about this new country was strange to me, from the very first day I had the feeling of having come home. I knew that we belonged here. Here, being a Jew was normal. We were not an unloved minority. Here, no one would shout 'dirty Jew' at our backs. No one would taunt us with 'Go home to Palestine.' We had come home."

---

* Years before resorting to mass murder during World War II, the Nazis first tried to rid the nation of Jews by "the Zionist emigration of the Jews from Germany by any means." Of the estimated 550,000 Jews living in Germany in 1933, 130,000 emigrated by 1938.

Thus, Hermann Aronheim was no more. The seventeen-year-old immigrant adopted the Hebrew spelling of his name: Zvi Aharoni.

A quarter century later, as he prepares to stalk Adolf Eichmann, the Mossad agent is haunted by the knowledge that his father had to die in order that his family might be safe. "If he had lived another year, I would have gone up the chimney at Auschwitz," Aharoni will recall.

And the man who would have sent him there is Adolf Eichmann.

⚡⚡

At almost the exact same time that Zvi Aharoni's family reached sanctuary in Palestine, Adolf Eichmann's personal war against the Jews began in earnest.

Working from his new office in Vienna, the newly christened Obersturmführer started the ethnic purification of Austria by brutally accelerating the emigration of the nation's Jews. Ironically, a year earlier he had traveled to Palestine to explore the option of forcibly relocating the Jewish population to that location, but the logistical and financial realities were too great. Now he just wanted them gone, leaving it to the Jews to figure out their own final destination.

Within eight months, almost one hundred thousand Jews were evicted from their homes and forced to leave Austria. The most influential Jewish leaders were sent to concentration camps. Others became refugees, wandering Europe as winter approached. Traveling with only the clothes on their back and a few minor possessions, they desperately searched for a nation willing to take them in. In a tragic act of misjudgment, the first choice for many was Poland, which would soon be home to more death camps than any other nation in Europe. But by the fall of 1938, even Poland had closed its borders.

Infuriated by the cruelty of these German deportations and forced emigrations, a young Jew living in Paris marched into the German embassy and assassinated a low-level diplomat named Ernst vom Rath on November 7, 1938. Two days later, enraged Nazis used the murder as a pretext for the night of terror known as *Kristallnacht*.

ᛋᛋ

Zvi Aharoni prepared himself to hunt Eichmann by meeting with Fritz Bauer. The interrogation was friendly but thorough. By the time Aharoni flew to Buenos Aires, he was convinced that Ricardo Klement and Adolf Eichmann were one and the same.

It has been established that Eichmann was recently employed by a corporation known as CAPRI, which specializes in hydroelectric power. He also owned a rabbit farm, which went bankrupt in 1958 due to crossbreeding issues.

The idea of Eichmann needing to work for a living is still confusing to the Israeli investigators, who labor under the belief that the Nazis smuggled large amounts of gold out of the country to secure the future of the Fourth Reich. In the final days of the war, the U.S. Army found gold coins, bundles of banknotes, and crated boxes of gold bullion and platinum hidden in the caves of the Merkers salt mines. Surely that was only one of many Nazi caches.*

Further suggestions of Eichmann's fantastic wealth came from a series of stories in the Austrian press in 1954. The newspaper *Der Abend* published reports that Eichmann was alive and well in Europe, eager to claim his stash of stolen Nazi gold. The rumors still persist, even in Argentina, among the expatriate Nazi community. It is not uncommon for fellow Germans to ask Eichmann about his gold after they've enjoyed a few lagers together at the ABC *Biergarten*.

Either Eichmann is not receiving any of the stolen Nazi wealth or he is under orders to lead a modest life until the Nazi hunters go away.

---

* On April 4, 1945, shortly after Gen. George S. Patton's Third Army crossed the Rhine River and advanced toward the German heartland, displaced persons told American intelligence officers about gold and other precious treasures being hidden in the nearby Kaiseroda potassium mine. The main shaft was twenty-one hundred feet below the surface. Upon entering the mine, American soldiers found long rooms filled with currency, gold, silver, platinum, and precious works of art. The Germans had been attempting to smuggle this wealth out of Berlin, to be hidden and later used to fund a resurgent Fourth Reich.

Time has not changed Eichmann's heart. Among the recently unearthed new research is a vignette Zvi Aharoni learns from a source close to Eichmann. The South American country of Bolivia has recently been enduring political upheaval. It was suggested by some in Argentina's Nazi community that Eichmann travel there to take a temporary position with state security services to help the Bolivian leaders, who are openly sympathetic to the Nazi cause.

"When I hear those words, 'state security services,'" Eichmann is said to have responded, "my appetite for killing is whetted all over again."

⚡⚡

Zvi Aharoni arrives at 4261 Chacabuco Street on March 3, 1960. The house is white, with a terra-cotta roof and ringed with a gated fence.

The apartments are empty. Rather than the Eichmann family, Zvi Aharoni encounters a team of house painters who have come to apply a fresh coat at the home owner's request. "The German," as the painters refer to Adolf Eichmann, moved three weeks ago.

That the case is moving so slowly is frustrating. But Zvi Aharoni now knows that Lothar Hermann, the blind man who first claimed to have located Eichmann, was essentially correct.

"I could not return to Tel Aviv without a conclusive answer," Aharoni will write. "I therefore had to accept calculated risks. It was clear to me that Harel would never have approved certain steps had he been informed. But now I was on my own and my own boss. I carried full responsibility for all my decisions and maneuvers."

Zvi Aharoni is certain of one thing: The war criminal *is* somewhere in Buenos Aires.

At least for now.

10

March 8, 1960
Buenos Aires, Argentina
5:15 p.m.

Zvi Aharoni sits in his rented Fiat on the corner of Avenida Santa Fe and Avenida Sarmiento. With him is "Juan," a young local man who has volunteered to help the Mossad at any time, no questions asked. These *sayanim*—"helpers" in Hebrew*— are Jews who live outside Israel and make themselves available to help the homeland. They are taught not to ask questions and do not receive payment for their services.

Juan does not know why he is sitting in this compact vehicle, nor does he know Zvi Aharoni's real name. Yesterday he sat with Aharoni for three hours. He has so far spent another sixty minutes holding vigil today. Aharoni has only told him that they are searching for a man who is thought to work as a mechanic in a shop across the street from where they now sit. Aharoni's investigation has led him to believe that Dieter Eichmann gets off work at 5:00 p.m., but thus far there has been no sign of him. If they do spot him, his next

---

* The singular form is *sayan* ("helper").

step is to follow Dieter home from work to the family residence, where Aharoni believes Adolf Eichmann is living under the name Ricardo Klement.

At last, two men emerge from the garage. One is a dark-haired man of roughly fifty years, wearing thick glasses. The other is blond and wears blue overalls, looking to be no more than twenty years old.

Believing the young man to be Dieter Eichmann, Aharoni turns the key in the Fiat's ignition and slips the car into gear. The two workmen sit one behind the other on a dirty black moped and drive away. The Israeli spy and his assistant follow at a discreet distance as the small motorcycle maneuvers down Avenida Santa Fe toward the section of Buenos Aires known as San Fernando.

Ten minutes pass.

Zvi Aharoni has extensive training in surveillance and knows to take care that the driver of the moped does not notice the Fiat traveling a few car lengths back. The Israeli allows a gap to open, sure that so long as he can see the moped there will be little difficulty tracking the vehicle.

But trouble arises as the road leads into the heart of San Fernando. A long and slow funeral procession meanders through the main square. All traffic comes to a standstill. Aharoni's Fiat is stuck.

The small and agile moped, however, has no such problems. Its driver nimbly weaves it through the traffic.

Forced to stop, Zvi Aharoni and his volunteer assistant can only watch hopelessly as the moped disappears.

When the traffic clears, the Fiat breaks down. It is towed back to the rental company, where the pursuers are told there are no more cars for rent.

⚡⚡

The killer Adolf Eichmann is now just days away from his fifty-fourth birthday, although his Argentinean identity card lists him as seven years younger. He has lived in South America for almost a decade. There is no record of what the former SS-Obersturmbannführer did with the gold and other wealth the SS stole from so many hapless Jews during the war, but he clearly does not possess it now. Since his arrival in Argentina, Eichmann has scraped by on a series of low-paying jobs doing manual labor. In his free time, he plays the violin and has an occasional drink at the ABC with other former Nazis in downtown Buenos Aires. There, Eichmann enjoys a level of notoriety and respect for his wartime atrocities.

But as time has passed, and many Germans have secretly moved back to Europe, Eichmann's status has begun to change. He complains about feeling abandoned. His eldest son, Nick, will one day claim that much of this is the work of a fellow notorious war criminal. "Dr. Mengele had spread the word: avoid Eichmann. Getting close to him could be dangerous," the young Eichmann will bitterly recall.

Now Mengele is gone, running off to hide in Paraguay, leaving Eichmann as the most wanted SS murderer in Argentina. The tension continues to escalate as prosecution of Nazi war criminals by German authorities like Fritz Bauer has raised awareness about the Holocaust. The West German government is still being secretive about former Nazi war criminals, but it is reluctantly taking steps to find and prosecute men like Eichmann. This is not being done out of a moral imperative but because the Soviet Union has provided East Germany with captured Nazi documents. The West German intelligence community has reason to believe that it is the intention of the East Germans to smear their West German counterparts and in the process portray West Germany as soft on vicious Nazi war criminals.

In Germany, Adolf Eichmann has been the subject of numerous books and magazine articles. In Argentina, in an attempt to maintain his low profile, Eichmann's sons are forbidden to talk about their father or the family in public. Adolf Eichmann is known to impulsively throw a hard slap at their cheeks to keep them in line.

In late 1958, resigned to his dreary life in Argentina and sensing that the statute of limitations on his millions of murders would never expire, Eichmann sought to make a more permanent life for his family. He paid 56,000 pesos for a plot of land on Garibaldi

Street in the Buenos Aires suburb of San Fernando.* Lot no. 14 is a half mile wide by a half mile long. It is isolated, undeveloped, swampy, and has no access to electricity, running water, or sewage lines. But during a short period of unemployment, Eichmann threw himself into building a new home on the site. Working obsessively, he drained the land and constructed an impregnable bunker with walls several feet thick.

The house was unfinished in March 1959, when Eichmann took a job working in a Mercedes-Benz factory earning 5,500 pesos a month sorting replacement parts in the company warehouse.† Some of his fellow employees immigrated to Argentina from Germany and Austria after the war. Many were in the SS, but one of the supervisors is a Jew. One female coworker will remember Eichmann as "very polite and pleasant. Every time he saw me, he said hello, and every evening when he left he said, 'See you tomorrow!'"

The bus ride to work is two hours each way. Eichmann does not arrive home until 8:00 p.m. most evenings, so he and his sons could only work on developing their new property on the weekends. But just over a year after starting construction, Eichmann is able to move his family the half-dozen miles from Chacabuco Street into the flat-roofed, one-story brick structure. It is not the same luxury to which he grew accustomed during the war, living in villas and luxury hotels, pampered by servants, his every whim attended to. But the door and shutters are made of thick wood, in the Bavarian fashion. Kerosene lamps substitute for electricity, and running water is still nonexistent. The home sits on a small rise, with a front porch and living-room windows specially designed to give Eichmann a clear view hundreds of yards in every direction.

So it is that Adolf Eichmann hides in plain sight, walking to and

---

* About $650 American dollars at the time. This is an estimated $5,500 in modern money.

† Roughly $65 dollars, or $550 in today's currency. This was actually slightly higher than the average Argentine wage earner, leading some historians to believe Eichmann was given a preferential salary due to his SS connections in Argentina.

from the bus stop each morning. He doesn't go into the city much, preferring to spend his weekends puttering around the house and playing his violin. To the casual observer, he is nothing more than a middle-aged man determined to live out his life in his new home. Few of his coworkers at Mercedes know his real name or past. Not a single one suspects that he is proud to have been the notorious "Czar of the Jews" who brazenly executed a war within a war, striving to murder as many Jews as possible within German-held territory.

Now, he is simply Ricardo Klement, the illegitimate son of Anna Klement from Bolzano, Italy; Argentine identity card number 1378538.

But that figure is a sham. The numerals by which Eichmann is rightly identified are 45,326—the digits designating his Nazi Party membership number.

He may have a new job, and he may have built a new home, but Adolf Eichmann's past will have far more bearing on his future. And unbeknownst to the former Obersturmbannführer, those who wish to make him pay for those transgressions are closing in.

⚡⚡

It is March 11, three days after Aharoni and Juan got stuck in the funeral procession and lost sight of Dieter Eichmann. The two men have tried unsuccessfully to follow the black moped every night since. Both men are uncertain if they are even tailing the proper individual.

In a burst of inspiration, Aharoni instructs Juan to pay another visit to 4261 Chacabuco Street. On his last visit, one of the carpenters had let slip the address of Dieter Eichmann's place of work. Perhaps Juan might get him to elaborate further.

It is 4:15 in the afternoon as Juan knocks on the door of Eichmann's former apartment. Just as Sylvia Hermann did so many years ago, he steps inside. A group of workers tell him that the carpenter he is looking for is upstairs.

"I met him on the second floor where he was presently working," Juan's report to the Israeli embassy will read. "I asked him for the new address of the former tenant."

The carpenter is a bachelor in his midfifties who speaks with a thick European accent. He tells Juan that he has been to the new Eichmann house, where he did work for which he has not yet been paid. He gives Juan detailed directions, right down to which bus number goes past the house and how many pesos the ticket costs.

"Are you absolutely certain?" Juan asks.

"I am," replies the carpenter.

This should be the high point of Juan's short career as a *sayan*. Yet when he returns to Buenos Aires to brief Aharoni on his new findings, he also brings some disappointing news.

"What's the matter?" Aharoni asks. "Come on, let's have a drink."

Juan shakes his head.

"I'm sorry. I have bad news for you," Juan tells Aharoni. "All our work so far has been in vain. We have been following the wrong man."

"What wrong man?" replies Aharoni.

"Dito," he begins, referring to Dieter Eichmann in his thick Spanish accent, "is not the man we are looking for."

Aharoni refrains from saying anything. He has divulged just a small amount of information to Juan, only enough to move the operation forward in clandestine fashion. He has never uttered the word "Eichmann" to his *sayan*.

"His name is not Klement," Juan tells his spymaster. "It's Aichmann."

Aharoni will later write of that moment. "'Aichmann' and 'Eichmann' are clearly the same name. It took a great effort for me to remain calm."

Instead, the Israeli reassures his young charge. "Don't worry. You've done a fantastic job. Don't bother about the name. In the end, we'll get the right man and we will remember how much you helped us. Until then, if you still want to be helpful, don't talk to a living soul about this."

Dismissing Juan, who promises to maintain his silence, Zvi Aharoni hastens back to the embassy. He cables a message back to

Tel Aviv. The words are in code, but the subject matter is unmistakable: Adolf Eichmann has been found.

The address is 14 Garibaldi Street.

⚡⚡

It is nearing evening as Zvi Aharoni drives alone down Route 202 in the unincorporated northern suburbs of Buenos Aires. His rented Fiat has been replaced by a station wagon—chosen specifically for its unobtrusive appearance. The area is run-down, even poor, in Aharoni's estimation. He makes note of the lack of telephone poles and power lines. As he passes by the Eichmann residence, which is set fifty yards back off the road, he notices a short, heavyset woman with black hair standing on the porch. She is shabbily dressed. Zvi Aharoni no longer thinks that Eichmann would never live in such a run-down neighborhood or allow his family to dress in such a disheveled fashion. Without even having to take a second look, he is certain the woman is Vera Eichmann.

There is no sign of her husband.

Aharoni drives away, not wishing to draw attention to himself. With Eichmann so close to his grasp, the last thing the spy wishes to do is behave suspiciously and force the Nazi to run.

Aharoni returns to this sleepy section of town after dark, parking the car and slowly walking through an adjacent field toward the house. He is relieved that he isn't threatened by any barking dogs. When the day comes to kidnap Eichmann, the Israelis will be able to approach the house without advance warning of their arrival.

The intricacies of capturing Eichmann and returning him to Israel to trial are many. He is a legal resident of Argentina, making it illegal for the Israelis to kidnap him, no matter how heinous his crimes. Also, no extradition treaty exists between Argentina and Israel. Handing him over to Argentinean authorities would most likely mean that Eichmann would not be prosecuted. And finally, there is no regular air service between Israel and Argentina. Eichmann would have to be smuggled out of the country on board an Israeli freight ship.

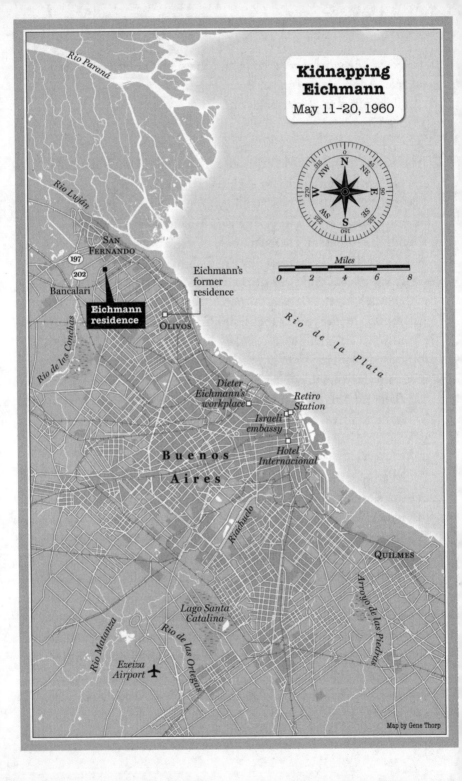

Those details will have to be sorted out in the future. For now, Aharoni simply wants to see Adolf Eichmann in the flesh and ensure that this is the man he is hunting. He walks back to his car in the dead of night and drives away without being detected. Every day thereafter, he returns to Garibaldi Street, becoming more and more familiar with the neighborhood.

But day after day passes with no sign of the killer.

Finally, Eichmann appears.

"Nineteen March," Aharoni will long remember. "On this day I saw him for the first time."

The spy expected to witness a man of monstrous physical proportions. Instead, he is stunned that the SS bureaucrat who murdered millions is thoroughly average—"a man of medium size and build, about fifty years old, with a high forehead and partially bald."

Aharoni writes an urgent report back to his superiors in Tel Aviv: "I am of the opinion that we should now begin with the next phase of the operation. I have no doubts that I have seen Eichmann."

But just to be sure, Aharoni returns to the Eichmann home and secretly photographs the man living at 14 Garibaldi Street.

On April 9, 1960, Zvi Aharoni returns to Tel Aviv. Exactly two weeks later, he once again lands in Buenos Aires. This time the spy affects a new look, growing a mustache and letting his hair grow longer while affecting the disguise of a German businessman. He will have no contact with any of the *sayanim* who helped him on his earlier visit. Indeed, a new level of secrecy is in place. Aharoni will not even be allowed to visit the Israeli embassy or stay in the same hotel as on his last visit. For this time, the spy has not returned to Argentina to track the movements of Adolf Eichmann, and he does not plan on flying home alone when he returns to Israel.

Zvi Aharoni and the Mossad are here to snatch the Obersturmbannführer. Somehow, someway, they will smuggle him out of Argentina and take him back to Israel to stand trial for his crimes.

Of course, it is illegal.

Of course, it must be done.

11

May 3, 1960
San Fernando, Argentina
Afternoon

Isser Harel sits in the passenger seat of Zvi Aharoni's rental car. The vehicle is "large, dependable," in Aharoni's words, easily capable of carrying several members of the ten-man Mossad hit team that has come to abduct Adolf Eichmann.

Right now it is just Aharoni and Harel, cruising slowly up and down the many roads on Route 202 leading to the Eichmann compound. The Mossad director is among the last Israeli operatives comprising Operation Eichmann to arrive in South America. Harel will leave the actual surveillance and snatch to the others, instead working logistics behind the scenes. It is a task perhaps as important as the proposed kidnapping itself. The man who once closed the Eichmann case for lack of evidence is now consumed by the small details of making this illegal operation succeed.

Aharoni points out the railway line whose raised bed offers a hidden place for observation, and the small kiosk where Eichmann steps off bus 203 each night at 7:40. He tells Harel of how

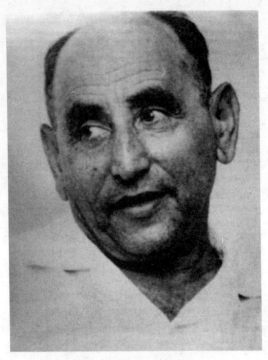

Isser Harel, the Mossad director who led the capture of Adolf Eichmann

Eichmann uses a special two-colored flashlight with red and white beams to guide himself home.

For Aharoni, this day represents the summation of his work. He is not merely showing Harel the details of Eichmann's neighborhood but showing off the results of countless hours of investigation. In the top-secret world in which both men live, there are few people with whom Aharoni can share his accomplishments.

As a final grand gesture, Aharoni turns a corner and deliberately slows his speed. He drives past the house itself, letting Harel take a long look. It is a brazen, though calculated, gesture on Aharoni's part. It is Tuesday, a working day. Eichmann will not be home for hours. Aharoni is gambling that Vera Eichmann is not as observant as her husband and will not notice the large vehicle driving slowly past the home, nor the two men staring carefully at her residence.

"I could sense that the cool, impenetrable Harel was deeply impressed," Aharoni will write of this moment. "However, he did not utter a word, not even when we saw the house from close up." But Isser Harel has also done his part, acquiring many items vital to the actual kidnapping. These include a forgery kit, wigs, makeup, false teeth, pocket cameras, and handcuffs. A doctor has been found to operate as a member of the team, and the proper drugs with which to sedate Eichmann have been placed under his care.

So it is that the sequence of events vital to kidnapping Adolf Eichmann have fallen into place: Aharoni's successful identification and confirmation of the Nazi's location; assemblage of the Operation Eichmann task force; arrival into Argentina; and acquisition of items necessary for the capture.

In the few short weeks that the team has been in Argentina, they have also rented two safe houses, code names *Tira* and *Doron*. They have purchased vehicles large enough to stage an abduction, and even fashioned two-sided license plates so that registration numbers can easily be reversed

"If we succeed," Isser Harel has commented to one of the operatives, "this will be the first time in history that a court of justice of the Jewish people will judge a man who slaughtered multitudes of Jews. That is why I see in this action a humane and moral significance that cannot be applied to anything we have ever undertaken before."

Yet, as vital as each of those actions have been, the next two steps are the most crucial. Harel will meet with members of the team each day to coordinate activities, giving or refusing approval of plans as he sees fit.

The most important action, of course, is taking physical possession of Eichmann. Even as he drives past the house on Garibaldi Street with Zvi Aharoni, Harel can only guess at how this will take place. He has assigned one of his top operatives, Mossad agent Rafi Eitan, to be in charge of this phase. It was Eitan, the Israeli-born commando who led many famous operations during the nation's postwar struggle for independence, who saw the need for handcuffs and sedatives to subdue Eichmann.

But what comes after the kidnapping—should it be successful—will be the most daring action of all. Overpowering, subduing, and imprisoning Adolf Eichmann will mean nothing if the Mossad director cannot find a way to smuggle the Nazi out of Argentina.

And for that, Isser Harel has a plan.

⚡⚡

The distance between Buenos Aires and Tel Aviv is almost eight thousand miles. The Atlantic Ocean, equator, and continent of Africa stand between the two capital cities. Harel has just two options for transporting Adolf Eichmann: ship or plane.

Out of necessity, Israel has a thriving cargo shipping industry. The new nation borders several hostile Arab nations sworn to its destruction. However, Israel also possesses a significant coastline on the Mediterranean Sea. All goods being imported or exported from Israel travel by ship, through the two major ports at Haifa on the Mediterranean and Eilat on the Red Sea. During the early years of Israel's statehood, Israeli cargo ships were largely responsible for transporting the hundreds of thousands of new Jewish emigrants eager to flee Europe and make a new home in the Promised Land.

So it is natural that Isser Harel's first inclination is to smuggle Adolf Eichmann out of Argentina by cargo ship. Discreet inquiries are made to the ZIM Integrated Shipping Services, to see if coincidentally an Israeli ship might be sailing in South American waters during the month of May. Harel believes that diverting such a ship into the port at Buenos Aires would be suitably covert.

But no Israeli ships are scheduled to be in Argentinean waters. More daunting, such a diversion might go unnoticed to the world at large, but it would set off alarm bells throughout the oceanic cargo shipping industry.

When Harel inquires about the possibility of hiring a ship especially for the purpose of transporting Eichmann, perhaps disguised as a freighter taking on a load of frozen Argentinean beef, the results are just as discouraging. Such a ship would require at least one month to reach Buenos Aires and waste valuable time by stopping at ports along the way in order not to appear suspicious.

"I decided that transportation by sea would be too slow and might delay the operation by some vital weeks," Harel will write. "So I applied myself to a thorough investigation of the possibilities of air transport."

Even more than the sea, Israel is a country dependent upon air travel. The day after the nation's founding in May 1948, its Arab neighbors declared war and blockaded Israeli ports. Israel's air and ground defense force repelled an invasion, but with access to the Mediterranean cut off, the nation was forced to rely upon aircraft to import the munitions necessary to wage war. Foreign airlines refused to fly into Israel during the hostilities, forcing the fledgling nation to rely completely on their own civil aviation as a means of survival. In this spirit, Israel founded its own airline, El Al, whose name means "to the skies" in Hebrew.

In addition to regularly scheduled air travel, El Al is often called upon to perform missions of national interest. Operation Magic Carpet secretly transported 49,000 Yemenite Jews into Israel in 1949, while Operation Ezra and Nehemiah in 1951 flew almost 130,000 Iraqi Jews from that nation as part of a broader Jewish exodus from Muslim nations. El Al pilots taking part in these missions, as well as other covert operations, take great pride in their roles. Secretly, they refer to themselves as "the monkey business crews."*

However, more than a decade after El Al's founding, Israeli airplanes are still not in the habit of flying to South America, let alone to a nation that has openly shown sympathy for Adolf Hitler and the Third Reich. El Al can make the journey, having recently purchased two state-of-the-art propeller-driven Bristol Britannia air-

---

* A significant example of a secret venture was Operation Solomon, an airlift of 14,325 Ethiopian Jews to Israel on May 25–26, 1991. The political climate in Ethiopia at the time was unstable, and it was feared that a widespread massacre of these Jews was imminent. Thirty-five aircraft took part in the thirty-six-hour operation, including El Al luxury 747s.

craft capable of nonstop transatlantic flight. But El Al's current routes are restricted to Europe, Turkey, Iran, and New York. Isser Harel, however, is not deterred. He arranges a meeting with airline executives, asking if it would be possible to send a plane to Buenos Aires as a means of showcasing El Al's transatlantic capability, while pretending to be interested in opening a new route from Tel Aviv.

The Mossad director's timing could not be worse: May and June are the start of the tourist season. El Al will lose an extraordinary amount of revenue by loaning the Mossad a plane.

But fate intervenes. Ironically, it is the nation of Argentina that comes to Harel's rescue.

⚡⚡

From May 18 to May 25, 1810, Buenos Aires was the site of an insurrection that would go down in history as the May Revolution. After hundreds of years of oppression and colonization by Spain, the people of Argentina sought independence. The ruling Spanish naval viceroy was toppled and replaced by a local governing body known as the Primera Junta—the first junta. It would be years before Argentina was truly independent, but that exciting week in May was a turning point in the country's national history.

The festivities to celebrate the 150th anniversary of the revolution will begin on May 20, 1960. A wave of patriotism engulfs Argentina. Invitations have gone out to nations around the world to share in the moment. Much to its surprise, Israel is asked to participate. Through contacts within Israel's Ministry of Foreign Affairs, Isser Harel learns that his country's diplomats plan to attend.

Harel pounces. Carefully, so as not arouse suspicion, he inquires as to whether these diplomats would like to travel by plane.

They would, indeed. Israel's Department of Latin American Affairs considers traveling by air to be far more prestigious than a long voyage by ship. One representative even tells Harel that the arrival of an Israeli airplane in Buenos Aires would "enhance the prestige of the state still further, especially in the eyes of the Jewish community in South America."

With this knowledge in his grasp, Harel turns once more to El Al.

The Mossad director asks Mordechai Ben-Ari, the airline's deputy director, to come to his headquarters. Isser Harel's true occupation is unknown to most Israelis, but Ben-Ari is an insightful man. The Mossad offices are nondescript and nothing about Harel's spare suite screams that he is a spy. But Ben-Ari knows that Isser Harel is not in the business of arranging air travel for diplomatic legations. However, Ben-Ari does not voice objections, even when Harel informs him that the flight crew must be entirely of his choosing.

Mordechai Ben-Ari goes along with Harel's request, even though Ben-Ari's stomach is churning about the financial repercussions. El Al is still a young company and has yet to turn a profit. Abruptly altering its timetables and refunding airline tickets is not the best way of doing business. Yet the executive agrees.

Ben-Ari rises to leave. He gets as far as the door. With his hand resting on the knob, he turns to Harel. Ben-Ari wavers for a moment, a nervous smile crossing his face.

"Does it have anything to do with Eichmann?" he asks.

Isser Harel pauses. He is not allowed to confirm or deny such a question. Should the secret get out, the ramifications would be enormous. Harel himself might lose his job for this act of gross incompetence. But he is desperate for the help of Mordechai Ben-Ari and knows full well the burden he is placing on El Al.

Harel nods.

12

May 10, 1960
Mossad "Safe" Apartment, Buenos Aires
Late Evening

Adolf Eichmann has less than twenty-four hours of freedom—if all goes well.

"All honors should go to Zvi Aharoni," says Isser Harel, starting tonight's dress rehearsal for tomorrow night's kidnapping. "Without him we would not be sitting here."

Aharoni is shocked—and a little embarrassed. "The Old Man," as the agents have taken to calling Harel, is not prone to handing out compliments. Aharoni does not look to the right or left in this room filled with his fellow Israeli operatives, preferring to gaze straight forward until this awkward moment passes.

Harel continues laying out the scenario: The kidnapping will take place as Eichmann steps off bus 203 at 7:40 p.m. A secluded country road offers a better chance of capturing him without incident. Grabbing Eichmann from his home is too much of a liability—not only has the house been designed to keep out intruders, but there is also the potential that Eichmann's wife or sons might be armed.

The team will use two cars. One will park on the side of the road with the hood up, as if suffering from engine problems. Its headlights will remain on, shining at oncoming traffic to blind the drivers who might provide eyewitness testimony about the kidnapping.

The second vehicle will be filled with Israeli agents who will subdue Eichmann as he walks toward home. "At the moment of the snatch," Zvi Aharoni will later write, "[Eichmann] would only be able to see two of our people: Zvika standing next to the open driver's window and possibly me as driver . . . Rafi was to lie down on the floor in the back. As soon as Zvika and Zeev had overpowered Eichmann, [Rafi] would open the back door and help pull our captive inside. We then intended to tie him up and hide him under a blanket. After that, the run to the safe house could begin."

The plan is bold, yet has the potential to fail in a hundred different ways. Harel looks around the room at this elite group of operatives. They are all male, a fact that disturbs Harel enough that he is flying a female Mossad agent in from Tel Aviv to pose as a spouse to one of the spies. Harel feels this will attract less attention to the safe house. Yehudith Friedman was told of her assignment just four days ago and was due to arrive tonight. But as an example of how anything that can go wrong, *will* go wrong during a covert operation, she missed her connecting flight in Spain and will not arrive until tomorrow night—by which time the snatch will have either succeeded or failed.

Harel has already delayed the kidnapping of Adolf Eichmann by one day, which troubles him greatly. He is a strong believer that once an operation is set to go, even the slightest change in plans can prove costly. A nosy gardener at the *Doron* safe house, a secluded mansion two hours outside Buenos Aires once intended to hold Eichmann until he could be smuggled onto the El Al flight, makes that sanctuary unusable. So today has been spent transferring the cots, heaters, bedding, cookware, and canned food required for a lengthy stay into the *Tira* safe house. In a move designed to ensure complete redundancy in the event of problems, the team has rented a total of seven apartments or houses on which they can rely if *Tira*'s cover is blown. Isser Harel is normally very tightfisted with his operational budget, requiring his agents to stay in modest hotels and eat in inexpensive restaurants. But the Eichmann grab is too important to be done on the cheap.

One of the two large sedans leased for the abduction suffers a blown transmission and is in the garage for the day. Rather than being disturbed by the vehicle's problems, the agents are relieved that it happened before the kidnapping. An expensive luxury vehicle broken down on the side of the road would surely attract police attention. This might give Eichmann the chance to cry out for help. At the very least, the police would be sure to look inside the vehicle and ask about the bundle on the backseat floor.

But it is the exhaustion of his men that concerns Harel most of all. "Operators dare not undertake an action that demands supreme physical and mental exertion without every certainty they are fit to stand up to it," he will later explain.

Since their arrival in Buenos Aires two weeks ago, the Operation Eichmann team has worked around the clock, driving enormous distances to shadow Eichmann and canvas prospective escape routes. Their physical fatigue, however, is enhanced by mental anguish. The thrill each man felt upon seeing Adolf Eichmann in the flesh while performing their many reconnaissance missions is now replaced by the fear of failure. Many in the room worry they are just one day away from being arrested and sent to an Argentinean prison. Some wonder if they will ever see Israel again.

And even if the kidnapping goes off without issue, all of the men know that they won't be able to relax for at least ten days. The El Al flight that was supposed to arrive in two days has been delayed for a week. Thus, they will be forced to hide Eichmann for a while. A manhunt is sure to take place once police are informed of his kidnapping. Between now and the time their flight clears Argentinean airspace, the already drained team must practice around-the-clock discipline and vigilance.

"How long do you think we'll have to sit in prison if we're caught?" asks one agent.

"A few good years," replies Harel.

Silence fills the room.

※

As the team puts the final touches on their plan, startling news arrives from Israel. The Mossad is reporting that Dr. Josef Mengele is currently visiting Buenos Aires. Can it be possible for Isser Harel's agents to capture both Adolf Eichmann and Mengele in one amazing coup? Putting both men on trial in Israel would be an unprecedented triumph for Jewish justice.

Isser Harel secretly begins planning a second operation.

※

It is time to catch a war criminal.

Zvi Aharoni eases the sedan onto the shoulder of the country road. World War II ended fifteen years and four days ago, thus beginning Adolf Eichmann's long flight from justice. If all goes well tonight, the manhunt for this unrepentant killer will come to an end just moments from now.

Aharoni and his fellow Mossad agents peer at the bus stop and wait for the 203, which always arrives punctually at 7:40 p.m.

In the distance, Aharoni sees the second Israeli vehicle parked alongside the road. The Israeli agent wears a suit and tie in his disguise as a foreign diplomat. This cover allows him to explain the expensive car in a section of Buenos Aires not known for its wealth.

Aharoni turns off the ignition and releases the catch on the front hood. Mossad agents Peter Zvi Malkin and Zeev Karen get out of the vehicle, raise the hood, and bend over the engine, as if fixing it.

Rafi Eitan, the fourth agent traveling with Aharoni and a member of the "snatch team," lays low in the backseat, where passing cars cannot see him.

No one speaks.

A teenage boy riding past on his bike stops and asks if he can help.

"Get lost," Aharoni barks in Spanish.

The Good Samaritan immediately does as he is told.

Silence resumes as cars come and go along the road. Night has descended, with a full moon rising. There are no streetlights.

At 7:42, Eichmann's bus stops at the small local station. The team tenses for the grab. Peter Malkin will make initial physical contact, distracting the Nazi, then grabbing him. Unwilling to directly touch a man he considers the embodiment of evil, Malkin has chosen to wear gloves on this warm spring evening.

But as the bus doors open, Eichmann does not step off.

The team is deflated. To avoid compromising the mission by lingering on-site too long, they have a deadline of 8:00 p.m. If they do not capture Eichmann in that time, they will try again tomorrow night.

But 8:00 p.m. comes and goes with no sign of the Nazi. Both Mossad vehicles remain in position. "Do we leave or continue to wait?" Aharoni whispers to Rafi Eitan, who is in charge of the physical abduction.

"We wait."

Five minutes pass. Zvi Aharoni lifts a pair of binoculars to his eyes and searches for a sign of Eichmann getting off the next bus.

As if on cue, the second Mossad vehicle switches on their headlights, clearly illuminating Adolf Eichmann as he steps down and begins his nightly walk home to his family.

"Watch out for a weapon," Aharoni whispers to Malkin, still bent low over the engine.

Eichmann walks toward the car, approaching from behind. Aharoni watches in his rearview mirror. When Eichmann is ten yards behind the sedan, the Israeli starts the car.

Eichmann passes by Aharoni's window.

Peter Malkin stands up from inspecting the engine, blocking Eichmann's path.

"Un momentito, señor," he says in thickly accented Spanish. Peter Malkin is an expert in the martial arts and explosives. Though his family escaped from Europe prior to the war, his sister, her children, and more than one hundred close relatives were murdered in Nazi extermination camps. Thirty-two years old, with dark hair and piercing brown eyes, the handsome Polish-born Malkin will one day be known for his sensitivity as an artist. But tonight, there is none of that on display. He is considered the team's "strongman," in Aharoni's words, and will be as brutal as needed to get the job done.

Eichmann stops in his tracks. He has stayed late at work for a union meeting and simply wants to get home and enjoy a glass of red wine. But curiosity gets the best of him.

Believing that the Nazi might have a gun in his pocket, Malkin leaps at him, trying to pin his arms. Eichmann yells out, stepping quickly backward. Aharoni revs the engine, hoping to drown out Eichmann's cries. By now Malkin has grabbed the Nazi. The two men are rolling in a ditch off the side of road. Malkin's gloved hands strain to subdue Eichmann, who is now kicking and screaming.

Agent Zeev Karen joins the scrum, grabbing at Eichmann's legs.

"Help them!" Aharoni screams at Rafi Eitan, who is following orders by remaining out of sight in the backseat. Aharoni will later write that the "well-planned and carefully exercised operation" had become "an unholy mess." But once Eitan jumps into the ditch to wrestle Adolf Eichmann, the plan gets back on track.

The Nazi is thrown into the car, whimpering. The exhausted Israeli agents struggle to catch their breath after the intense wrestling match.

"If you resist you will be shot," Aharoni yells at Eichmann in German.

There is no response. Aharoni repeats the threat.

Again, silence.

Three minutes pass.

Then, in perfect German, come the first words the agents will hear Adolf Eichmann speak: "I have already accepted my fate."[*]

---

[*] Almost thirty years later, the gloves Peter Malkin wore on the night of Eichmann's kidnapping would be cast in bronze and displayed in Israel as a work of art.

13

May 11, 1960
Tira Safe House, Buenos Aires
9:00 p.m.

A terrified Adolf Eichmann is led from the garage into the kitchen, his eyes covered with motorcycle goggles. His body is tense as members of the abduction team support him on both sides. Unable to control his actions, Eichmann opens and closes his fists as if in spasm.

Eichmann suspects that it is the Mossad who have taken him prisoner, but he cannot know for sure because the lenses of his goggles are taped over, making it impossible for him to see his captors. The original plan called for Eichmann to be sedated upon his capture, but the team physician thought that too dangerous—a pharmaceutical injection after drinking alcohol or even eating a big meal prior to his kidnapping would not combine well and might sicken or even kill the prisoner. Thus, Eichmann was bound, trussed, and blinded to keep him disoriented. The twenty-five-mile drive from the kidnapping site to this house in the Quilmes region of Buenos Aires has gone without incident; the Nazi has remained silent throughout the journey.

The only voice Eichmann has heard since being bundled into the backseat is the fluent German of Zvi Aharoni. Now, the Israeli agent helps guide Eichmann up a back staircase to a second-floor bedroom that has been soundproofed to serve as the Nazi's prison cell. It will be nine days until the El Al flight departs from Buenos Aires to Tel Aviv. Eichmann will remain in this room the entire time. Such a lengthy imprisonment will give the experienced interrogator Aharoni multiple opportunities to grill Eichmann. There will also be ample time for the Argentinean police to locate the safe house, so the agents are on high alert. In case of such a police intervention, two small hiding places within the house—one in the crawl space beneath the veranda and the other in a storage cavity above the ceiling—have been stuffed with pillows to muffle any sound should Eichmann be hastily relocated.

In the second-floor bedroom in which Eichmann will spend his final days in Argentina, mattresses cover the windows and thick wool blankets have been nailed to the walls, meaning his screams will go unheard. The room on the second floor is just ten feet by twelve. A single iron bed dominates the center. A table and two small chairs will serve as a point of interrogation and a place to sit for Eichmann's around-the-clock guards. The cell is never allowed to go dark. Every aspect of the abduction is designed to confuse Eichmann, dulling his senses. The goggles are never removed. The Nazi cannot know the date, the time, or whether it is night or day. He will eat only kosher food—among the items: chicken soup, boiled chicken, omelets, mashed potatoes—all prepared by a Mossad agent whose family was murdered at Eichmann's behest during the war.

The Mossad agents standing guard will maintain utter silence. Only Aharoni will communicate with Eichmann. Should the Argentinean police find this safe house, Eichmann will not have seen or heard the voices of his captors and will thus be unable to testify against them.

Eichmann is stripped. His workman's clothing and boots are old and frayed. His undergarments are threadbare.

The team doctor performs a thorough physical examination of Eichmann. The prisoner's mouth is checked for a cyanide capsule, even though it has been so many years since the war's end that it would be unlikely for him to still conceal a suicide vial in his teeth. When no poison is discovered, Eichmann's dentures are removed as an added precaution.

On the Nazi's left arm is a cigarette burn; the scar under Eichmann's armpit covers up his SS blood-type tattoo.

The Israelis dress Eichmann in pajamas purchased to his measurements. His left ankle is handcuffed to the bed. At 9:15 p.m., little more than an hour since he was snatched, Eichmann's interrogation begins. Zvi Aharoni's specialty was never surveillance or driving a getaway car, though he has handled both those aspects of this operation with professional élan. The same cannot be said of interrogation—the art of breaking a man down to extract information is not only Aharoni's specialty but also a job he enjoys a great deal. In addition to his work during the war, he has spent time in America working with the CIA to learn their interrogation methods. Physical force is not part of Aharoni's repertoire. Instead, he maneuvers to outwit his subjects, allowing them to ensnare themselves in a circle of lies.

To prepare for the coming round of questions, and the most important debriefing of his life, Aharoni has read every available file on Eichmann, committing to memory facts and vignettes that will allow him to question the Nazi in a manner suggesting he already knows the answers to the questions he is posing. It is vital that Aharoni convince the prisoner to admit his true identity—flying home to Tel Aviv with the wrong man would make Israel—and Mossad—an international laughingstock.

"What is your name," Aharoni begins in fluent German—"Was ist dein name?"

"Ricardo Klement." Eichmann shows no sign of fear.

"Wie würdest du vorher genannt?" Aharoni counters—"What were you called before?"

"Otto Heninger."

"What is your membership number in the NSDAP?"*

"Eight-nine-nine-eight-nine-five."

"What was your number in the SS?"

"Four-five-three-two-six."

"What is your date of birth?" Aharoni continues, noting that each of Eichmann's answers thus far confirms his true identity.

"Nineteen March 1906."

"Under what name were you born?" Aharoni has come full circle with his questioning but now hesitates. The correct answer will mean he can proceed with a more in-depth line of interrogation about Eichmann's role in the Holocaust. A false answer means the two men might spend the entire night engaged in a mental chess match.

After fifteen years of hiding, and spinning elaborate tales to conceal his true identity, the proud Nazi now prefers to tell the truth.

"Adolf Eichmann."

⚡⚡

Nick Eichmann, the former boyfriend of Sylvia Hermann, is working in an elevator shaft. He is now married to an Argentinean girl and no longer lives at home. It is the morning of May 12, just hours after his father's kidnapping. Using a screwdriver, the twenty-four-year-old mechanic makes adjustments to the elevator's control panel. Without warning, his younger brother Dieter steps into the small space.

"The old man is gone," eighteen-year-old Dieter says breathlessly.

The brothers immediately drive toward Garibaldi Street. Along the way, they stop briefly at the home of former SS officer Carlos Fuldner to give him the news. It was Fuldner who arranged their father's immigration to Argentina. Together, they come up with

---

* The National Socialist German Workers Party, also known in German as Nationalsozialistische Deutsche Arbeiterpartei—more commonly referred to simply as the Nazi Party.

three possible scenarios to explain the disappearance: Eichmann has been arrested by Argentinean police, perhaps for being drunk in public; Eichmann was injured in an accident and is in a local hospital; or, the Israelis snatched him.

Two days of fruitless searching of morgues, hospitals, and police stations give them their answer. When the Eichmann boys retrace their father's likely steps home from the bus station, their attention is drawn to mud and flattened grass alongside the road, indicating some form of struggle. Bending down to inspect the area more carefully, Nick Eichmann finds his father's eyeglasses in the mud.

It is the Israelis.

Now there is urgency: the Eichmann boys must find their father before he can be smuggled out of Argentina.

ᛋᛋ

The wait is agonizing. As he counts down the days to the El Al flight, Isser Harel obsessively scans the newspapers for signs of a manhunt. He is certain that Vera Eichmann became concerned when her husband failed to arrive home but doubts that her first thoughts would be a kidnapping. More likely she would think that he hurt himself in an accident and was in a hospital. He doubts she would go directly to the police. "Was Klement often drunk?" Harel asks himself, placing himself in the mind-set of a police investigator. "Were there fights? Arguments? Was he mixed up with another woman?"

Harel decides that Vera is not a concern. She would not dare reveal her husband's true identity or past to local law enforcement, almost surely meaning that her appeal for a search would be ignored. "Like police the world over, they would finally tell her that husbands disappear and return, and all she had to do was wait patiently until homesickness brought him back."

Also, should Vera Eichmann foolishly tell officials that her husband is the infamous war criminal Adolf Eichmann, the news would flash around the world in an instant. Rather than rescuing her husband, she would confirm once and for all that he is alive in Argentina.

No, Harel decides. Vera Eichmann will never go to the police.

The local Nazi population, however, will do anything within its power to rescue Adolf Eichmann. Indeed, as Isser Harel awaits the arrival of El Al flight 601, a network of former SS agents is taking action. Vera Eichmann and her youngest son Ricardo have been removed from the house on Garibaldi Street and spirited into hiding.

"Another friend of my father's, also an SS man, organized an observation network over all the seaports and airports. [There was] no airport, no harbor, no major railway station, no important crossroads that was not being watched by our people," Nick Eichmann will boast to a German journalist five years later.

Help also comes in the form of the Tacuara, a militant anti-Semitic Argentinean organization. Its members greet one another with the raised arm of a Nazi salute, and worship Adolf Hitler and his Fascist policies. The members are exclusively Catholic and anti-Communist, with the mission of remaking Argentina as a nation "free of politicians, free of demagogues, and of Jews." They are in alliance with the Arab League of Buenos Aires, a group determined to wipe Israel off the map. Pope Pius in Rome has learned of the hatred spread by the Tacuara group and ordered one Catholic priest to tone down his anti-Semitic rhetoric.

So it is that Dieter and Nick Eichmann join forces with the SS and Tacuara to find their father. They believe he is being hidden somewhere in Buenos Aires, most likely in the cellar of a synagogue. Existing on just a few hours of sleep every night, they canvas the city in a frantic search. With Buenos Aires already caught up in the 150th anniversary celebration festivities, the aggressive behavior of these passionate young men goes unnoticed.

"We knew with certainty," Nick Eichmann will explain years later, "that he had not yet left Argentina."

⚡⚡

It is the evening of May 19, 1960, as the El Al turboprop approaches Buenos Aires's Ezeiza Airport. "The Whispering Giant," as flight 601's Britannia has been nicknamed, flew from Tel Aviv to Rome, then on to Dakar, Senegal, then westward across the Atlantic from Africa to the Brazilian coastal airport at Recife. It is the first time any of the crew has been to South America. The charts for the Britannia aircraft used by chief navigator Shaul Shaul have been purchased in New York City specially for this flight.

In Recife, the two pilots were given a lesson in the idiosyncrasies of South American bureaucracy during the refueling stop. A short visit turned into a frustrating delay when an air traffic controller refused to recognize their right to fly over Brazilian air space, even though all the proper permits had been arranged. Three hours and a hefty bribe later, the El Al flight lifted into the sky.

Descending into Buenos Aires, the crew learns a second hard truth about South American thinking. The Argentinean control tower gives them landing instructions in meters instead of feet. Told to level off "when reaching 2,000," the flight crew is stunned to see clouds at treetop level. Sudden death is just seconds away. The startled pilots quickly pull the nose up to gain altitude, barely averting a crash.

Thus, as El Al 601 finally lands in Buenos Aires, the drained crew eagerly awaits their mandatory twenty-four-hour rest period. They will need it—as arduous as the flight into Buenos Aires was, the return to Tel Aviv tomorrow night will be even more demanding.

⚡⚡

A red carpet is rolled out as Israel's highest-ranking diplomat steps off the plane. Israeli and Argentinean officials make welcoming speeches. The leaders of local Jewish community organizations wait patiently inside the terminal, eager to greet Abba Eban, Israel's foreign minister. None of the diplomats or locals know anything of the Eichmann plot.

While it is just one day until the final phase of Eichmann's kidnapping is due to transpire, the planning for the Nazi's extraction continues at a furious pace. Airport security is the greatest stumbling block, with customs agents bound to ask numerous questions and scrutinize the identities of all travelers. Thus, as the entourage moves from the tarmac into the terminal, the Britannia is towed to the far side of the airfield. The Mossad have specifically requested that the El Al flight be parked near Argentinean airplanes. It is felt that this will lower the level of scrutiny when it comes time to depart.

Despite the presence of the El Al Britannia aircraft, Zvi Aharoni has not given up on the possibility of utilizing a cargo ship for the evacuation. Pretending to be an avid water-skier, he rented a speedboat and journeys out into the Rio de la Plata estuary, where he sees for himself that an oceanic exchange is very possible. However, there is still the difficulty of diverting a cargo ship from its regularly scheduled route. Indeed, officials at the ZIM line confirm that a vessel will not be passing the South American coast until June at the earliest.

This is hardly ideal. However, it is the fallback plan should all go wrong with air travel. Eichmann would have to be sequestered in the safe house for at least another month, a situation Aharoni cannot possibly imagine. The Mossad agents already feel like prisoners in *Tira*. They have passed the time playing chess, reading the few available books, and listening to the radio, but the sheer boredom of guarding Eichmann is wearing them down. The agents shave the Nazi, help him shower and go to the bathroom, and spoon-feed him the kosher meals prepared by the newly arrived female Mossad operative. With every passing day it becomes harder and harder for them to believe this simple man masterminded the deaths of millions or was once arrogant enough to boast to Adolf Hitler that he would present the Führer with a *Judenrein* (Jew-free) Vienna for his birthday.

The sooner Eichmann is placed on trial in Tel Aviv, the better. The Mossad agents are chafing at the claustrophobic conditions of the safe house and at being in such daily proximity with a man they revile. With every passing day that he is held in their custody, the notion of waiting another whole month to place him aboard a cargo ship becomes more repugnant.

A local Jewish carpenter performing yet another *sayan* function has constructed a special crate for the flight. The box is large enough to hold a man, allowing the Nazi to be secretly loaded on board like a piece of cargo. Four heavy leather straps are screwed to the interior, to which Eichmann's arms will be bound so he cannot move around. Fifty air holes are drilled into the wood so that the prisoner will not suffocate. To ensure that no airport security guard attempts to open the crate, the words "Diplomatic Post" are stenciled to the outside, granting the package official immunity.

Simultaneously, an Israeli tourist is confronted by the Mossad at his hotel. He has nothing to do with the Mossad but asks no questions when told that his government would consider it an act of patriotism if he would check himself into a local hospital. Though obviously not injured or ill, the tourist is to feign a concussion from a phantom automobile accident. Just to ensure he plays the part perfectly, the Operation Eichmann team doctor briefs the tourist on the symptoms of a concussion.

Bound by national duty, the tourist tells the Argentinean doctors about the crash and how he was thrown violently forward, smacking his head on the front seat. He is tested for vertigo. Neurological exams are carried out and his skull is X-rayed.

Once the patient is admitted to the hospital, the Mossad secures his passport. The agents do not explain why. Nonetheless, the tourist obliges. With the insertion of a new photograph by the Mossad team's very capable forgers, the passport will soon bear the image of Adolf Eichmann.

The tourist—whom Harel will give the code name of Rafael Arnon—plays his part in the deception perfectly. He tells the doctors that all normal flights to Europe are fully booked and that he is hoping the El Al plane will have room for a sick Israeli who wants to make it home as soon as possible.

On the night of May 19, just hours after the El Al flight lands, a member of the Mossad team visits the tourist in the hospital.

He instructs the patient to tell the doctors that he has been granted a seat on the return flight to Israel. Upon his release from the hospital, the Mossad will find some other way to get him home to Israel, but his passport now belongs to Adolf Eichmann.

ᛋᛋ

It is not just Adolf Eichmann who needs official clearance to depart Argentina. The Mossad team made their way into the country wearing various disguises and under false identities, traveling on separate flights and arriving through different points of embarkation. Some traveled through Paris, while others made stops around South America before arriving in Buenos Aires. And this is the way they must leave. Only a handful of agents will be on board the El Al flight. The others must make a clandestine exit from Argentina, knowing all the while that they will be hunted should the Eichmann kidnapping unravel.

So it is that the Operation Eichmann team spends its last night in *Tira*. As the El Al Britannia stands alone on the tarmac, bathed in the white-hot beams of security floodlights, the Operation Eichmann members prepare their new identities and break down the safe house.

The cover story is that *Tira* was rented by a husband and wife, so all traces of the prison cell must be dismantled. "A great deal of work also went into restoring the house to its former condition. Everything that was in it when we rented it was put back in place," Isser Harel will write. "Everything that was added during the tenancy was destroyed . . . the inspectors worked with exact lists in their hands to make sure they wouldn't forget the most minute detail."

The work continues through the night. By dawn, the plan is ready for execution.

"It finally came, the twentieth of May," Harel will write. "The last day, and for me, the longest and most dramatic day of Operation Eichmann."

But one unanswered question remains: will Eichmann attempt a last-minute escape?

14

May 20, 1960
Ezeiza Airport, Buenos Aires
7:00 p.m.

Isser Harel sits alone in an airport employee café. The air is thick with cigarette smoke. Outside, the weather is cold and raining. Harel has chosen this location carefully, hoping for a discreet place where he will go unnoticed as he awaits the midnight departure for Tel Aviv. Harel is surrounded by uniformed security guards and mechanics in coveralls, all waiting impatiently for an open seat in this overcrowded hall. It is here that he will meet with members of the Mossad team, who will brief him through the night as the plan unfolds.

Harel is not just thinking about Adolf Eichmann. He has ordered a group of Mossad agents to comb Buenos Aires for the location of Josef Mengele. It is a risk to divert manpower to that task so late in Operation Eichmann, and the Mossad agents involved are unhappy about the assignment, believing it might doom their carefully designed plan. But it is a gamble Harel is willing to take.

Soon, Zvi Aharoni joins Harel. The two men can barely hear each other over the terminal noise. Harel finds a seat with a group of hungry Argentine soldiers who are too busy eating to pay any attention to the Jewish agents. Aharoni's information is simple: the roads from *Tira* are clear. Despite the heavy airport security and many flights arriving for the 150th anniversary celebration, there are no signs of roadblocks. Also, much to both men's satisfaction, there is nothing in this afternoon's Buenos Aires papers about Eichmann.

"Execute plan Number One," Harel instructs Aharoni, sending him back to *Tira*. With that, the fallback plan of waiting a month to depart by sea is set aside. Aharoni breathes a sigh of relief, knowing that his fellow Mossad agents will be very glad to hear this news.

Plan Number One also means that the specially designed crate will not be necessary, because Eichmann will actually walk onto the plane.

At 8:30 p.m., the El Al pilots depart their hotel in downtown Buenos Aires. They are driven to the remote corner of the airport where the Britannia is parked and begin preflight planning.

At the same moment, Zvi Aharoni steps inside Adolf Eichmann's cell in *Tira*. The Nazi has not had food or drink since lunch. His hair is dyed gray and thick makeup has been applied to his face to make him appear much older. He wears a false mustache. Eichmann is dressed in the same crisp white shirt, blue tie, and pressed blue pants of the El Al crew members. Perched atop his head is a matching hat, bearing the emblem once worn by Eichmann's millions of victims: the Star of David.

The two men have spent hours together since the kidnapping. Aharoni has extracted a great deal of damning information from Eichmann. The Israeli has always been professional, though never overly friendly. Earlier in the day, before meeting with Isser Harel, Aharoni had informed Eichmann that this is the night they would depart for Israel, where he will stand trial for his crimes. The Nazi has known this day is coming and has even signed a document stating that he is complying willfully with his extraction.

"Remember your promise," Aharoni reminds Eichmann.

"You have nothing to fear," says the mass murderer, still wearing his goggles covered in tape. "I am going with you voluntarily, and I will keep my promise."

Eichmann seems comfortable wearing the same uniform as the Jews. In fact, he even asks for a matching uniform jacket, but his request is denied.

"The doctor had to be able to reach his arm and a vein at any time," Aharoni will write. The team doctor is among the best anesthesiologists in Tel Aviv and will soon return to that profession, never to give his name as a member of Operation Eichmann. "He would inject his patient with a certain amount of medication and then leave the needle sticking into the vein. In that way, he could increase the dose at any time. The shirt would hide the needle but not hamper the doctor. This would be much harder with a jacket."

The injection is administered at 9:00 p.m.

"We are ready to travel," announces the doctor, as the drugs take hold. Eichmann is incapable of coherent speech but still able to walk. His goggles are removed. Two Mossad agents also dressed as flight crew members walk him into the garage, where the Nazi is once again placed in the backseat. The sedan has been fitted with diplomatic license plates to guarantee it will not be searched.

Once again, Zvi Aharoni is the driver. He knows the roads to the airport better than anyone, as well as side streets should the need arise for a secondary route. It is 9:30 as he engages the clutch and drives away from *Tira* for the last time.

⚡⚡

At the same moment, outside the Hotel Internacional in the heart of Buenos Aires, the pursers and stewardesses comprising the remainder of El Al's flight crew board a small bus. Their arrival at the airport must coincide perfectly with that of the vehicle containing Eichmann. It is only just this morning that the cabin crew was informed that a special passenger wearing an El Al uniform would be joining them this evening. They were not told his name, only that the individual in question was a man of "paramount national importance." The crew was "flabbergasted," in the words of Isser Harel, but not completely surprised. Too many curious incidents have accompanied the planning of this flight.

The return journey, for instance, will not be going through the Brazilian town of Recife, as on the inbound. Instead, the route will immediately swing across the Atlantic heading to the city of Dakar in Senegal, even though the distance is slightly beyond the Britannia's fuel capacity. The pilots will need the assistance of favorable following winds to make the crossing without incident.

The veteran El Al staff have been doing their jobs long enough to spot these little irregularities.

※

Isser Harel remains in the employee cafeteria. He spies the two leaders of the Josef Mengele search party making their way through the crowd. Many of Harel's men thought that trying to grab the Angel of Death so late in Operation Eichmann was overly ambitious. "When I have a bird in my hand, I don't start looking for the bird in the bush," one agent has warned Harel. "I'll take the bird in my hand, put it in a cage, and then deal with the one in the bush."

But the Mossad director is certain that if Eichmann is successfully transported back to Israel, a panicked Mengele will go back into hiding. It is an amazing coincidence that the Nazi doctor has returned to Buenos Aires at the same time the Mossad has arrived to grab Eichmann. Better to take advantage of this moment, than to let it pass—the chance to grab Mengele might not ever happen again.

But as the two agents take a seat at the small table where Harel has held covert meetings throughout the evening, he immediately senses that something is wrong. Both men are hours late. The spark of excitement they might display if the operation were proceeding smoothly is nonexistent. Instead, they look tired and defeated. Earlier, the agents approached Mengele's known residence in two separate acts of deception: one time as a parcel delivery man and the other in the guise of handyman seeking to gain entry for the purpose of fixing the water heater.

Both agents report the same outcome to their gambit: a woman answered the door.

She spoke English with no discernible German accent. In fact, she spoke no other language, not even Spanish. The woman freely gave her name, explaining to the Mossad agents that she had just moved to Buenos Aires, the house was a recent rental, and she had no knowledge of where the previous owner might have gone. Furthermore, she insisted that there was nothing wrong with her water heater, and thus no reason to let them inside.

The agents persisted, asking leading questions to verify the truth of her story. In the end, both men decided that the woman was telling the truth.

The Mossad agents now tell Isser Harel that the Angel of Death has vanished. There will be no double kidnapping on this operation.

⚡⚡

Klaus Eichmann and his little brother, Dieter, are still prowling the streets of Buenos Aires, searching for their father's abductors. Their Tacuara allies are keeping a close watch on the train stations, ports, and the airport but have grown restless. The Tacuara have proposed a radical plan to kidnap the Israeli ambassador to Argentina and hold him hostage until Adolf Eichmann is returned.

The Eichmann boys find that option extreme at this point in time, but in the end they may have no other choice.

⚡⚡

Zvi Aharoni drives slowly, knowing that any abrupt turns or stops will cause the needle to be yanked from his prisoner's arm. He takes back roads. The main autoroutes are filled with police and other security for the many visiting dignitaries, for while Argentinean officials have little problem harboring Nazi war criminals, they fear that their national reputation will be tarnished should the sesquicentennial celebrations be interrupted by violence of any kind.

Already, terrorist groups seeking the return of Juan Perón to power have attempted to blow up the national telephone company. The likelihood of a suspicious vehicle being stopped and searched to find the bombers is high.

Aharoni's caution pays off—the Mossad sedan arrives at Ezeiza Airport without incident. Security officials wave the vehicle through the gate without so much as a stop, thanks to the diplomatic plates. The guards do not pay any attention to the three men sitting side by side in the rear seat. They will leave such scrutiny to customs officials during passport control.

As Aharoni steers across the tarmac, the crew bus looms out of the darkness on schedule, falling in behind his car. The El Al departure will be the last flight of the night, so there is little activity in the Aerolineas Argentineas hangar area where the Britannia is parked.

Aharoni comes to a stop at the base of the gangway. A crew member appears in the door at the top of the steps, giving the thumbs-up signal. Immediately, the rear doors of Aharoni's sedan are opened and Eichmann is guided up the steps into the aircraft. The doctor is at one side, a Mossad agent on the other.

To maintain the appearance that this is standard employee boarding procedure, the remainder of the crew pile out of their airport minibus and follow Eichmann up the ramp. "Form a circle around us and follow us up the steps," commands agent Rafi Eitan.

The seven pursers, radio operators, and stewardesses obey orders.

Suddenly, an airport security guard shines a floodlight on the stairway, giving the group a start. But no one approaches to question the odd behavior of the man who cannot stand on his own two feet or the crowd milling around him. The crew can only hope that the guard assumes one of them has had too much to drink.

The gangway is too short for the Britannia. Eichmann must be lifted and pushed the last step up into the fuselage.

The Nazi is immediately lowered into an aisle seat in the front row of first class. A blanket is placed across his body. There is an empty seat next to him, but the Mossad doctor has no intention of spending the entire flight home seated next to a Nazi war criminal. Instead, he sits directly behind Eichmann, prepared to administer another dose of sedative, should it be required.

"You should try to get a bit of sleep," Aharoni tells Eichmann. Unable to speak, the prisoner complies.

The El Al crew settles into the remaining six seats in first class. The lights in the forward cabin are off. A curtain is drawn. Everyone is told to pretend they are sleeping, just in case Argentinean officials demand to come on board.

Thus far, every aspect of Operation Eichmann has gone according to plan.

Now the Mossad and their prisoner must clear passport control—but the Argentinean customs authorities who will usually board a plane are nowhere to be seen.

The Britannia's engines roar to life. The plane taxis toward the main terminal, there to pick up passengers. Isser Harel is among those in the terminal, but he has not decided whether it would be best to immediately board the flight or wait until the last minute. Should the operation fall apart, it will be crucial that he escape. Harel knows far too many secrets to be arrested by foreign officials.

Just before midnight, a bearded Argentinean passport officer finally steps into the passenger lounge. He is embarrassed for being late due to a scheduling mistake. "Please excuse me. I am sorry!" he says, quickly stamping everyone's passport. Zvi Aharoni is among them. There is no attempt by the official to board the flight and check the crew's documents. The intense forgeries and deceptions required to get Eichmann out of the country have become unnecessary. The deception of the Israeli tourist giving up his passport and enduring a stay in the hospital was also unnecessary. But Aharoni knows it is always better to err on the side of taking every precaution possible.

"Bon Viaje," the Argentine says warmly, nodding toward the flight.

It's time. Isser Harel hands his passport to the bearded customs agent, hears the resounding thump as it is stamped, then steps out onto the tarmac to board the flight home.

※

In the cockpit, pilot Zvi Tohar makes a mental checklist of what to do in event of emergency. Nicknamed the "Tall Captain with the Well-Kept Mustache," for his dapper good looks, the German-born Tohar was a fighter pilot in the Royal Air Force during the war and has been instrumental in bringing aviation to Israel. Should Argentinean fighter planes be scrambled to shoot down the El Al flight, he plans to drop to treetop level and evade the attack until he can get out over the ocean.

Tohar radios the tower. "El Al is ready to taxi."

"El Al, proceed to runway," comes the reply.

Tohar releases the brakes. The Britannia begins a gentle roll across the tarmac.

Zvi Tobar, whose cool behavior under pressure prevented catastrophe during the Eichmann operation

But then, a shock—the tower issues another command.

"El Al, hold your position. There is an irregularity in the flight plan."

Isser Harel's stomach lurches as the airplane brakes to an abrupt halt. Without a hesitation, he gets out of his seat and steps into the cockpit. Harel is certain that Vera Eichmann and her sons have guessed that their patriarch is on board the one and only Israeli aircraft leaving Argentina and have finally alerted the police. The Mossad director orders Zvi Tohar to ignore the tower and take off.

Throughout his long career, Tohar has earned a reputation for being cool under pressure. Now, despite Harel's command, the pilot refuses the order.

"There's still one more option," he tells Harel. "Before having the Argentinean air force put on our tail, we should check and see if they really know Eichmann is on board. Let's not create a problem that doesn't exist."

Stairs are wheeled to the plane. Navigator Shaul Shaul steps outside and walks to the tower. Harel has given him precisely ten minutes to ascertain the situation. If he does not return in that time, Zvi Tohar will have no choice but to take off—and face whatever consequences may come.

Shaul is thirty-two. He has two children. There is nothing he would rather do than return home safely. But as he climbs the steps to the control tower, Shaul wonders if a set of handcuffs awaits him. "What is the problem?" he asks, searching out the air traffic controller.

"There is a signature missing," says the controller, pointing to the flight plan.

Not wasting any time, Shaul politely signs the document and says his good-byes.

Back at the El Al Britannia, Shaul climbs the steps and settles back into the cockpit.

"Everything's OK," Shaul tells Zvi Tohar.

The pilot radios the tower. "This is El Al, may we proceed?"

"Affirmative."

Zvi Aharoni will remember that moment the rest of his life. "I was still unable to relax. Then the aircraft began to move. The runway was clear. At the end of the runway, the Britannia lifted off. It was four minutes past midnight."

Retribution is in the air.

15

April 11, 1961
Jerusalem, Israel
9:00 a.m.

The noose is getting closer for Adolf Eichmann.

It is Tuesday. Passover has just ended. After ten months in captivity, and hundreds of hours of interrogation, Eichmann stands trial. He sits surrounded on three sides by bulletproof glass. Since his arrival in Israel, Eichmann has been guarded around the clock, with a police officer stationed inside his cell, another seated outside, and a third sentinel standing by to make sure that no one communicates with the prisoner. Now, that vigilance continues. Two unarmed sentries stand on either side of Eichmann within his protective glass dock. For good measure, two more guards stand just inches away. In the name of judicial impartiality, they have all been specially chosen, not just for their strength or skills but because none has lost a family member in the Holocaust.

The trial spectators clamor loudly, awaiting the arrival of the judges. The room is brightly lit and the air-conditioning too strong, but few complain. Such is the demand for seating that Eichmann's trial is not taking place in a normal courtroom but in the cavernous

Adolf Eichmann in the exercise area outside his cell in Israel, awaiting trial

new Israeli cultural center of Beit Ha'am. Workers were still rushing to complete construction last night. It is the only building in Jerusalem capable of holding the hundreds of international journalists and Holocaust survivors here to witness evil on display. In a year that has seen the world stunned by great headlines, no news story can match that of Eichmann's capture.* The trial is such an international sensation that even this great auditorium is

---

* Among the world-changing news stories of 1960–1961 are an American U-2 spy plane being shot down by the Soviet Union; Fidel Castro expanding his power in Cuba; and the inventions of the laser, pacemaker, and contraceptive birth control pill. One lesser-known incident was an unknown band named the Beatles appearing live in the German city of Hamburg.

not big enough. In addition to the journalists in the courtroom, hundreds more will watch on closed-circuit TV in two other nearby locations. Television cameras stand ready to beam the trial live to the people of Israel. The transmission will also be sent to the United States each day, where it will be aired on national television.

Awaiting testimony, the crowd cannot help but stare at Eichmann. They struggle to reconcile that this thin elderly man dressed in a cheap suit, constantly sucking on his dentures and blowing his nose into a large white handkerchief, is the same leader of Sondereinsatz-Kommando Eichmann who zealously oversaw the death of millions.*

"The normal reaction to a man alone, in trouble, is pity," journalist Martha Gellhorn writes in her notebook.† "Yet this man in the dock arouses no such feeling, not once, not for an instant."

"His voice is ugly, with a hard R, a sound that makes one think of a hammer and a knife. Neither by voice, accent, nor vocabulary is he an educated men," writes Gellhorn, covering the trial for the *Atlantic Monthly*. "Eichmann's voice sharpened: the cold snarl, the bark that many of the eyewitnesses remembered, was there.... From the first day of his testimony, we could imagine Eichmann clearly as an old Hungarian Jewish aristocrat had described him: 'an officer in boots, with one hand on his pistol, in all the pride of his race.'"

Yet despite the repulsion most feel, a minority are on Eichmann's side. A worldwide wave of anti-Semitic violence followed the news of his kidnapping from Argentina. Israel was roundly attacked in the worldwide press for its aggressive behavior, and the United Nations Security Council cast a resolution condemning the Eichmann

---

* Eichmann Special Commando Unit.

† Gellhorn was married to the writer Ernest Hemingway from 1940 to 1945. She is considered one of the great journalists of the twentieth century, having covered almost every important conflict of her time. She lived to be ninety, before taking her life with a cyanide pill rather than endure the ravages of ovarian cancer.

kidnapping—a response that many in Israel also considered an act of anti-Semitism.*

Another criticism of Israel comes from an unlikely source: Lothar Hermann, the blind concentration camp survivor who first helped the Mossad find Eichmann in Buenos Aires. He now lives in poverty and is angry about the lack of financial compensation he received from Israel. Just a few weeks ago, on March 23, 1961, Hermann suffered a nervous breakdown and was taken to a police station to explain his erratic behavior. Hermann claimed to be Josef Mengele, an admission that promptly saw him arrested. It would take twenty-four hours before the truth came out, but in that time, news flashed around the world that Mengele had finally been found.

But the Angel of Death is still very much a free man. Meanwhile, Eichmann was transported one hundred miles from a prison cell in Haifa to the city of Jerusalem one week ago. He now lives in a jail built especially for his incarceration on the top floor of the Beit Ha'am facility. A ten-foot-high fence surrounds the building. Elaborate security measures are in place for all in attendance at the trial, as well: everyone entering the building must step into a cement cubicle for a complete physical search. No personal baggage is allowed in the courtroom.

Finally, the trial begins.

"Beth Hamispath," booms the voice of the court usher—"House of Justice." He is an older gentleman who delivers the words with polished theatrical flair. The Israelis are intent on avoiding the absurdity of a show trial, but the power of those opening words cannot help but remind Adolf Eichmann that this court will be completely unlike the Nuremberg Trials. There, the crimes against the Jews

---

* The United States voted in favor of the resolution, taking the side of their postwar allies Britain and France. In an attempt to save face with the nation of Israel, the United States stipulated that their vote was predicated upon a UN acknowledgment that the Jews had suffered greatly at the hands of Germany, and a second amendment wishing for greater peace and understanding between Argentina and Israel. Meanwhile, the Soviet Union and Poland voted against the resolution, then took the subsequent action of making it a propaganda issue.

were just a portion of the war crimes being prosecuted. The Eichmann trial will focus completely on atrocities—and it is the Jews who hold the fate of this *Schreibtischmörder* in their hands.*

As the three Israeli judges, all dressed in black robes, enter the makeshift courtroom through a side door, each of the 756 spectators rises to their feet. The judges take their seats on a platform near Eichmann. Below them sit court stenographers and two translators. Eichmann himself occupies the lowest row on the stage, so the Nazi must twist his head awkwardly up and to the right in order to see the men who will decide his fate.

"Are you Adolf, son of Adolf Eichmann?" asks presiding judge Moshe Landau, a balding man with a solemn disposition.

"Jawohl!" confirms the defendant, now standing at sharp attention.

"You are accused before this Court in terms of an indictment containing fifteen counts. I shall read the indictment to you and this indictment will be translated for you into German. This is the indictment against you on behalf of the Attorney General," says Judge Landau.

Eichmann remains standing as the charges against him are read aloud. His defense attorney, a thickset German named Robert Servatius, listens from his table across the room. Servatius, a World War II soldier in the German Wehrmacht whose fee is being paid by the Israeli government, has brought his pretty blond secretary with him from Cologne. She now sits to his left.

Each charge in the fifteen counts is read aloud by Judge Landau, then reiterated with a lengthy list of details. It is a recitation that lasts for almost ninety minutes.

ϟϟ

"Did you understand the indictment?" Landau asks once all counts have been thoroughly explained.

"Jawohl!"

---

* Translation: "killer behind the desk."

Yet defense attorney Servatius spends the next three days of court engaged in a series of stalls and delays to gain a tactical advantage. It is not until Monday, April 17, that Judge Landau is allowed to ask for Eichmann's final plea. In that time, the world's attention has been diverted from the proceedings by the stunning launch of a Soviet rocket that sends astronaut Yuri Gagarin into orbit around the earth. But as amazing as that might be, the spotlight remains fixed on the Eichmann trial—and the courtroom at Beit Ha'am packed with journalists eager to witness every word.

"The defendant will rise," Landau tells the former SS commander.

Eichmann does so but no longer does he snap to attention. The many hours in court are making him weary. The smart military bearing is missing from his countenance.

"You have heard the indictment," says Judge Landau.

Eichmann knows the charges all too well. His most recent interrogator was not Zvi Aharoni, who is now engaged in other undercover activities, but police inspector Avner Less. The two men have met on ninety different occasions, culling 270 hours of testimony. All of Eichmann's words have been taped so that they can be replayed. The text version comes out to 3,564 typed pages. Inspector Less has not only shown this transcription to Eichmann, but he has also allowed the war criminal to make changes. So as Judge Landau asks the accused man whether or not he is innocent, Eichmann is thoroughly aware of each and every damning word he has spoken over the last eleven months. A less arrogant man would meekly submit to the power of the evidence against him: not Eichmann.

"I am not guilty," the Nazi replies in German.

⚡⚡

More than twenty years have not diminished the horror. Heinrich Grüber was a German Protestant theologian who was outraged by the ongoing harassment and deportation of German and Austrian Jews to concentration camps. He had petitioned Adolf Eichmann and Hermann Göring, trying to protect Jews and Christians of Jewish descent. On December 19, 1940, as he made ready to travel to a death camp to offer encouragement to the afflicted, the Gestapo surrounded Grüber's office and arrested him.

More than two decades later, he has traveled to Israel to offer his testimony in court. He takes the stand against Adolf Eichmann on May 16, 1961:

> PRESIDING JUDGE MOSHE LANDAU: What is your full name?
> WITNESS HEINRICH GRUEBER: Heinrich Karl Ernst Grueber.
> Q: What was your occupation before the outbreak of the War in 1939?
> A: In 1939 I was a parson in an eastern suburb of Berlin, at Karlsdorf.
> Q: Dr. Grueber, do you know the Accused?
> A: I know his name and I used to know him, but I would not be able to identify him now.
> Q: You did meet him in Berlin, did you not?
> A: Yes.
> Q: In his office at Kurfuerstenstrasse 116?
> A: Yes.
> Q: What were the subjects discussed when you appeared in Adolf Eichmann's office?
> A: I went there very often and raised all the questions of importance to us. Questions about emigration, questions about treatment of the Jews and everything of importance—I raised them all in the office, unless they were matters concerning other authorities.
> Q: How did Adolf Eichmann behave?
> A: Well, I had the impression—and I hope the Accused will not take it badly—but quite honestly, I must say, having come here without any hatred or feelings of revenge, the impression I had of him was that he was a man who sat there like a block of ice, or a block of marble, and everything you tried to get through to him just bounced off him.

Q: Did you sometimes manage to achieve your purpose in going to see Eichmann?

A: As far as I remember, either I heard a "no," or I was told you will receive a reply, come back. But I do not ever remember being given a decision with a "yes." I do not remember any such instance where I left the room with a positive decision, normally it was a "no" or a reply to the effect "you must wait, you will receive a reply."

Q: Mr. Grueber, do you remember whether during these meetings or conversations the Accused ever referred to his superior's instructions, which he had to ask for or receive?

A: As far as I remember, everything was in the first person, i.e., I order, I say, and I cannot; I am not aware of a single instance in which he may have said: I have to consult a superior authority.

Q: Towards the end of 1940 you were arrested, Dr. Grueber, were you not?

A: I was arrested on 19 December 1940.

Q: You told the court that you were transferred to the Sachsenhausen camp. Was that an SS concentration camp?

A: Yes, all concentration camps were under the SS.

Q: When did you leave Sachsenhausen?

A: October 1941.

Q: Where were you transferred to?

A: To Dachau.

Q: Who were the people with you in the Dachau camp?

A: Do you mean the people in charge, or my fellow prisoners?

Q: Your fellow prisoners.

A: There were about 700 clergy in the special camp: The Jews and the clergy were isolated from the other prisoners.

Q: My first question about the Dachau camp concerns the conditions in which you and your fellow clerics lived.

A: Just like everywhere else, it was an existence of utter uncertainty, because we were totally at the mercy of the SS troops, without any protection or rights. If someone was shot, it was of no consequence.

Q: Can you tell the Court about transports of prisoners from Dachau for killing by gas?

A: I had already experienced that in Sachsenhausen, particularly with a theologian with whom I was friendly, who was with one of the first "transports of invalids"—i.e., of people not capable of working. People were selected, usually some 300 for each transport, they were taken to the gas installation; the relatives were notified shortly afterwards that the person in question had died, and in spite of all medical efforts it had not been possible to save him.

Q: When you were in Dachau, did you hear of Majdanek and Auschwitz?

A: Not only did we hear about them, we also saw something of them, lots of clothing of those gassed in Auschwitz was sent to Dachau for sorting. Whole wagonloads arrived. When in the first consignment we found a pair of tiny children's shoes, we were all shocked to our inner souls by this, and we men, for all that we were used to terrible things, had to struggle with our tears, because it brought all the suffering of these children before us. Then more and more children's shoes arrived, and that was something which was part of the most bitter suffering we went through.

Q: Dr. Grueber, can you tell the Court about the various medical experiments carried out on the inmates of Dachau?

A: Yes, I myself almost underwent something of the sort. Many of my friends and colleagues were—I cannot say used—abused in such experiments. There were all sorts of experiments, injections of Phenol, malaria, cold-water experiments where they were thrown into ice-cold water, air-pressure tests, where people were placed in a bell jar and air was pumped in or out, and many died. They were normally people not capable of working, who were used as what we called guinea pigs.

ϟϟ

Dr. Grüber's testimony lasts for approximately two hours. His words are immediately transmitted by the press all over the world. He has received threats against his life by unnamed forces of evil for agreeing to testify, but the people of Israel are so moved by his selfless behavior that hundreds write him letters of thanks. But this is just the beginning. There will be no letup in the accusations against Adolf Eichmann.

ϟϟ

On August 2, 1941, one year after France surrendered to Nazi Germany, occupied Paris swarmed with German soldiers, combing the streets, looking for Jews of all ages. A particular focus was the 11th arrondissement, an administrative center of the city where the Jewish population was most dense. Soldiers went house to house and business to business, checking personal documents. Georges Wellers, a Jewish Russian-born scientist who became a naturalized French citizen in 1938, bore witness as four thousand Jews are arrested.

Wellers was the father of two children. His wife was not Jewish. He knew this would only protect him from arrest for a short period of time. Nevertheless, he remained in Paris. Twenty years later, sitting on the witness stand at the Beit Ha'am courtroom, Georges Wellers recounts that day.

> STATE ATTORNEY GABRIEL BACH: When were you arrested, Mr. Wellers?
> WITNESS GEORGES WELLERS: I was arrested on 12 December 1941.
> Q: By whom?
> A: By a single policeman who came to my home at five or six in the morning.
> Q: A policeman?
> A: One single German policeman.
> Q: When were you deported to Auschwitz?

A: On 30 June 1944.

Q: How did you arrive there?

A: I arrived in Auschwitz on the 2nd or 3rd of July; I no longer remember. There was one small detail, but it was a very special detail, because I was in a wagon where there were only men. There were no women, and I had a group of friends; there were a dozen of us and we had decided to escape, to slip away in the course of our journey. We had already prepared this; we had sawed away at part of the wagon. To our misfortune, at a certain point, not very far from Paris, the train stopped and the Germans noticed what we had done.

Q: In what kind of train were you deported?

A: It was a goods train, as was always the case. Only one convoy left in a passenger train, the first convoy of 27 March 1942. All the others always left in goods trains. We were seventy and eighty in a wagon, shut in, and, throughout the whole journey, we were never given anything to eat. We were given something to drink once in the course of the journey.

PRESIDING JUDGE MOSHE LANDAU: How many days did the journey take?

WITNESS WELLERS: Four days.

STATE ATTORNEY BACH: How many people were there in the train altogether?

WITNESS WELLERS: The convoy consisted of 1,000 people. If there were sixty to seventy people in a wagon that means there were twenty to twenty-five wagons.

Q: When the convoy of 1,000 reached Auschwitz, was there any sort of selection?

A: Yes, of course. When the train arrived, the wagons were opened and everyone on the train had to get off. We formed a sort of column, or Indian file, and we had to pass before two officers in German uniforms who did not ask any questions. This happened very quickly. We hardly slowed our pace before these two officers, and one of the two officers made us a sign to go to the left or right.

Q: In this selection, how many people out of the 1,000 have remained alive?

A: In my convoy, I think there are three or four of us.

Q: When you tried to escape from the train, did you know where the train was going?

A: No, I had no idea, and I had no idea what was going on at Auschwitz itself.

Q: Until you actually reached Auschwitz, you had no idea that the deportations to the East were for the purpose of extermination?

A: No, I did not know this and we did not know it. We knew very well that the London radio spoke about the gas chambers, but we didn't take it at all seriously. We thought it was propaganda—we didn't believe it was really so.

⚡⚡

But the horrors of the death camps were all too true. Kalman Teigman, a survivor of the Warsaw ghetto, was shipped to a Polish compound known as Treblinka on September 4, 1942.

PRESIDING JUDGE MOSHE LANDAU: Did you believe that you were in an extermination camp?

WITNESS KALMAN TEIGMAN: At the beginning I did not believe it. When I arrived, I saw what was going on there. Later on, the train again moved on, and we continued our journey for almost the whole night. Towards morning, we reached the station at Malkinia. By then, I was standing near the window, and I noticed that Polish men, railway workers, were making signs to us that we were travelling to our deaths. They drew their hands across their throats, as a sign for being slaughtered. At all events, no one wanted to believe it. "How could it be that they could take young, fit people and send them straight to their deaths?" We did not want to believe this.

Once again, the carriages moved, and we came to a certain place. Suddenly we heard shouts in German: "Everybody out, and take all your possessions and parcels with you." Of course, they began immediately hitting people with their rifles and clubs, shooting people who did not manage to get out quickly, most of them elderly people, sick persons, and those who had fainted, and those met their deaths in the freight cars or near the platform. And then we assembled on the platform, and they made us run in the direction of the gate. The gate led into a large yard.

Q: Was this already inside Treblinka?

A: Yes, this was inside the Treblinka camp.

Q: You arrived at the platform. What happened to you at the platform?

A: As I have already said, they opened the freight cars and shouted at us to come out and take with us our personal belongings and parcels. A large number of people were killed on this platform or inside these freight cars, such as those who fainted or those who were not quick enough. On the double, at lightning speed, they made us run towards the courtyard in which those two huts stood. Next to the gate, men were standing, men of the SS and Ukrainians, and here, right away, the sorting began. They shouted to the women to go to the left, and to the men to go to the right. I did not want to part from my mother so soon. Precisely at the gate, I received a blow on my head from something, I think it was from a stick, and I fell down. I got up immediately, for I didn't want to receive another blow, and by then my mother was no longer at my side.

Q: After that, did you see your mother again?

A: After that, I did not see her again.

Q: How many young people were there with you?

A: When we entered the camp, out of the entire transport, they took four hundred people—of course, after sorting, after selection. Two hundred remained in Camp 1, and two hundred young people were sent to the camp where there were the gas chambers. This I learned afterwards, for I did not know about it at the beginning.

Q: Do you want to add something about the Lazarette? Did

something happen in connection with the Lazarette immediately after you arrived?

A: Yes.

Q: Where was that?

A: I see it here. [He points it out.] And, in fact, it was here, at the end of the camp, next to the second gate. This Lazarette was a pit that had been dug out and fenced with barbed wire, and near it, at the entrance, stood a hut painted white, with markings of the Red Cross, and there was also a sign there: Lazarette.

All these people who were killed on the platform, or those who fainted or who still showed signs of life but were unable to walk, we had to carry them to the Lazarette. They cynically gave it this name, as if they were going to the doctor. There was this pit, and we had to throw all these bodies into the pit. Those who were still alive were shot at the edge of the pit and were thrown inside.

ATTORNEY GENERAL GIDEON HAUSNER: On the following day, you went out to work?

WITNESS TEIGMAN: Yes.

Q: What kind of work?

A: At first, we had to take logs of wood and to carry them from place to place. Afterwards, they sent us to sort out personal effects.

Q: What personal effects?

A: The personal effects of the people they had brought there, the victims who had gone to the gas chambers. They left all these articles in our camp, Camp 1, before they entered the ...

Q: What was the quantity of personal effects that you saw, when you first came there?

A: An enormous quantity. There were actually heaps outside on the ground, several storeys high.

Q: Clothes, personal possessions?

A: Clothes, personal possessions, children's toys, shoes. I think there was nothing that ... everything that one could see was there—medicines and instruments, everything.

Q: Meanwhile, did further transports arrive on the day following your arrival?

A: Yes, all the time.

Q: Transports were arriving all the time?

A: At first, there were many transports, almost every day. There were also instances of two transports a day. Later on, after a number of months, the number of transports decreased, there were less.

Q: And so, you say, your work was to carry logs of wood?

A: It was only at the beginning that they gave us that work.

Q: Afterwards, what was your work?

A: We worked in sorting personal effects. There were also people whose work was in preserving fur coats; we also worked on renovating aluminum ware.

Q: Where did all these articles go to?

A: As far as we knew, as the talk went in the camp, all of it went to Germany.

Q: Who shot the people at the Lazarette?

A: There were SS men: Scharfuehrer Mentz or Minz—I do not remember his exact name; they called him Frankenstein, since he had a face which really was frightening to look at—I think his name was Scharfuehrer Minz. The second was Scharfuehrer Miete, he was from Berlin. The third was Scharfuehrer Blitz. And they were helped by one of the Ukrainians, but I don't remember his name.

Q: Once a transport of children arrived, do you remember?

A: Yes. A transport of children arrived. There were two freight cars. The children were almost suffocated, actually. We had to remove their clothes and take them—that is to say, we transported them—into the Lazarette, and there the SS men whom I have mentioned shot them. It was said that these were orphans who came from an orphanage. I don't know.

Q: Generally speaking, what was the size of the transports?

A: Generally, sixty freight cars would arrive, and into each freight car they put about one hundred persons. I imagine that there were up to six thousand persons, or even more.

Q: Was it always Jews only?

A: No. There was also a transport of Gypsies.

Q: One?

A: In fact, there were two, but I remember one well.

Q: Apart from the Gypsies, were all the others Jews?

A: They were Jews.

Q: Do you remember a transport of Jews from Grodno?

A: Yes.

Q: What happened?

A: The transport of Jews from Grodno arrived, that is to say, it was already the second transport. It arrived towards evening.

Q: Before that, was it preceded by another transport?

A: The transport that preceded it was much larger, apparently from the environs of Warsaw—I don't know.

Q: Did they go to the gas chambers?

A: They went to the gas chambers. After that, came the transport from Grodno. This was already towards the evening, and the people who entered the courtyard between those two huts refused to undress. They were told to remove their clothes, to tie their shoes well together; they were given rope, wire, and they were strict about that.

Q: That they should tie their shoes together?

A: That they should tie their shoes together.

Q: Were the people there told why they were being asked to do this?

A: Yes.

Q: What did they tell them?

A: There was also a large notice in the yard which said that all the people were going to take a bath, that they would be disinfected, and all their papers, valuables and money should be handed in to the camp safe which was there on this path that led to the gas chambers. They called it Himmelstrasse (Road to Heaven), or Schlauch (hosepipe), or Himmelallee (Avenue to Heaven). This building was a small hut. These people who had to receive all the papers, all the money, and all the documents stood there.

Q: Can you point out where this Schlauch or this Himmelallee was situated?

A: Yes. I can see it [points to the sketch]. Here we see a certain line, these two buildings. And here is the Schlauch, this Himmelallee.

Q: And here [pointing] the people walked after they had already undressed?

A: Yes. Here the people entered this path, it was called Schlauch or Himmelstrasse.

Q: Can you identify it in the second picture also?

A: In the second picture, one sees it differently from here [points to it]. The people inside the small building who received all the documents and money used to be called *Goldjuden* (gold Jews). The person in charge was someone named *Scharfuehrer Suchomit*. I believe he was from Sudetenland, for he spoke with a Viennese or Austrian accent.

Q: Was it there that they told the people that they would be taken to work, and that they had to take a bath?

A: First of all, they were going to take a bath, and afterwards they should come to retrieve their belongings, and then they would go out to work.

Q: Did the people who reached that point still believe that this was the truth?

A: There were some who, I think, still believed, for at first there was no reaction.

Q: Even after the blows at the railway station, after the whipping?

A: People were confused, for it was done at tremendous speed. I think the people did not even have time to think. Each one fled and ran fast, so as not to receive blows. But perhaps we can pass on to the transport from Grodno.

Q: Let us go back now to the transport from Grodno.
A: Amongst them there were men who called out to the others not to get undressed. Apparently, they realized what was going on and they knew. And so they refused. Then the Germans and the Ukrainians began beating them. They also shot them. I also remember SS men and Ukrainians who were sitting on the roofs on the two huts I mentioned, with automatic weapons, and they also fired into the crowd. Despite all this, the people were not ready to undress. We stood some distance away and saw it all. We were near the yard. Later we heard an explosion. Apparently, someone had thrown a grenade or I don't know what. At any rate, they removed a seriously wounded Ukrainian from this yard. Afterwards, the Germans somehow overpowered them and put them onto this path by force. But most of them walked in their clothes.
Q: When was this?
A: This was several months after I reached Treblinka. I don't remember exactly when.
Q: In 1942?
A: Still in 1942.
Q: What did they do to the women, to the women's hair?
A: The women who came to the camp, as I have said, had to go to the left and to enter one of the buildings in the yard. There they had to undress and to continue walking. There was also a room there. In a section of the room, there were men who were called "barbers." They had to cut off the hair of these women before they entered this path.
Q: Please tell me, did the people who were brought in the transports undergo some kind of selection in the camp, either for work or dispatch?
A: There was no selection, apart from those who were taken out for work. Each time they took a number of people for work.
Q: Work in connection with the extermination?
A: Exactly.
Q: Was there no other work in this camp?

A: There was no other work. It was all connected with the extermination.

⚡⚡

Despite the horrors recounted by close to a hundred witnesses, Adolf Eichmann sits implacable behind his bulletproof glass shield. He shows no emotion, occasionally shifting in his seat and cleaning his glasses. Until Eichmann's trial, it was considered wrong for Holocaust survivors to rehash their terrible memories. The war has been over for sixteen years and the past cannot be changed. But as the testimonies move into the third month, the survivors' remembrances are allowing a catharsis. Eichmann was not personally present for many of the atrocities these men and women describe, but the sheer scope of the Jewish extermination has become startlingly clear.

The former SS officer certainly knows that. But, still, his face displays no emotion. But his constant blowing of his nose and the irregular twitch of his mouth are minor tics giving away his nervousness.

Finally, on June 6, 1961, a man named Avraham Lindwasser is sworn in to give testimony. He survived Treblinka only because he was strong enough to dispose of the bodies. He was fourteen when separated from his mother at the gates after their train arrived at the death camp in Poland—whereupon he watched as she was sent directly down what the Nazis jokingly called the *Himmelstrasse*—the barbed-wire "path to heaven," which led directly to the gas chambers.

Lindwasser delivers his testimony in a crisp voice. He speaks in slow, measured tones, determined to remain calm and direct. But the emotion in each syllable cannot be missed, and his words cause many in the gallery to openly weep.

PRESIDING JUDGE MOSHE LANDAU: What is your full name?
WITNESS AVRAHAM LINDWASSER: Avraham Lindwasser.
Q: On 28 August 1942, you arrived at Treblinka from Warsaw?
A: Correct.
Q: Was there some notice at the station, in German and Polish?

A: Correct.

Q: What did it say?

A: "Jews, after you have bathed and changed your clothes, the journey will continue to the east, to work."

Q: Did they allow you to alight quietly?

A: No.

Q: What happened?

A: They opened the freight cars, we heard the order: "Get out." There were shouts. We began getting off. They struck us with clubs all the time we were getting off, so that they did not give us an opportunity to understand where we were or what was happening; we were chased straight away to the square, and there we were ordered to hand over our money and jewelry; we were then told to remove our shoes.

Q: Who gave the orders?

A: Germans, SS men.

Q: How many people were there in that transport?

A: It is hard for me to say, but more than one thousand.

Q: When you came there, did you know what was the place you had arrived at?

A: No. I knew it was Treblinka, but we did not know the purpose.

Q: Had you heard about Treblinka in Warsaw?

A: We had heard about Treblinka.

Q: Did you know that Jews were being exterminated at Treblinka?

A: We did not believe it.

Q: You did not believe it. Why?

A: Why? This would, perhaps, be difficult to answer. Possibly, it is an individual matter for each person. One simply could not grasp that such a thing was possible—actual extermination. Rumors reached Warsaw that the Germans were sending people out to work. And simply, it was better to cling to this idea.

ATTORNEY GENERAL GIDEON HAUSNER: Did you, already on that day, notice corpses?

WITNESS LINDWASSER: At the beginning, when I entered the place—I was brought in by a German, also one of the SS—

whose name I subsequently learned was Matthias. He took me inside, and we were immediately ordered to take hold of bodies and drag them towards the graves. At first, I thought that the corpses came from the freight cars, people who had died, who were suffocated in the cars, and I was certain that they were undergoing some kind of disinfection here and then buried.

Q: This was adjoining the gas chambers?
A: Next to the small gas chambers.
Q: Before the men transferred the bodies to the pit?
A: Before they were taken to the pits.
Q: And you did this?
A: Yes. I was occupied in this work for approximately one month, a month and a half, perhaps less, perhaps more, until once I recognized my sister's body.
Q: She was lying there, dead?
A: Yes.... I could not stand it. I tried to commit suicide. I was already hanging by my belt, when a bearded Jew—I don't know his name—took me down. He began preaching to me, that while the work in which we were going to be engaged was contemptible and not the kind of thing one ought to do, nevertheless, we should tolerate it and ought to make efforts, so that at least someone should survive who would be able to relate what was happening here, and this would be my duty, since I had light work and would be able to go on living and be of help to others.
Q: Were you working near the gas chambers?
A: Yes.
Q: Did you notice anything at the entrance?
A: The entrance to which chambers? For while we worked at the gas chambers, inside the corridor of the small gas chambers, we also could see the gas chambers at the end. On one occasion, I was even taken—again by that Matthias—to the first camp, in order to fetch pairs of forceps for extracting teeth, since extra men had been added to our group.

We passed by the large chambers and, on the way back, I saw a big curtain at the entrance to the large chambers, a curtain used to cover the Ark containing the Torah Scrolls with the Shield of David on it, and on the curtain there was the inscription: "This is the gate of the Lord, through which the righteous shall enter."

⚡⚡

It is June 20, 1961, when Adolf Eichmann finally takes the stand. He seems shrunken by the months of the damning testimony against him. In that time, he has rarely turned his head to gaze directly at the spectator gallery. Eichmann is deferential to the court, presenting himself as a small cog, and as someone interested in Jewish emigration. But when it finally comes time to speak, Eichmann is once again the proud unrepentant Nazi. "I had no special positions or privileges," he tells the court, establishing his line of defense that he was merely an inconsequential bureaucrat. "They gave me instructions."

But as the courtroom drama turns from examination to cross-examination, the real Eichmann emerges—efficient, arrogant, defiant, and true to his Nazi roots.

⚡⚡

The trial continues until August 14, 1961—114 sessions in all. It is 2:30 in the afternoon when Judge Landau declares the session closed and directly addresses Eichmann. "The trial will now be adjourned for judgment. At any rate, as it looks now, judgment will not be given before the month of November of this year. You will receive approximately two weeks' notice before the date when judgment will be given."

In fact, it is not until December 11, 1961, that the three judges read their decision. There is no jury.

The courtroom is packed as Judge Landau announces his final verdict. As the presiding jurist, he has exacted strict courtroom discipline from all in attendance, despite the emotional severity of the testimony. Applause and catcalls have been forbidden.

Four days later, speaking solemnly, from a lengthy prepared text, he begins the proceedings of December 15 by immediately addressing Eichmann's sentence.

"Now that we have reached the end of the long proceedings in this trial, we must pass sentence on the Accused.

"We started from the assumption that it is within our discretion to determine the penalty in this case.

"The dispatch of each train by the accused to Auschwitz, or to any other extermination site, carrying one thousand human beings, meant that the accused was a direct accomplice in a thousand premeditated acts of murder, and the degree of his legal and moral responsibility for these acts of murder is not one iota less than the responsibility of the person who with his own hands pushed these human beings into the gas chambers. Even if we had found that the Accused acted out of blind obedience, as he argued, we would still have said that a man who took part in crimes of such magnitude as these over years must pay the maximum penalty known to the law.

"This court sentences Adolf Eichmann to death."*

---

* The proceedings of the Eichmann trial are available for viewing on YouTube.

16

May 31, 1962
Buenos Aires, Argentina
Late Evening

Zvi Aharoni may soon confront the Angel of Death.
The Israeli spy nervously fingers his passport, just moments away from entering Argentina for the first time in two years. He will do so illegally, under a false name—and not by choice.

Since returning to Israel he has transferred from Shin Bet to work full-time for the Mossad. Isser Harel has placed him in charge of a new division within the agency focused on hunting for Nazi criminals. Now Aharoni is returning to South America to find and capture the brutal Nazi killer Dr. Josef Mengele. Acting on a tip from a former SS officer, Aharoni has reason to believe the heinous murderer is hiding in the pro-Nazi country of Paraguay—Aharoni's intended destination tonight.

But bad weather has forced a change of plans. Because of wind shear, Aharoni's plane could not land at his scheduled stopover in Montevideo, Uruguay, and has set down in Argentina. The Mossad forbids any agent involved in the Eichmann kidnapping from returning to that country. Some Argentineans are still bitter about Israel's aggressiveness and are eager for revenge. The arrest and subsequent trial of a Mossad agent would be a scene of humiliation for both Aharoni and Israel itself.

Yet Zvi Aharoni has no choice. Buenos Aires's Ezeiza Airport is closing. There are no other flights until morning. So Aharoni must spend the night in Argentina.

On the ground, Aharoni waits to present his fake passport to the Argentinean authorities.

Mossad forgers have been meticulous in preparing his papers, so Aharoni's chances of getting caught are small. Yet as he steps forward in the customs line, the spy cannot help but feel a twinge of nervousness: there is always the chance something might go wrong.

Zvi Aharoni should not be here at all. He was invited to be an eyewitness at the Eichmann execution, which is due to take place any day now. He attended the trial, where he sat in the front row and locked eyes with the man he so famously kidnapped. "I am not sure whether Eichmann recognized me," Aharoni will admit in his autobiography. "He looked directly at us several times, but did not give any sign that he knew who I was."

The spy is satisfied with the guilty verdict but has no wish to attend the hanging. Aharoni recognizes the evil within the former Nazi, but he has also come to know Eichmann very well and might be haunted by the sight of the condemned murderer dangling from a gallows.

"Fortunately, I was spared the dilemma," Aharoni will write, referring to his new Mengele assignment.

In Buenos Aires, the customs agent motions for Aharoni to step forward.

The spy does as he is told.

⚡⚡

Although Aharoni will not witness it himself, danger lurks for Jews in Argentina.

University of Buenos Aires science major Graciela Narcisa Sirota learns this while waiting at a bus stop in June 1962. Fascist militant groups such as the Tacuara have become more active in their persecution of Jews since the Eichmann verdict, making telephone threats, setting fire to schools, and toppling headstones in Jewish cemeteries. In all, there have been more than thirty such incidents in the last month—so many that Argentinean police are reluctant to make arrests for fear of inflaming even more violence. Yet that tactic is failing, for on this very day a Jewish restaurant will be sprayed with machine-gun fire for a second time.

Graciela stands on a busy public thoroughfare, not knowing that she has been targeted, when a gray sedan screeches to a halt at the small kiosk. The doors open and three young members of the Tacuara jump out. One carries a wooden club. He knocks Graciela to the ground with a savage blow to the head. No bystander bothers to help as she is dragged into the backseat of the car, which leaves as quickly as it came.

Unconscious, Graciela is taken to a remote location, where she is stripped and tied to the top of a table. She wakes up to a symphony of pain as her captors take turns punching, molesting, and burning her body with lit cigarettes. "This is in revenge for Eichmann," they tell the nineteen-year-old Jewish student.

Her torso bruised and face swollen, Graciela is helpless to stop the young hoodlums as they carve a swastika into her right breast with a razor blade.

Once again, Graciela passes out from the pain. Her naked body is dumped on a suburban street, in full view of passing cars. She is alive, but barely.

Graciela's horrified parents attempt to file a police report, but it is two days before the Argentinean authorities allow them to press charges. Even after a police physician completes a thorough examination corroborating Graciela's story, federal police chief Horacio Enrique Green claims she brought it on herself, citing her attendance at a leftist protest. Graciela's kidnappers, Green announces, are "moved by a deep and purely nationalistic sentiment, which assumed the form of hurt pride and was evidenced by means of a few anti-Semitic incidents."*

⚡⚡

But Zvi Aharoni knows nothing of this violence.

Instead, he is now tailing a suspect's vehicle from a respectful distance. He has been lucky so far, evading arrest in Argentina and successfully flying to the Brazilian city of São Paulo in his quest to capture Dr. Josef Mengele. The sickening specifics of Mengele's atrocities are well known to Aharoni, for he has committed the Mossad's thick, decades-old file on the death camp doctor to memory.

Aharoni is following a car driven by Wolfgang Gerhard, a forty-year-old fervent Nazi who was once in charge of the Hitler Youth in Austria. It is believed that Josef Mengele lives on a property owned by either Gerhard or an associate. Aharoni's best hope is that the Nazi will lead him to the Angel of Death. There have been a half-dozen alleged Mengele sightings in the last year, but this is the closest Aharoni has come to a genuine lead.

The journey takes them outside the city, onto a highway. Aharoni steels himself for a long ride, hoping he can avoid notice the entire length of the drive. One hundred miles later, upon reaching the Serra Negra region, Gerhard turns onto a small dirt road leading up a hillside. The track is rutted and unpaved, and Aharoni knows all too well that he will attract attention by following Gerhard.

So the Israeli agent turns around and drives back to São Paulo. Three days later he returns to the jungle road. This time he travels with two Mossad agents who have come to aid the hunt for Mengele.

---

* The Tacuara claimed responsibility for the attack on Graciela Sirota. Two weeks later, on July 6, 1962, a seventeen-year-old Jewish girl named Soledad Barrett was attacked in a copycat crime by pro-Nazi thugs. When Barrett refused to repeat the pledge "Long live Hitler," they used a knife to carve a swastika into both her thighs. Barrett was so traumatized that she became a pro-Communist revolutionary and traveled to Moscow for Soviet training. She was shot and killed on January 8, 1973, while trying to overthrow the Brazilian government.

Aharoni arrives at the dirt road once again but this time makes the turn. His rental car absorbs the ruts and bumps for several miles before arriving at a small group of heavily fortified farm buildings. A three-story cement block tower with a red tile roof is the most prominent feature, manned by a solitary individual holding binoculars.

Aharoni's plan of action for what will come next is absurd, but it is important that he make a visual confirmation that the suspect is truly Josef Mengele. So the Mossad agent has no other choice. Stepping out of the car with the other two agents, Aharoni sets out a picnic lunch of sandwiches.

Almost as soon as the men begin eating, three individuals step from the farm to challenge them. Two are dark-skinned and appear to be Brazilians. Wolfgang Gerhard is known to have spoken contemptuously about the locals, referring to them as "half monkeys."

The third man walking toward Zvi Aharoni and his Mossad companions has the pale skin of a European. Aharoni is familiar with the many photographs in Mengele's file, and by all appearances, it is him. Though this man the Brazilian farmhands refer to as "Pedro" tries to conceal his identity by pulling his broad-brimmed straw hat down low over his eyes, the mustache, the height, even the gap between the two front teeth—all match the photographic evidence. Yet now is not the time for a kidnapping. There is no airport nearby for a quick escape from the country and Israel cannot afford another diplomatic fracas in South America. Aharoni must gather proof that this is Mengele, then seek proper official approval to launch a plan of action to capture the Nazi.

Aharoni has a camera within arm's reach, but Mengele is standing too close for the spy to surreptitiously snap a picture. Instead, Aharoni and his companions allow themselves to be chased off the property. His only proof is his gut instinct. "I thought the man may well be Mengele," Aharoni will later write. "In fact, I was sure of it."

A cable is immediately dispatched to Mossad headquarters in Tel Aviv: "Zvi saw on Gerhard's farm a person who in form, height, age and dress looks like Mengele."

Aharoni flies from Brazil to Paris to personally discuss the matter with Isser Harel, who has traveled there on business. "I was certain that in a little while we would be able to bring Mengele to Israel to be tried," he will later remember.

But Harel refuses to approve a kidnapping plan. He has just received news that the same German scientists who devised rockets capable of attacking London during the war are now working for Egypt, Israel's sworn enemy. Until that crisis is solved, all of the Mossad's threadbare resources must be devoted to defeating the threat.

Isser Harel's single-minded focus does not allow him to pay attention to more than one mission at a time. As Aharoni will remember while discussing the history of Mossad, "when Isser began dealing with something, he dealt only with that."*

Zvi Aharoni is experienced enough to know that Josef Mengele will now remain a free man. In fact, the Nazi has been operating in Brazil under his real name, although he sometimes introduces himself as a native of Switzerland named Peter Hochbichler. Recently, however, Mengele has become nervous about whether or not he will be protected by Brazilian authorities, and he has started to take the same secretive precautions as Adolf Eichmann.

The Angel of Death is, indeed, living on the farm twenty-five miles outside of São Paulo, growing tropical fruit, coffee, and rice and overseeing a large herd of cattle. Mengele also consorts with Nazis all over the world. The Mossad suspects he travels extensively to cities like Rome and Milan.†

So it is that one of the most notorious and brutal Nazi war criminals lives a fairly normal life, protected by state and local authorities in Brazil and Paraguay, where he frequently travels.

But that situation will soon change.

---

* It was all about money. Mossad could barely afford to protect the borders of Israel, so international operations were shut down.

† The Mossad's file on Josef Mengele was released to the public in September 2017. Reports of Mengele's European travels were wildly exaggerated.

17

May 31, 1962
Ramleh Prison, Israel
7:00 p.m.

"You will be hanged at midnight," Israeli prison commissioner Arye Nir informs Adolf Eichmann.

It has been six months since the death sentence was passed. Eichmann's attorney immediately filed an appeal, giving the condemned murderer time to write his autobiography while awaiting the outcome. Two days ago, a five-judge panel of the Israeli Supreme Court upheld the decision. Eichmann's final hope was a plea for clemency to Yitzhak Ben-Zvi, president of Israel.

"There is a need to draw a line between the leaders responsible and the people like me forced to serve as mere instruments in the hands of the leaders," Eichmann wrote to Ben-Zvi.

"I was not a responsible leader, and as such do not feel myself guilty. I am not able to recognize the court's ruling as just, and I ask, Your Honor Mr. President, to exercise your right to grant pardons, and order that the death penalty not be carried out."

That request was quickly denied.

The execution will take place here in this prison outside Jerusalem.

Israeli law dictates that the death penalty must be carried out by hanging, but until recently, a working gallows did not even exist in the country. During the time of British rule it was common to hang Jews convicted of terrorism against the Crown, but the gallows once used has been relocated to a museum as a reminder of Israel's painful struggle to become a nation.

So a former guards' quarters in Ramleh has been converted to a place of execution. A hole was cut in the third floor and a special wooden platform and trapdoor were built over the opening. The frame from which the rope dangles is made of iron. A button controls the trapdoor. Once it is sprung, Eichmann will plummet straight down into a darkened room on the second floor. Witnesses to the execution will be able to see Eichmann as the noose is draped around his neck. However, once the Nazi drops through to the level below, onlookers will be spared the aftereffects of a hanging—swollen tongue jutting from the mouth, eyes popping from the skull, the final release of the bowels as the sphincter muscle relaxes.

The new gallows have been inspected by a police commissioner and engineer. The rope has also been tested, utilizing a bag loaded with weight to match Eichmann's own body mass. By Israeli law, the execution must take place between midnight and 8:00 a.m. A black flag must be raised over the prison immediately afterward.

Eichmann is well aware that many considered the appeals process to be a formality. He also knows that Ramleh Prison has been preparing for his execution. The gallows are just fifty yards from his cell and the sounds of construction have been impossible to ignore.

Prison commissioner Nir now asks Eichmann what he would like for his last meal. But Eichmann prefers not to eat. Instead, he requests a bottle of Carmel, a kosher Israeli wine. He also asks for cigarettes, along with pen and paper.*

---

* A 2014 study by researchers at Cornell University examined the last meal choices of 247 death row inmates. Those who maintained they were innocent were far more likely to reject a final meal.

Over the next four hours, Adolf Eichmann writes to Vera and their sons. She has refused to admit to his crimes, still believing that her husband was just following orders. Since Eichmann's kidnapping, Vera has left Buenos Aires and returned to Germany. But she has had trouble adapting after such a long absence and is eager to return to South America. Just one month ago, on April 30, Israeli authorities allowed Vera and Adolf Eichmann one final visit. The meeting was so secret that Israeli authorities will not acknowledge it for forty-five years.

Vera was smuggled into Israel via Zurich, using a passport in her maiden name of Vera Loebel. She was then escorted into the prison shortly after midnight and visited her condemned husband from 12:20 to 1:43 in the morning.

One month later, Eichmann chain-smokes and sips half the bottle of wine while writing his final letters. In preparation for his execution, he brushes his teeth and shaves. The Nazi has become obsessed with cleanliness during his time in prison and is prone to washing his hands compulsively.

At 11:20 Eichmann is visited by Rev. William Hull, a Canadian missionary who has made it his goal to convert Eichmann to traditional Christianity. The task has been futile, with Eichmann labeling the Old Testament as "Jewish fairy tales" and refusing to ask forgiveness for his crimes under the premise that he is not guilty.

"Why are you sad?" Eichmann asks the minister. "I am astonished that *I* have such peace."

Twenty minutes before midnight, the men are joined in Eichmann's cramped cell by two guards and prison commandant Nir. They have come to take the prisoner to his death. Eichmann prays alone in a corner for a brief moment, then submits to the guards, who tie his hands behind his back.

The unrepentant Nazi is led from his second-floor cell and marched down the hall, then upstairs to the execution chamber. The group enters the room containing the gallows, where four members of the press, a policeman, and Agent Rafi Eitan await. It was Eitan who helped subdue Eichmann on the night of the kidnapping. Just one hour ago, he was sitting at home when he got the call to witness Eichmann's execution. Now the two men look across the small room at each other. They are less than thirty feet apart.

Adolf Eichmann is led to the wooden platform and made to stand over the trapdoor. He wears brown trousers, a matching shirt, and slippers with a checkered design. The guards tie his legs together. This will prevent him from kicking and fighting the rope once the trapdoor is sprung.

The Nazi looks across the room, focusing his gaze on Rafi Eitan. "I hope, very much, that it will be your turn soon after mine," Eichmann coldly tells him.

The hangman steps forward. His name is Shalom Nagar. A short Yemenite Jew, he is one of twenty-two men specially chosen to guard Eichmann during the previous six months at Ramleh. He has seen Eichmann in his most intimate moments and was tasked with tasting Eichmann's food to ensure it was not poisoned and with preventing the condemned man from committing suicide.

Now it is no longer Nagar's job to keep Adolf Eichmann alive, but to ensure that he dies.

Nagar offers to place a black hood over Eichmann's head. The Nazi refuses.

Eichmann now speaks directly to the gathered journalists. "Long live Germany," he tells them. "Long live Argentina. Long live Austria. Those are the three countries with which I have been most connected and which I will not forget. I greet my wife, my family, and my friends. I was required to obey the laws of war and my flag. I am prepared."

Nagar places the noose over Eichmann's head and tightens the knot around his neck. The rope has been lined with leather to prevent friction burns.

Nagar and another guard step behind a blanket that has been draped over the trapdoor's electrical release mechanism. Two buttons are hidden behind the curtain, but only one activates the actual release. Both guards will depress their buttons at the same time, neither man knowing whether his is the lethal device.

Eichmann's face goes pale. The peace he professed forty minutes ago is nowhere to be seen.

"Gentlemen, we shall meet again soon, so is the fate of all men. I have believed in God all my life, and I die believing in God," says Eichmann, uttering his final words.

"Ready!" barks prison commandant Arye Nir.

Adolf Eichmann's pallor turns to gray. He looks down at the trapdoor beneath his feet, his lips pursed.

"Action," orders Nir.

The two guards behind the blanket press their buttons. Eichmann immediately drops from sight as the trapdoor falls open.

For the rest of his life, Shalom Nagar will claim it was his button that sprang the mechanism. In fact, he will contradict some accounts and say that he was the only man sent to execute Eichmann and that it was a lever instead of a button that did the job.

What is certain is that one hour later, Nagar is sent downstairs to the second floor to remove Eichmann's body from the rope. "His face was white as chalk, his eyes were bulging and his tongue was dangling out. The rope rubbed the skin off his neck, and his tongue and chest were covered with blood. I didn't know that when a person is strangled all the air remains in his stomach. So when I lifted him, all the air that was inside came out and the most horrifying sound was released from his mouth—'baaaaa,'" Nagar will long remember.

"For years I had nightmares of those moments."

⚡⚡

Adolf Eichmann's body is placed on a stretcher and carried to a crematorium just outside the prison walls. A jailer who was once an inmate at Auschwitz, where he was forced to operate the ovens that burned the bodies of murdered Jews, has been given the task of incinerating Eichmann. One of the observers is police inspector Michael Goldman-Gilad who still bears the telltale tattoo given to all Auschwitz prisoners. It was once his job to spread ashes of the dead on icy Auschwitz walkways in the winter to prevent the SS guards from slipping on the slick paths.

The task of burning Eichmann's dead body takes two long hours.

Adolf Eichmann's ashes are then placed inside a small urn and driven one hour to the port city of Haifa. Police patrol boat *Yarden* waits at the dock. The ashes are motored six miles out into the Mediterranean. The Israelis are determined that neo-Nazis not portray Eichmann as a martyr and raise a memorial to his place of burial. Instead, the Nazi murderer's ashes are dumped at sea without ceremony.

At long last, justice has been served.

18

February 28, 1967
São Paulo, Brazil
Evening

The trap is set.

For fifty-nine-year-old Franz Stangl, one of life's simple pleasures is ending his workday by joining his youngest daughter for a beer at a local tavern. Like many Germans who immigrated to South America after the war, the Stangl family works for a company with ties to the Fatherland. Franz and Isolde both have jobs at Volkswagen. In addition, Franz's wife, Theresa, who prefers to call him by his middle name of "Paul," is one of the head bookkeepers at the local Mercedes-Benz plant.

Unlike Stangl's old friend, Adolf Eichmann, the former SS commandant does not live in poverty. Stangl and his family reside in São Paulo's well-to-do Brooklin residential district. He owns a car, in which father and daughter commute the fifteen miles to and from the Volkswagen facility each day.

The beer is cold and the time with Isolde, in her early twenties, a welcome respite. Afterward, the two pull up to the house and park, knowing Theresa has a hot meal waiting inside.

But something is not right.

As he opens his car door, Stangl hears footsteps. In a flash, a half-dozen strong hands grab him, throwing him onto the street. Isolde is also being wrenched from the car, but the attackers now ignore her—she cries out in panic as she falls to the side of the road.

Stangl tries to fight back. Although a strong man in his youth, with a square jaw and imposing physique, he suffered a near-fatal heart attack last year. The aging Nazi is easily pinned to the ground. His arms are yanked behind his back and he feels steel handcuffs tightening around his wrists. Inside the house, Theresa Stangl has heard the shouting of men's voices and the screams of her daughter. She now looks on helplessly as her husband is pushed into the back of a black-and-white Volkswagen police car and driven away.

Incredibly, this is not a moment of shock to Franz Stangl. "I wasn't surprised," he will later admit. "I had always expected it."

Ever since the Israelis executed Eichmann, Stangl feared this day might come. As the former commandant of the Treblinka and Sobibór death camps, the Austrian was personally complicit in the deaths of nine hundred thousand Jews. His tactics while commanding Treblinka are now known worldwide, having been detailed in Kalman Teigman's eyewitness testimony at the Eichmann trial.

At first, Stangl could not come to terms with the daily mass executions he oversaw. Before going to bed at night, he would drink a large glass of brandy in order to sleep. But after a few months on the job, that changed. Stangl grew to consider Jews nothing more than "cargo" and marveled at the enormous trust he saw in their eyes before they went to their deaths.

"I rarely saw them as individuals," he will explain to a journalist. "It was always a huge mass. I sometimes stood on the wall and saw them in the tube. But—how can I explain it—they were naked, packed together, running, being driven with whips.... This was the system.... It worked and because it worked, it was irreversible."

Cramped in the backseat of the police vehicle, Stangl believes he has been kidnapped by Mossad agents, who have disguised themselves as Brazilian cops. Everything from their uniforms to their Portuguese is perfect. It's almost as if they're real police officers.

Franz Stangl is terrified. He knows he was foolish to continue living in Brazil under his real name, particularly after what happened to Eichmann. Relatives back home in Austria even have the Stangl mailing address. The former Nazi never told his wife the truth about his wartime activities; thus, changing his name would have caused Theresa to ask too many uncomfortable questions.

Now Stangl is regretting his mistake.

As the VW patrol car slows and turns into the São Paulo Office of Public Security, the Nazi grows confused. The Mossad would never drive him to the federal police who are not sympathetic to Israel.

Right now, Franz Stangl desperately wants the answer to one simple question: who has captured him?

⚡⚡

If there is one man in the world who annoys Mossad director Isser Harel more than any other, it is a fifty-nine-year-old death camp survivor living in Austria. The man's name is Simon Wiesenthal, and he is currently taking full public credit for the capture of Adolf Eichmann. Even though he was not part of the abduction plot, Wiesenthal claims he located Eichmann for the Mossad. Even though it's not true, there is nothing Harel can do about it.

For political reasons, Israeli prime minister David Ben-Gurion has prohibited the Mossad from acknowledging their role in the Nazi's kidnapping—a period of silence set to last fifteen years.

So Wiesenthal has stepped boldly into that void, basking in the acclaim. His sensational tell-all book, *I Chased Eichmann: A True Story*, was published in Hebrew six weeks before the trial began. Wiesenthal survived several Nazi death camps and has endured the near-death experience of being stripped naked in preparation for being shot dead at point-blank range. While attending the trial, he unfailingly spoke to reporters about his role in the kidnapping. Privately, Israeli officials disparage Wiesenthal as a "publicity hound."

Some even call him "Sleazenthal."

But most galling of all to Harel is that while Simon Wiesenthal promotes himself as the world's greatest Nazi hunter, he is secretly on the Mossad payroll, using the code name Theocrat. It is the undercover nature of Wiesenthal's role that allows him to take credit, even as the true spies cannot even tell their spouses what they have done.

The Nazi hunter's penchant for embellishment is well known. For instance, the number of death camps in which Wiesenthal claims to have resided seems to increase with every passing year. But in truth, no other individual has been more devoted to finding and prosecuting the SS than Simon Wiesenthal, and for good reason. An architect before the war, he was irrevocably changed by his own experiences during the Holocaust. One such moment came while he was interned at the Mauthausen death camp. SS leader Heinrich Himmler arrived to pay a visit. In an effort to entertain him, the camp guards engaged in an activity they liked to call *Fallschirmspringen*— parachute jumping. Wiesenthal bore witness to the sight of more than one thousand Dutch Jews being thrown over the edge of a quarry, falling 165 feet to their deaths.

Another horror occurred on April 12, 1943, when SS guards lined up Wiesenthal and forty other men along the side of a burial pit. Just a few feet away, six other SS men aimed submachine guns at the group. Wiesenthal and the captives were ordered to strip. But just before they were all shot, a corporal came running to the edge of the pit to pull Wiesenthal away. With Adolf Hitler's birthday coming up, the camp commandant needed someone to paint a large mural celebrating the Führer. Wiesenthal, thanks to his drawing prowess, was that man. He quickly dressed and raced away from the burial pit, even as the sound of submachine gunfire quickly announced the death of his fellow inmates.

As Wiesenthal learned, no atrocity was considered too vile. Wiesenthal witnessed fellow camp inmates being lashed with bullwhips, knifed, pushed into pits of hot lime, burned alive in bonfires, or simply shot for allegedly trying to escape. If a prisoner actually did escape, twenty-five men were shot as retribution.

But the true turning point for Simon Wiesenthal came in the

waning days of the war. A German corporal named Merz asked how Wiesenthal would describe the atrocities to those who had not witnessed them.

"I believe I would tell people the truth," Wiesenthal replies.

"You know what would happen, Wiesenthal?" Merz responds with a smile. "They wouldn't believe you. They'd say you were crazy. Might even put you into a madhouse. How can anyone believe this terrible business—unless they lived through it?"

Thus inspired, Wiesenthal spent the first few years after the war working with American prosecutors building evidence for the Nuremberg Trials. But that was just the beginning. Working first out of an office in Linz, Austria, a few blocks from Eichmann's prewar residence and just miles from the former Mauthausen death camp, Wiesenthal became the self-proclaimed voice of the six million Jews murdered in the Holocaust. Throughout Europe, there is a growing belief that reconciliation and forgiveness are the best way to deal with Nazi atrocities. Yet Wiesenthal and his wife, Cyla, have roundly rejected this philosophy. He has devoted his postwar life to tracking down as many Nazi war criminals as possible. Shortly after the Eichmann trial in 1961, Wiesenthal relocated his headquarters to Vienna. There, in a three-room office cluttered with card files, yellowing newspapers, and photographs of Nazi killers, he keeps track of hundreds of missing war criminals. His secretary simply refers to Wiesenthal as "the Engineer," in a nod to his former life as an architect. He lives off donations coming in from around the world and off his small Mossad stipend. For Simon Wiesenthal, this meager living is enough.*

Wiesenthal often depends upon tips from informants to crack a case. Most suspects are simple men: camp guards, police,

---

* While in a concentration camp early in the war, Cyla Wiesenthal became separated from her husband. Afterward, she wrote to a lawyer friend in Kraków, Poland, asking him to help locate her husband's remains. Coincidentally, Wiesenthal had also written to the same lawyer with a similar request that he help find his wife's body. Thus, the two were reunited. When they calculated how many members of their immediate families had survived the war, they were shattered to find that the answer was none. In all, eighty-nine of their relatives had been murdered.

functionaries. Their capture might create a local stir, such as that of Karl Silberbauer, the Austrian police inspector and former SS official who personally arrested the family of Anne Frank in 1944.*

But Wiesenthal is most obsessed about catching the top echelon of the SS. On that list is Martin Bormann, Adolf Hitler's personal secretary. Long before President Harry Truman signed an order on June 16, 1948, authorizing America's Federal Bureau of Investigation to track down this Nazi villain, Wiesenthal had been investigating his whereabouts. The Nazi hunter is convinced that Bormann escaped from Berlin in the final days of the war and has been living in South America. There is no doubt that Bormann's plan to resurrect the German economy following the war is succeeding brilliantly, with German businesses around the world prospering at record levels. Since 1948, there have been a number of unverified Bormann sightings in Argentina, Uruguay, Brazil, and Paraguay. In 1961, allegedly masquerading under the last name of Bauer, Bormann was reportedly spotted at the Ali Baba nightclub in Asunción. At his side was Josef Mengele.†

Bormann's current location is unknown to Simon Wiesenthal. He is thought to have massive landholdings in the cattle-growing region of Argentina, and to be fond of visiting the resort city of Bariloche, where he operates under a Jewish alias, believing this will throw any Israeli commando off the scent.

ᛋᛋ

---

* Anne Frank was a fifteen-year-old German-born Jew who spent the war in hiding. She kept a journal of the experience that would later be turned into a bestselling book, *The Diary of Anne Frank*. When a stage version of the book was performed in Linz, Austria, in 1958, a group of Holocaust deniers picketed the show, proclaiming it to be fiction. To disprove this belief, Wiesenthal spent five years searching for the officer who arrested the Frank family. Anne Frank died in Bergen-Belsen prison just three weeks before it was liberated by Allied troops. Though Karl Silberbauer admitted his guilt in the Frank arrests, he was exonerated of all charges by the Austrian courts.

† CIA and FBI documents declassified as part of the 1999 Nazi War Crimes Disclosure Act contain extensive details about the ongoing U.S. pursuit of Bormann and the many sightings of him decades after he had allegedly died.

Of all the high-ranking SS still at large, Simon Wiesenthal is most obsessed with capturing Dr. Josef Mengele—and feels he is getting closer by the day.

Just prior to the start of the Eichmann trial in 1961, Wiesenthal received a tip from his network of global informants that the Angel of Death was vacationing on the Greek island of Kythnos with his wife, Martha—with whom Mengele had allegedly split two years earlier.

In an unusual move, though one suiting his fondness for publicity, Wiesenthal did not inform Greek officials. Instead, he told editors at the German magazine *Quick* about the Mengele sighting. Two days later, a reporter arrived, only to find no trace of Mengele. In the six years since, Wiesenthal has had reason to believe the Angel of Death has been sighted in Peru, Brazil, and Chile.

By 1967, Wiesenthal has publicly stated that he knows Mengele's location "quite exactly." In a separate statement, Wiesenthal will claim that Dr. Mengele and Martin Bormann are actually neighbors.

In truth, the Nazi hunter is chasing rumors and hunches. He has absolutely no proof of anything. Simon Wiesenthal is not any closer to capturing the elusive Josef Mengele or Martin Bormann in 1967 than he was in 1948.

⚡⚡

The same cannot be said for Franz Stangl.

Simon Wiesenthal has been pursuing the death camp commandant for three years. Stangl's middle daughter, Renate, married an Austrian named Herbert Havel in 1957. The marriage ended badly—so terribly, in fact, that Havel sought revenge against the Stangl family. After reading in the Vienna newspapers about the horrors of Treblinka, Havel went to Wiesenthal's office and revealed Stangl's location.

It took three years, but Wiesenthal convinced the Austrian Ministry of Justice and officials in West Germany to work with Brazilian authorities to arrest and extradite Franz Stangl. There would be no Israeli-style kidnapping.

When Brazil balked, Wiesenthal enlisted the aid of New York senator Robert F. Kennedy to apply pressure. "What's at stake is justice for enormous crimes," Kennedy said in a phone call to Brazil's U.S. ambassador. "Brazil now has an opportunity to gain millions of friends."

On June 8, 1967, the Brazilian Supreme Court ruled that Franz Stangl should be extradited to West Germany to stand trial for crimes against humanity.

Two weeks later—now having his answer as to who arrested him—Stangl leaves Brazil forever.

He is taken to Düsseldorf, Germany, where he stands trial for war crimes. The incarceration and trial drag on for three years. Stangl is convicted and sentenced to life in prison.

Within six months, a heart attack kills him.

19

December 7, 1972
Berlin, Germany
Morning

It has been twenty-eight years since aerial bombing by the British and Americans, as well as artillery fire from the Soviet army, destroyed the main hall of the Lehrer railway station in Berlin and rendered its tracks useless. Construction workers now pick through the rubble, selecting bricks and other items that can be utilized in the ongoing rebuilding of Berlin. It was here, just north of the river Spree, where Adolf Hitler's chief aid, Martin Bormann, was last seen alive in 1945. Time and again, investigators searched for his remains. No stone or track was left unturned. Yet the Bormann mystery remains unsolved.

Berlin has changed dramatically since the Reichsleiter disappeared. A stone wall twelve feet high now divides the city into east and west—Communist and capitalist. More than three hundred East German sentry towers line the wall. Those trying to escape from the austerity of East Berlin to the sex, drugs, and rock-and-roll lifestyle of West Berlin are shot on sight. This division is a visible scar reminding the Germans that they are a conquered people. It seems unlikely the Berlin Wall will ever come down, but the emotional resolution of solving the Bormann mystery might mitigate some of the frustration the people of Berlin feel about this division of their city.*

Yet on December 13, 1971, the West German government declared the hunt for Martin Bormann over. Chancellor Willy Brandt was tired of reliving the Nazi past. Jewish groups, led by Simon Wiesenthal, were outraged, declaring that the search would not end until Bormann was found, dead or alive. At the same time, neo-Nazi radicals inside Germany used the announcement to push propaganda that Bormann was indeed alive, preparing to launch a Fourth Reich.

The chaos surrounding the announcement shook the West German government in Bonn, causing the hunt for Bormann to be reopened.

Which is why, despite the mundane nature of sifting through rocks and dirt, the Berlin workmen press their shovels into the earth with a glimmer of hope. This rail yard is famous for being the site of Bormann's disappearance. In July 1965, West German officials had authorized yet another hunt for his remains on this very spot. Once again, nothing was found, despite two days of digging. So the odds of finding Bormann's body are slight. The ground is hard, thanks to the autumn frost. Progress is slow.

Suddenly, one worker is shocked to unearth a human skull. Then another. All work stops as the crew wipes away the soil from their discoveries. The skulls are exhumed first, followed by the remainder of the skeletons. Curiously, though the Berlin dirt is known for being a unique pale yellow color, the corpses are encased in clay of a deep red hue. Both skulls also contain glass shards embedded in the jaw, a possible sign of the use of cyanide capsules.

---

* There is no accurate count of how many were shot and killed trying to cross the wall into West Berlin, but the figure is thought to be somewhere between 180 and 200. On the other hand, the number of individuals shot trying to escape into East Berlin is well known: zero.

Then, another extraordinary find: a military pass is discovered near the taller of the two skeletons, identifying it as the remains of Dr. Ludwig Stumpfegger, Hitler's personal physician—the same man who had fled the bunker with Martin Bormann that May night in 1945. Somehow this document remains intact and legible after more than a quarter century in the dirt—but there is little trace of the clothing or shoes the men must have worn. Those garments have disappeared.

Also suspicious is that the skeletons are discovered just yards from the site of the very thorough 1965 excavation. Nevertheless, at a press conference in Frankfurt two weeks after the find, West German authorities are quick to proclaim that the smaller of the two skeletons does indeed belong to Martin Bormann. In the future, police throughout Germany are informed, "If anyone is arrested on suspicion that he is Bormann we will be dealing with an innocent man."

But there is doubt. Simon Wiesenthal attends the official press conference and states that the skull does not look like that of Bormann. American reporter Paul Manning, who has been tracking the Bormann case for years, writes that the bodies are not that of the dead Nazi and Hitler's doctor but of two hapless inmates from the Sachsenhausen concentration camp. Manning opines that the men were killed because the shapes of their skulls were a perfect match for Bormann and Stumpfegger. He further claims that the bodies were disguised in Nazi uniforms, then buried in secret by a special SS team on April 30, 1945, anticipating that the remains would be located at some future date.*

---

* Manning utilized captured Third Reich documents, files from the OSS and FBI, British intelligence, and the United States Treasury Department while tracking Bormann and looted Nazi wealth, which Manning referred to as "the Nazi flight-capital program." Manning was very specific about the details of Bormann's location, yet provided scant evidence to back up his theories. Given his four decades in the business and wartime work with CBS News, Manning was taken seriously as a journalist, so this breach of protocol is unusual. However, publications such as the *New York Times* gave enough credence to his work that on March 3, 1973, shortly after the finding of the alleged Bormann skull in Berlin, the paper ran a Manning op-ed piece about Bormann's ongoing role in the revival of postwar Germany.

Another question lingers. In the mid-1960s, a retired German mailman named Albert Krumnow emerged from anonymity to make the startling claim that upon the fall of Berlin, he was forced by the Soviets to bury the corpses of two high-ranking Germans. This confession is what led to the fruitless July 1965 excavation. The veracity of Krumnow's story has never been disproved. But his reasons for emerging to tell it almost twenty years later are unclear, leading some to believe that it is fiction as part of an ongoing Nazi conspiracy.

※

On April 4, 1973, the Frankfurt State Prosecution Office releases their final report on Martin Bormann.

"Although nature has placed limits on human powers of recognition, it is proved with certainty that the two skeletons found on the Ulap fairgrounds in Berlin on December 7 and 8, 1972, are identical with the accused Martin Bormann and Dr. Ludwig Stumpfegger.

"The search for Martin Bormann is officially terminated."

But instead of handing the bones over to Bormann's remaining relatives, including his namesake son who serves as a Jesuit priest, the skeleton of Martin Bormannn is locked in a cabinet, and there it will remain for more than a quarter century.

Unguarded.

※

Even as the skeleton and skull molder over the years, there is one detail that West German officials cannot explain: the dental work. In May 1945 Dr. Hugo Blaschke, Adolf Hitler's personal dentist, dictated the contents of Bormann's dental history by memory to Allied interrogators who were trying to locate Bormann.

Blaschke's recollections prove to be exact. The skull thought to be Bormann's is an almost perfect match with the dental records. However, there is one significant problem: extensive dental work had been performed on the skull since 1945, including the addition of several crowns and fillings, using dental techniques that were not available in 1945.

This stunning revelation is not publicized until 1976—three years after West Germany declared Bormann dead.*

So it is that Simon Wiesenthal and others are certain that the Martin Bormann "discovery" in Berlin is a fraud. Wiesenthal is sure the heinous Nazi is alive and prospering with the help of ODESSA.

But Simon Wiesenthal must prove it.

He believes that Argentina is the place to do that.

---

* The dental investigation was performed by Dr. Reidar F. Soggnaes, founding dean of the UCLA School of Dentistry. Results were published in the *Legal Medicine Annual, 1976*. Another of the examining pathologists, Dr. W. H. Thomas of Wales, noted of the discovery: "The dental records, while proving the identity of Bormann, displayed worrying anomalies which suggested that much dental work had been carried out after 1945 . . . there is, therefore, considerable proof that Bormann's remains were taken back to Berlin for discovery." Dr. Thomas puts forth his belief that Bormann had actually died in Paraguay, date unknown. The Welsh doctor based that opinion on soil found on Bormann's skeleton.

20

May 16, 1976
São Paulo, Brazil
Afternoon

The Angel of Death is not in Argentina. Nor is he in Paraguay. Or Uruguay. Or any of the places Simon Wiesenthal claims Josef Mengele has been spotted.

Instead, he lives alone in a two-bedroom bungalow at 5555 Estrada Alvarenga in the seedy Brazilian neighborhood of Eldorado Paulista. Mengele's roof leaks and he has painted the interior yellow and green. "My cage becomes more comfortable," he wrote after laying tile on sections of the cracked hardwood floor, "but it is still a cage."

The sixty-five-year-old SS officer is racked by loneliness. He never drinks, for fear of slipping up and saying something incriminating that will lead the authorities to his door. The regular flow of funds being smuggled to him through the family business in Günzburg, Germany, is drying up. A new generation has taken over the company and is reluctant to entangle its livelihood with an infamous butcher. Hans Sedlmeier, the company go-between who acts as Mengele's contact, is still active in caring for the Angel of Death,

Josef Mengele's Residences in South America
1949–1979

1. 1949—Boarding house in the suburb of Vicente López
2. 1949—Moved to the neighborhood of Florida
3. 1953—Apartment in the center of Buenos Aires
4. 1954—Rented house in Olivos suburb
5. 1960—On a farm near Hohenau
6. 1960—On a farm at Serra Negra
7. 1961—Bought a farm in Nova Europa
8. 1969—Bought a farmhouse in Caieiras
9. 1974—Rented a bungalow in Eldorado
10. 1979—Mengele dies at a resort near Bertioga

Map by Gene Thorp

but the small envelopes of money now contain less than $150 per month.

Mengele no longer risks using his own name, preferring a number of aliases to protect his identity. Sometimes he goes by "Don Pedro," sometimes "Wolfgang Gerhard." The real Wolfgang Gerhard, the Hitler Youth leader so fanatic he adorns his Christmas tree with swastikas, and who protected Mengele for so many years in Brazil, has returned to Germany to be with his wife as she dies from cancer. He has gifted Mengele with his Brazilian identity card, even though the Angel of Death is fourteen years older and six inches shorter than Gerhard.

Mengele's own wife, Martha, still keeps in touch but never visits from her home in Germany. Back when he lived on the farm outside São Paulo, Mengele sated his longing for feminine companionship by having an affair with the married woman for whom he managed the property. Blue-eyed Gitta Stammer is Hungarian. She came to Brazil with her husband, Geza, in 1948.

Mengele had purchased half the farm, so their finances were intertwined. Their relationship grew strained as the Nazi began criticizing the way the Stammers were raising their two sons. Upon learning his true identity, Gitta furiously challenged him: "You're such a great man, so why do you live in hiding? At least your colleagues had the guts to live openly and stand trial. Sure, some were hung . . . but they were real men. They didn't hide."

But now Mengele's days on the farm are over, as is his affair with Gitta Stammer. He has an enlarged prostate, degenerative discs in his back, and digestive problems caused by hair balls in his intestines from the nervous habit of chewing and swallowing the ends of his large mustache.

Mengele's only companion is a sixteen-year-old neighbor named Luis Rodriguez, who sometimes stops by to watch the *Wonderful World of Disney* on the doctor's black-and-white television. A homesick Mengele bought the TV specifically to watch the 1976 Winter Olympics, being held in the Austrian Alps just 150 miles south of his hometown. Lonely, he hopes that his thirty-two-year-old son

Rolf, a lawyer in the German city of Freiburg, might soon make the journey from Europe to pay him a discreet visit.

On this Sunday afternoon, Mengele is elated to have several guests from the old country. Ernesto Glawe is an engineer from Germany who has come, along with his fiancée and son, to pay his respects. But this is not a social call, as Mengele believes. It is a visit arranged by the doctor's contacts back in Europe, checking up on his state of mind. Glawe has been told that "Don Pedro" is a lonely widower.

Ernesto Glawe does not know Mengele's true identity. He believes the lie that "Don Pedro" is the nickname for "Peter Gerhard," who once served as a sergeant in the Wehrmacht infantry.

The visit is friendly, but when it comes time to say good-bye, Mengele abruptly grabs the right side of his head as if struck a hard blow. When he tries to explain what is happening, the doctor is unable to speak. Mengele then falls hard to the floor; the muscles on the left side of his body completely paralyzed.

But he is not dead.

⚡⚡

"If I could get this man, my soul would finally be at peace," Simon Wiesenthal tells *Time* magazine, for an issue that will go on sale September 26, 1977. Wiesenthal's interview is conducted in the Vienna offices of the Jewish Documentation Center, as he now calls his company. The Nazi hunter would consider the capture of Dr. Josef Mengele to be the summation of his life's work, but he is also comfortable with what he calls the "biological solution"—or simply, Mengele's death by old age.

These are not good times for Simon Wiesenthal. He is sixty-six and in failing health because of a heart condition. The bank holding all his finances has failed, rendering him and the Jewish Documentation Center without monetary resources. And he has become the subject of ridicule in Austria, thanks to an ongoing feud with Chancellor Bruno Kreisky, a Socialist and Jew whom Wiesenthal has publicly charged with appointing Nazis to his cabinet.

"Two old Jews fight," Wiesenthal tells *Time* magazine, referring to himself and Kreisky, "and the SS men laugh."

For now, Wiesenthal has all but given up the search for Martin Bormann. He has continued to seek out lesser Nazis, but in his financial distress the aging hunter finds that Josef Mengele has become his unlikely ally. The public is fascinated by the Angel of Death's whereabouts. Wiesenthal's ongoing publicity campaign about Mengele's likely location fuels this mystery—and results in the thousands of dollars in donations required to keep Wiesenthal's foundation afloat.

So even though the Nazi hunter has no real clue about where to locate the Angel of Death, he goes on record as stating that Mengele now lives in Paraguay, in the village of San Antonio. Wiesenthal tells *Time* that Mengele also has a villa in Puerto Stroessner, a city named for the Paraguayan president Alfredo Stroessner, who is offering the Angel of Death refuge. Wiesenthal talks about Mengele's drinking problem and fondness for sunglasses. He claims that instead of ODESSA, the doctor is now protected by the Nazi group Die Spinne (The Spider). Like ODESSA, the actual existence of Die Spinne has never been proven. Sadly, Wiesenthal reports, Mengele is working with Stroessner and Die Spinne to subjugate the Aché Indians of Paraguay, using the same "German methods" once utilized in the concentration camps.*

Wiesenthal cannot prove any of these theories that he presents as facts. The Nazi hunter would like to share another sliver of information about Mengele's location, but he holds back. This is uncharacteristic but necessary. Wiesenthal has received a tip from a very good source that Mengele's son, Rolf, is traveling to Brazil to see his father for the first time in twenty-one years.

But there is no money in the bank to send a team to follow Rolf. Wiesenthal attempted to raise funds by contacting a Dutch newspaper with this secret, asking for an $8,000 advance in exchange for

---

* Die Spinne allegedly did work with the Paraguayan government to subjugate the Aché Indians, but Mengele played no role.

exclusive rights to the story. Even though the information is accurate, Wiesenthal has raised a false alarm too many times in the past.

ᛋᛋ

On October 10, 1977, Rolf Mengele lands in Brazil. He carries $5,000 in cash for his father and travels on a stolen passport with the name Wilfried Busse. One day and three taxi rides later, the young attorney stands on the front porch at 5555 Estrada Alvarenga. Rolf is the exact same age as his father was during his murderous time in Auschwitz.

Dr. Josef Mengele answers the door. His left hand is twisted into a claw, the residue of his recent stroke. He is ecstatic to see his son. Tears in his eyes, Mengele raises his arms in a hug.

Rolf is exhausted from his long journey and anxious to have a serious discussion with his father about Auschwitz. But rather than encountering the powerful man he remembers from his teenage years, Rolf greets a pathetic figure: "a broken man, a haunted creature," Rolf will later recall.

Rolf Mengele wraps his arms around his father just the same.

ᛋᛋ

The clandestine visit lasts two weeks. In slurred words brought on by his stroke, Josef Mengele explains to his neighbors that his "nephew" has come to visit, and they will long remember the young man who spoke German and Italian fluently.

Mengele takes his son on trips to various locations in Brazil where he has lived over the past seventeen years. The two men go swimming at a favorite beach at Bertioga, a resort town fifty miles southeast of São Paulo where Mengele likes to relax for a few days each summer. The sand is flat for hundreds of yards out into the ocean, allowing them to walk far away from shore into the small waves.

The Angel of Death takes his son to see the farm and watchtower in Serra Negra, where Mossad agent Zvi Aharoni came so close to capturing him in 1962.

Rolf is impressed that his father is mentally alert, despite his physical frailties. Mengele is passionate about classical music and lapses fluently into Latin and Greek. He shows great consideration for his son, insisting that Rolf sleep on the bed each night while he sleeps on the floor.

Rolf Mengele has some hard questions for his father, as he is horrified by his reputation. "These facts left me speechless," he will later recall about the stories he has read about Auschwitz. "I tried to tell him that his presence in Auschwitz alone was unacceptable to me."

Each night, the two men square off in an intellectual debate. The topic is always the same. "I told my father I was interested in hearing about his time in Auschwitz," Rolf will recall. "What did he do there? Did he have a role in the things he was charged with?"

Josef Mengele is unrepentant. He swears that he was there to help the inmates and that he "never personally harmed anyone in his life." He says that he was just doing his job and that he would have been harshly punished if he failed to do so. When asked about the gruesome experiments he performed on twins, Mengele claims that he was saving them from an even more horrible fate—that, in fact, he "rescued the twins," who now owe him their lives.

The Angel of Death compares himself to a triage surgeon on the battlefield: "If ten wounded soldiers are brought into the hospital in critical condition, the doctor must make almost instantaneous decisions about whom to operate on first. By choosing one, then necessarily another must die. When people arrived at the railhead, what was I supposed to do? People were arriving infected with disease, half dead.

"My job was only to classify those able to work and those unable to work. I was as generous in my assessments as I needed to be," Rolf will remember his father saying.

The rambling arguments often make no sense to Rolf, which only infuriates his father. "Don't tell me you, my only son, believe what they write about me? On my mother's life, I never hurt anyone."

Mengele's insistence on innocence, and the passion for which he argues his case, confounds his son. Many days, Rolf does not know what to believe. But as the two weeks come to an end, Rolf realizes one true fact: Josef Mengele will never admit any wrongdoing.

"Why didn't you turn yourself in?" Rolf finally asks.

In words that will eventually provide Simon Wiesenthal with the peace for which he so desperately longs, Josef Mengele admits his grave fear of the Nazi hunter: "There are no judges, only avengers."

※

Rolf Mengele says farewell to his father at the São Paulo Airport. It is an enormous risk for Josef Mengele to even appear in such a public place, but he is sad to see his son leave and is already planning their next visit.

Mengele wraps his son in a final embrace. "We shall try to meet again very soon," he promises.

That will never happen.

For the *real* angel of death is coming.

21

July 29, 1978
Itatiaia, Brazil
10:00 a.m.

A German shepherd bares its fangs at the journalists gathered in front of the Hotel Tyll. The dog's handler keeps a tight hold on the leash but makes it clear the animal will be allowed to attack if the press attempts to enter the establishment. At his side, a fellow neo-Nazi taps a coiled whip against his thigh.

A photographer raises his camera to take a picture of the hostile duo. This is a vital moment in the history of Nazi hunting, for inside the hotel is a gathering of the Kamaradenwerk, the highly secretive organization that counts the ODESSA and Die Spinne among its networks that continue to assist the Nazi cause. An estimated eight thousand to ten thousand Nazi fugitives are indebted to this group for smuggling them into South America after the war.

"The Kamaradenwerk is anything but fiction," a São Paulo rabbi named Henry Sobel recently told the local media. It is a brave act, for the rabbi knows that reprisal might mean death. "It is the international umbrella group that shelters all its subgroups and keeps them in touch with each other."

The Kamaradenwerk uses code phrases in its communiqués to identify its membership. Sometimes they call themselves "friends of the 20th of April," in honor of Adolf Hitler's birthday. One invitation to a previous meeting at the Hotel Tyll referred to the attendees as "friends who have embarked from the same station."

Brazilian police received an anonymous tip about that meeting three months ago. Nazis are not illegal in this nation, where Communists are considered the true threat. So the tipster misled the authorities into believing they would be raiding a Communist gathering. In the subsequent report, police noted that the guests were drunkenly singing the "Horst Wessel" song, a Nazi Party anthem. The dragnet picked up Gustav Franz Wagner, a former camp guard at Sobibór who was once fond of throwing Jewish babies into the air and impaling them on the tip of a bayonet. Wagner was known as the Human Beast. He came to Brazil with former compatriot Franz Stangl and has lived in fear of arrest ever since. Wagner is terrified of the Mossad—but not so fearful of the Brazilian police who arrested him.

Inside the Hotel Tyll's dining room, unseen by the journalists waiting on the lawn, the walls are lined with swastikas. A poster of Adolf Hitler is displayed prominently. "Songs of Germany" spins on a record player. On a side table, magazines with titles like "Quotations from the Führer" and "The End of the Lie of the 6 Million" are arranged alongside stickers proclaiming Nazi dominance. "Kauft Nicht Bei Juden," reads one—"Don't Buy from Jews."

Far more chilling is the banner proclaiming "We Are Back: The Day of Vengeance Is Come."

Outside, as the photographer snaps his photo, the small man with the whip lashes out. Two short flicks of his wrist send the unbraided end of the bullwhip quickly toward the paparazzo's forearm. The tendrils tear away flesh, opening a pair of deep bloody wounds.

Simultaneously, the man who calls himself only "Magno" releases his German shepherd, which bounds toward the media. "Swine," he calls out as the reporters run. "Filthy bastards."

"We are not Nazis," Magno lies to the press. "And even if we were, it wouldn't be a crime."

That fact is clear from the treatment accorded the arrested Gustav Franz Wagner. Despite his proven record of atrocities during the war, Brazilian authorities refuse to extradite him. Israel, Austria, Poland, and West Germany all request that Wagner be sent to their country to stand trial. They are refused.

Wagner is released—a free man, safe from the long arm of justice. Or so it seems.

Two years later, on October 3, 1980, an assassin comes for Gustav Wagner. Though his attorney will later claim it was suicide, the Human Beast's corpse is discovered with a knife blade buried to the hilt into his heart, a feat impossible for a man to do to himself.

No one takes credit for the murder.

⚡⚡

In the words of one Wehrmacht soldier now living in Brazil, "The Nazi spirit is merely sleeping in a good number of inhabitants of this region. All it needs to be awakened is one intelligent leader."

That man may be presently in the Bolivian capital of La Paz. Klaus Barbie is sixty-four years old, the son of a schoolteacher. He owes his life and fortune to the Kamaradenwerk. To the casual observer, Barbie is a kindly, white-haired old man who enjoys reading the newspaper in the Plaza Murillo, near the presidential palace. He takes his coffee at the Café La Paz, where he always sits with his back to the wall. But in reality, Klaus Barbie is secretly working with the Kamaradenwerk to overthrow the Bolivian government and install a new president sympathetic to the Nazi cause. Earlier this year, Barbie flew to Germany to recruit mercenaries. He is also involved with terrorist groups and intelligence organizations trying to bring regime change to La Paz.

Despite the nickname "the Butcher of Lyon" for his atrocities as a Gestapo chief in France during the war, Klaus Barbie has shown himself to be remarkably diplomatic in dealing with those who should be trying to arrest him. For years after the war, he was protected by the U.S. Central Intelligence Agency and its leader, Allen Dulles, who paid him a lavish $1,700 per month to spy on the new French government. Finally, when France demanded that Barbie be handed over for trial, the CIA lied, saying that he no longer worked for them. Using traditional ratlines, Dulles helped Barbie escape. Like so many other top Nazis, Barbie also received assistance from the Vatican and Red Cross, which arranged passports and Bolivian visas for himself, his wife, and their two children.

Like Josef Mengele and Adolf Eichmann, Klaus Barbie set sail from Genoa, Italy. He set sail on board the *Corrientes* on March 23, 1951. And just as those two assumed new names, so it is that Barbie goes by Klaus Altmann.

"In 1951, because of the French and German efforts to apprehend Subject," a U.S. intelligence report will state, "the 66th Detachment resettled him in South America. Subject was documented in the name Klaus Altmann and routed through Austria and Italy to Bolivia. Since that time, Army has had no contact with Subject."

The Butcher of Lyon disappeared into his new identity so completely that when a West German intelligence officer who had traveled to La Paz on business met him by chance at the city's German Club, the agent insisted to his Bundesnachrichtendienst (BND) superiors that they put "Klaus Altmann" on the payroll. He was given the code name Adler—eagle—and a monthly stipend to file reports on the Bolivian government. Barbie's cover was so good that he traveled freely to the United States and Europe. He built friendships with Bolivia's top generals and lived well on the proceeds of his many businesses—some legitimate, others not. It was Klaus Barbie—along with the CIA—who assisted those generals in locating and assassinating the famous Communist icon Che Guevara.* He also supplied guns to a nascent drug lord named Pablo Escobar, eventually helping the narco-terrorist build a $30 billion global empire. With those connections came great power. Barbie and his wife successfully pushed for a "no Jew" policy at the La Paz German Club, where they also distributed pro-Nazi literature.

Despite his high profile, it seemed as if Barbie's past would never be uncovered. Even when he stood in the German Club, threw his right arm up in a Nazi salute, and shouted "Heil Hitler," few suspected that Klaus Barbie was among the most vile of all war criminals.

All that changed in 1971. A French court had convicted him in absentia after the war, but thanks to CIA complicity, Barbie never served a day in a French prison.† Then came French Nazi hunters Beate and Serge Klarsfeld. The husband-and-wife team made it their life's work to document the Holocaust in France and spent decades tracking Klaus Barbie.

Serge Klarsfeld is a French Jew and can still remember the night police came and seized his father, sending him to Auschwitz. The little boy survived only because he was concealed behind a false wall in their home outside Nice.

---

* Che Guevara was born in Argentina but is best known as a pro-Marxist revolutionary who helped make possible the overthrow of the Cuban government. He trained military forces crucial to the Cuban victory at the Bay of Pigs invasion. For this, and later Marxist activities in Africa, Guevara became the object of a CIA manhunt. When Guevara attempted to overthrow the Bolivian government in the mid-1960s, a CIA team captured Guevara in the mountain village of La Higuera. Knowing he was soon to be executed without a trial, one of Guevara's last acts was to hand his Rolex to Felix Rodriguez, leader of the CIA squad. Che Guevara was shot dead by the Bolivian military on October 9, 1967. His body is buried in an unmarked grave. Rodriguez, who would go on to testify before Congress in the Iran–Contra scandal, still wears the watch to this day.

† "In absentia" takes place when the accused cannot be found and is thus unable to hear the charges in court. Martin Bormann was also convicted in absentia, though at the Nuremberg Trials.

Nazi hunters Beate and Serge Klarsfeld in Cologne, 1979

Beate is not Jewish. She is not even French. As a German woman whose father fought in the Wehrmacht, her motivation is atonement for the evils committed by her nation.

Despite their efforts, the Butcher of Lyon remains free and prosperous in Bolivia, protected by his cronies.

Meanwhile, Beate and Serge Klarsfeld continue to tell the world about the SS war criminal and the horrors he perpetuated, never flagging in their quest to bring him to trial.

⚡⚡

It is 1943. Jean Moulin is not Klaus Barbie's first victim, nor will he be the last. Just forty when the war begins, Moulin serves as the prefect of the Eure-et-Loir district just outside Paris. He is a patriot.

And although Moulin does not take up arms in World War II, he will become one of the great figures in that subversive band of warriors known as the French Resistance.

Moulin's story begins shortly after the German invasion of France. A small force of Sudanese soldiers fighting alongside the French army outside the city of Chartres manages to stop the Wehrmacht advance. It is an affront to the German war machine to be pinned down by supposedly inferior black troops, so much so that when the Germans finally burst through, the 180 Sudanese soldiers are not permitted to surrender. Instead, they are lined up against a wall and shot.

As the prefect, or chief local representative, Moulin is the symbolic leader of his district. In an attempt to persuade the local French population that the murder of the Sudanese was justifiable, the German leadership in France orders Moulin to sign a document stating that the Sudanese were shot for raping and murdering French women.

Knowing the truth, Moulin refuses to sign.

The Germans beat him savagely, then once again demand his signature.

Moulin will not sign the paper. So the Nazis beat him again.

What the Germans do not know is that Jean Moulin has a genetic streak of righteousness that prevents him from bearing witness to a lie. His father was the attorney defending Capt. Alfred Dreyfus, a French officer falsely convicted of treason and sent to the notorious penal colony on Devil's Island at the turn of the nineteenth century.* Dreyfus was Jewish, and much of the evidence presented against him was based on anti-Semitism rather than truth. Moulin's father later went on to also protest the criminal nature of Euro-

---

* Devil's Island was located off the coast of French Guiana and operated from 1852 to 1953. More than eighty thousand prisoners were sent there to serve out a sentence of hard labor. The harsh work and living conditions, tropical diseases, and lack of adequate sanitary facilities ensured that the vast majority never again returned to France. Devil's Island was made famous in the 1968 book *Papillon* and the subsequent movie of the same title.

pean imperialism—the very system that required the Sudanese troops to fight and die on a battlefield nowhere near their African homes.

Fortified by his father's example, Moulin defies the Germans for a third time. The Nazis brutally beat him yet again, then throw him in prison. In the depths of his pain, unable to hold out much longer, Moulin recites Hamlet's soliloquy "To be or not to be," then pens a suicide note on June 17, 1940.

"For seven hours I have been subjected to physical and moral torture," Moulin writes. "I know that today I reached the limits of resistance. I know that if it starts again tomorrow, I will sign in the end. The dilemma remains: to sign or to disappear. It is impossible to flee. Whatever happens, I cannot sign."

Resigned to his fate, Moulin slashes his throat with a broken glass bottle—but it does not kill him. For the rest of his life he will wear a scarf to hide the jagged wound. The cravat will become his trademark.

As the Sudanese murders recede into history, Moulin prevails. Released from prison, he returns to his position as local prefect, though not for long. He soon joins the French Resistance, often traveling to London to meet personally with Gen. Charles de Gaulle, the exiled leader of the Free French forces. For two years, Moulin evades Nazi capture while establishing a network of subversive cells throughout France. Other than de Gaulle, no Frenchman has more authority in the fight against Germany.

Jean Moulin's code name is simply Max.

ss

Meanwhile on the Eastern Front, SS police official Klaus Barbie is attached to a Gestapo unit specializing in the acquisition of information from prisoners of war captured in the German invasion of the Soviet Union. It is here that the young SS policeman learns the ways of torture. When he cannot extract the information he needs, Barbie simply resorts to murder. In those cases where he knows the names and locations of prisoners' families, he makes it a point to kill them, too—and burn their homes to the ground as a reminder of what happens to those who dare defy Adolf Hitler's Third Reich.

It is only a matter of time before Barbie's skills lead him to a promotion—and transfer. In November 1942, the SS-Hauptsturmführer is assigned to the French city of Lyon, where there has been a considerable disruption of the German occupation by an underground group of Frenchmen calling themselves simply the Resistance.

Barbie sets up his headquarters in the *centre ville*, at a lodging known as the Hotel Terminus. There he extracts information from suspects through some of the most barbaric forms of torture ever seen. Unknown to either man, he and Jean Moulin are destined to meet.

ϟϟ

On June 21, 1943, Jean Moulin is betrayed. The true identity of his Judas is never discovered. Klaus Barbie personally oversees the arrest of the exalted "Max." Barbie is just thirty years old at the time, a rising figure in the Gestapo. Rather than send the Resistance leader to his regional headquarters in Paris, he personally oversees the questioning and torture of Moulin.

Barbie conducts the interrogation, which goes on for a week. The beatings continue around the clock. Moulin's hands and feet are bound with tight metal cuffs so he cannot deflect the blows. Hot needles are inserted under his fingernails. Moulin is whipped and hit repeatedly with a truncheon. Handcuffs with spikes inside are affixed to his wrists and he is hung from the ceiling, whereupon Barbie repeatedly smashes a rubber bar into his torso and legs. Moulin becomes unrecognizable, his head wreathed in purple bruises.

"I saw Barbie in his shirtsleeves dragging a lifeless body down the steps," one fellow Resistance fighter remembers of the unconscious Moulin. "He stopped for a few minutes on the ground floor to get his breath back. Then he started dragging the body again down more steps toward the cells in the basement. The man had been badly beaten around the face and his clothes were torn."

And yet, Barbie has spared Moulin the worst of his tortures:

being skinned alive, being sodomized by a dog, having his head thrust into a pail of ammonia—but perhaps all that is to come. It is impossible to tell. Barbie is impulsive in his methods, constantly inventing creative ways of destroying a human being.

Upon emerging from the basement, Barbie makes known his plans to seal Moulin's fate. The Gestapo leaders in Paris are demanding that the Resistance leader be sent there for questioning. Moulin is the most prized catch in Gestapo history. Barbie plans to personally escort the Resistance leader by train. "If he doesn't die," Barbie vows, "I'll finish him off in Paris tomorrow."

But Jean Moulin survives Paris—barely. He is nothing more than a breathing corpse when he is placed on a stretcher, then loaded on board the train that will take him to a death camp. On July 8, 1943, as his train sits in the station at Metz, Moulin dies.

Despite Klaus Barbie's heinous interrogation techniques—methods he now uses occasionally in Bolivia as a thirty-year member of that nation's secret police—Jean Moulin did not betray a single piece of information about the Resistance. He goes to his death a hero.*

But to the SS, Barbie is also a hero. His role in the capture and torture of Moulin receives praise from the Nazi leadership in Berlin, where he is recalled to receive the Iron Cross First Class with Sword, the Nazi regime's highest military honor. The citation mentions his "indefatigable devotion to the battle against resistance organizations in France."

No less than Heinrich Himmler, leader of the SS, is the author of that commendation.

⚡⚡

French Nazi hunters Serge and Beate Klarsfeld continue to compile a list of witnesses prepared to tell their stories of Klaus Barbie's

---

* Moulin's remains were originally buried in a large Parisian cemetery. They were moved in 1964 to the Panthéon, a location reserved for France's greatest individuals.

sadism: the woman who watched him crush an individual's skull with the heel of his boot because he thought the prisoner was Jewish; the time he broke a prisoner's vertebrae by striking the prisoner on the back with a spiked ball; the beatings; the near drowning in frozen water known as the "bathtub torture."

It seems there is no method of brutal interrogation that Barbie has not attempted. Each witness remarks about the great pleasure he showed on his face while administering torture.

But to Bolivian authorities, Klaus Barbie is valuable—a necessary force in their fight to maintain power. So it is that Barbie seems to be untouchable. He certainly believes that.

He is wrong.

22

February 7, 1979
Bertioga Beach, Brazil
5:30 p.m.

The day has been demanding for Josef Mengele. The sixty-eight-year-old fugitive has traveled to this resort town at the peak of the Brazilian summer to spend a few days in the two-story stucco home of his friend Wolfram Bossert and his wife, Liselotte. Mengele is constantly depressed these days, bitter about his lack of money and his lonely life in exile. Fueled by that low mood, the doctor picked a fight with Wolfram late last night. Liselotte will testify that she does not know the reason but the two men argued well past 2:00 a.m., when exhaustion got the best of them.

Mengele spent the next morning hiking through a local forest with the Bosserts. The afternoon was at leisure on this broad, sandy beach under a blazing sun. As evening falls and the time nears to head back for dinner, the Angel of Death enjoys a final swim. In the distance, a line of black clouds portends a coming storm, but he is unworried. The waves are getting bigger as he continues to navigate the sea. Wolfram and Liselotte Bossert have already gotten out of the ocean. Mengele can see them in the distance, toweling off.

With a burst of energy Mengele swims as hard as he can toward the beach. He rises and falls with the incoming swells, letting the waves help him toward shore. All at once, Mengele's left arm stops functioning. The same is true of his left leg.

Mengele screams for help. The doctor knows the telltale signs of a stroke, and he battles with the right side of his body to keep his head above water. The waves wash over him, pressing him beneath the surface.

Wolfram Bossert hears Mengele's cries. He runs into the sea and swims to his friend. Bossert is frantic. Like the sedentary Mengele, Bossert's physical condition is not peak. The race toward his houseguest through heaving seas has Bossert fearing for his own life.

Wolfram Bossert's efforts are in vain. By the time he reaches Josef Mengele, the Nazi has drowned.

Bossert wraps an arm around the body and drags it back to shore. Lifeguards help him place Mengele onto the sand, whereupon Bossert himself collapses. Rain begins to fall. Growing colder by the minute, Mengele's corpse lies on the beach. An ambulance arrives to assist Wolfram Bossert, while Mengele's body is taken to a Bertioga aid station. Lifeguards pronounce him dead on arrival. Due to the intense thunderstorm, the body lays flat for five hours, until Brazilian officials manage to secure the corpse.

Wolfram Bossert is too exhausted to travel. So it is left to his wife, Liselotte, to accompany Mengele's body to the morgue. The storm has knocked over a tree, blocking the road, so the sixty-mile journey into São Paulo takes almost three hours.

It is past 2:00 a.m. The coroner is not interested in details at this late hour. The victim is quite obviously dead due to drowning, so there is no further investigation. The coroner also overlooks the need to take fingerprints or photos of the corpse, thus relying solely on Liselotte's testimony as to the victim's identity.

"Wolfgang Gerhard," she testifies, giving the name on Mengele's fake identification papers.

The coroner immediately releases the body for burial.

For as long as Josef Mengele has lived in São Paulo, Liselotte and Wolfram Bossert have known his true identity. Working closely with Hans Sedlmeier, manager of the Karl Mengele and Sons farm equipment company back in Germany, they have helped funnel money to the fugitive and conspired to keep his location a secret from the law. Liselotte does not know the specific crime she is committing, but she is well aware that her actions are illegal.

The Bosserts have long known this day would come. So they have devised a plan to keep the world from knowing that Josef Mengele is dead.

Liselotte arranges to have Mengele buried the first thing in the morning. The real Wolfgang Gerhard once purchased a plot at the Embu cemetery, and it is there where the burial takes place.* There is no service. Other than Liselotte, there are no mourners. At her direction, the coffin lid remains closed because the funeral director knows exactly what the real Wolfgang Gerhard looks like. When a cemetery administrator insists on opening the casket, Lisolette feigns a fit of grief-stricken hysteria. Out of respect for the bereaved, the administrator rescinds his request.

Dr. Josef Mengele, the Angel of Death, is lowered into grave 321 at Nossa Senhora do Rosario cemetery in Embu, sixteen miles south of São Paulo.

The deceit seems to have worked.

ᛋᛋ

"I cannot say where he is, but he has been seen five times recently," Simon Wiesenthal tells the media in 1980, speaking of Josef Mengele, now dead for almost a year.

"I am much closer to capturing him than I was a year ago. His capture could come in the next few weeks."

In truth, the Nazi hunter Wiesenthal knows nothing at all about the true fate of Josef Mengele.

ᛋᛋ

---

* Wolfgang Gerhard, the former leader of the Hitler Youth, died approximately one month before Mengele in Germany.

Three years later, the Butcher is finally held to account.

After more than a decade of frustration, Beate and Serge Klarsfeld have succeeded in getting Klaus Barbie placed behind bars.

The date is February 7, 1983. Barbie is locked in a cell at the Montluc prison, the same jail where he once sent prisoners like Jean Moulin forty years ago. "He must go to the place he committed his crimes," a French judge pronounced. "He must, in turn, spend the night in a cell there, awaiting his fate."

In late 1982, a new government was installed in Bolivia. Barbie was no longer protected and just one month ago, the former Gestapo chief was arrested on charges of fraud. The Bolivian government could not get rid of Barbie fast enough and almost immediately extradited him to French soil. He left Bolivia alone, for his wife had just died of cancer and his son was killed two years prior in a

Klaus Barbie, the Butcher of Lyon, on trial in France in 1987

hang-gliding accident. When the sixty-nine-year-old Barbie's flight landed in French Guiana, he was arrested by authorities and placed on board a military transport. Barbie did not know the plane's destination, but he hoped it was bound for his German homeland, where he believed he might find sympathy. When he learned the transport was taking him to France, a despondent Barbie "walled himself in silence," in the words of one newspaper report.

Now, Klaus Barbie sits in his stone cell on this cold winter night, alone with his conscience. This is where Jean Moulin was taken each evening after his days of torture and where the children of Izieu spent a single terrified night before boarding the trains to Auschwitz. So many men and women occupied these cells, bruised and broken at the hands of Klaus Barbie, knowing they would awake in the morning to more of the same. Even four decades later, a sense of horror and evil permeates each cell of this massive prison fortress.

Yet Klaus Barbie is not sorry for what he did. In fact, he remains proud of the work he accomplished for the SS.

For that reason, Klaus Barbie has decided to plead not guilty.

23

May 5, 1985
Bitburg, Germany
Early Afternoon

President Ronald Reagan holds a wreath as he steps somberly toward the brick memorial tower serving as the centerpiece of the Kolmeshöhe Cemetery near Bitburg, Germany. The sky is gray. The American leader is not wearing a hat, but a light rain has prompted him to don a beige trench coat. Orange marigolds and yellow daisies grow wild in the new spring grass as a trumpeter mournfully plays "I Had a Comrade," a German song dedicated to fallen soldiers.

Reagan's visit to Kolmeshöhe will be brief, but he feels an obligation to honor the German war dead. The president and his wife, Nancy, have spent part of their morning touring the site of the former Bergen-Belsen concentration camp. Along with thousands buried in mass graves on that premises are the remains of Anne Frank, the young Dutch girl who has become an iconic symbol of the Holocaust.

From Bergen-Belsen, the president next travels to Kolmeshöhe, where he will lay a wreath in yet another show of symbolism. The fortieth anniversary of the war's end has brought the American leader to Germany in an effort to display solidarity between the two nations. It is at the request of German chancellor Helmut Kohl that Reagan has chosen to pay homage to the young German soldiers who fought and died for their homeland.

All is quiet as Reagan and Kohl each place their circular bouquets at the base of the memorial tower. Outside the cemetery gates, a crowd of demonstrators who have gathered from the United States, Europe, and Israel to protest this ceremony also observe this moment of silence. These protesters have traveled to Bitburg out of outrage over an act they consider an obscenity.

For among those buried here in Kolmeshöhe Cemetery are dozens of SS personnel. Just a few short months after the United States Department of Justice announced it would be more aggressive in catching and prosecuting Nazi war criminals, President Reagan stands just a few feet away from two SS graves as he lays the wreath. Not a word is mentioned by Kohl or Reagan about SS atrocities.

"No one could visit here," Reagan will state to the press after the eight-minute visit to the cemetery comes to an end, "without deep and conflicting emotions."

⚡⚡

In Vienna, 550 miles to the east, Simon Wiesenthal is weighing in on Reagan's controversial decision to honor the German dead. His desk here in the Jewish Documentation Center, as always, is covered by a messy stack of old newspapers and filing cards. There is rage in the Jewish community about the laying of the wreath, with many predicting President Reagan will never again have the complete trust of their people. Wiesenthal's prominent position as an authority on the Holocaust and SS atrocities has attracted journalists to hear his perspective.

Strangely, Simon Wiesenthal does not concentrate on the cemetery exposition, preferring to change the subject to the location of Josef Mengele. Wiesenthal shamed the United States this past January by proving that the Nazi was arrested by the Americans after the war but subsequently released. His information was found in declassified documents made available through the U.S. Freedom of Information Act. The Pentagon responded quickly, stating that "none of the documents indicate any American units" had ever taken Mengele into custody, but Wiesenthal refuses to back down.

The Nazi hunter, like the rest of the world, has absolutely no knowledge that Josef Mengele died six years ago.

In fact, Simon Wiesenthal is confident that he will soon meet Mengele face-to-face. With that optimism has come more frequent updates to the media on the hunt. A few years ago, in 1982, he informed the public of the Nazi's residence in Paraguay, but a year later Wiesenthal announced that Mengele was on the move. The Angel of Death has relocated to Parral, Chile, and spends time at various locations in Brazil.

Now Wiesenthal tells the *New York Times*, among other publications, that he has hard evidence that Mengele was once again seen in Paraguay last July.

This is more than a mere hunch. Three different people have come forth to tell Wiesenthal about the sighting. These eyewitnesses do not know one another, and each lives in a different country, giving their admissions the feel of truth.

The Nazi hunter is so sure about the authenticity of these reports that he has written to German chancellor Helmut Kohl, requesting that he work in conjunction with Paraguayan president Alfredo Stroessner to bring Mengele to justice. Stroessner is actually of German ancestry, the son of a Bavarian father. He is soon due to return to his roots and visit West Germany on a diplomatic mission. Wiesenthal's letter to Kohl asks that he "raise emphatically" the topic of Mengele's extradition.

In fact, no one knows the location of Josef Mengele. Simon Wiesenthal's guesswork is not an act of deception but a desperate desire to see justice served, based on the same hunches and tips that have been the cornerstone of his Nazi hunting over the years—a form of detective work leading to hundreds of arrests.

Wiesenthal's willingness to indulge in rumor has also had the unlikely effect of motivating others to join the search. The United States, West Germany, and Israel announced just last week that they are now working together to locate Mengele. Any individual finding solid evidence leading to his capture will receive an award of $2.4 million.

For Simon Wiesenthal, whether the money is awarded to him or someone else is irrelevant. What's far more important is that this bounty finally yield the prize Wiesenthal has sought for so many years.

⚡⚡

Three weeks after President Reagan's trip to Bitburg, and ten days after Simon Wiesenthal announced that Dr. Josef Mengele is in Paraguay, Nazi hunter Beate Klarsfeld has flown to that country to demand that Mengele be turned over to West German officials. Standing on the steps of the Palace of Justice in the capital city of Asunción, Klarsfeld holds up a sign in Spanish. She has offered a $25,000 reward to anyone who will step forward with information that will help her capture Mengele. In the meantime, she is hoping to pressure the Paraguayan president into taking action during his upcoming trip to West Germany.

"Stroessner, you lie when you say you don't know where SS Mengele is," the sign reads. "Don't go to Germany without him."

This is not Beate's first public act of protest. In fact, she is becoming quite famous for the extreme tactics she utilizes to bring Nazis to justice. In 1968, at a meeting of Germany's Christian Democratic Union political party, she borrowed a reporter's press pass, walked onto the main stage, and slapped then German chancellor Kurt Georg Kiesinger, denouncing him.

For this, Klarsfeld was sentenced to four months in prison. According to reports, the act was not entirely selfless, for the East German secret police, a group known as the Stasi, allegedly paid her 2,000 deutsche marks to humiliate the West German leader as part of their ongoing effort to denounce the West as being pro-

Nazi—a charge that has some validity since a few Nazi leaders have actually prospered in West Germany after the war.*

Among these individuals is Kurt Lischka, the former commandant of the Gestapo in Paris. Lischka was responsible for the deportation of more than seventy thousand Jews to death camps. He was tried in absentia by a French court and sentenced to a life of hard labor but remains a free man because West Germany has a policy of protecting its Nazi past by not extraditing its citizens. This allows Lischka to live his life without fear of arrest and, incredibly, to also serve on the bench as a judge in Cologne, Germany, where he works under his own name.

In 1971, Beate and Serge Klarsfeld attempted to kidnap Lischka from his home in Cologne and take him to France for trial. The plot failed, landing both Klarsfelds in a German prison.

However, the attempted kidnapping was not entirely in vain. The notoriety of their actions led to a public outcry for Lischka's arrest. In 1980, he was finally charged for his wartime actions. The Klarsfelds traveled to Cologne for the trial, then led a group of two thousand French Jews through the city streets to spotlight Lischka's atrocities. Many of the protesters wore the striped prison garb of concentration camp inmates, emblazoned with a yellow Star of David. Thanks to the Klarsfelds, the seventy-year-old former Gestapo chief and West German judge was sentenced to ten years in prison.

Of course, these public demonstrations have not endeared Beate and Serge Klarsfeld to the Nazi underworld. In 1979, a bomb destroyed their family car. Nobody was in the vehicle at the time. Both Klarsfelds believe ODESSA was responsible.

And yet, Beate Klarsfeld remains fearless in her campaign against Germany's Nazi past. The arrest and imprisonment of Klaus Barbie two years ago was her crowning achievement. Here in Paraguay this morning, she is surrounded by a small band of young

---

* Equivalent to $500 at the time.

people who share her views. The protest is peaceful, by design, although one hundred armed police officers watch their every move.

Not everyone in Paraguay is sympathetic to Klarsfeld. Channel 13, a local television station with pro-government leanings, has accused her of "making a business" of Nazi hunting. *El Diario Noticias*, a prominent local newspaper, has written that "she is very clever and has turned her hunt into a career."

Another newspaper, *La Patria*, accuses Klarsfeld of trying "to kill the honor of Paraguay."

⚡⚡

Though he is at his office in Vienna rather than in Paraguay, Simon Wiesenthal is energized by his Nazi hunting rival, Beate Klarsfeld. Informed in advance of Beate Klarsfeld's intended protest, Wiesenthal's Jewish Documentation Center has taken out a half-page advertisement informing the people of Paraguay about the substantial reward money available to anyone who helps Simon Wiesenthal locate Dr. Josef Mengele.

Meanwhile, the West German government is publicly taking a skeptical approach to the search for Mengele. "We have assurances from the government of Paraguay that he is not here," an embassy spokesman tells the Paraguayan press. "There are no reasons to disbelieve these reassurances."

For the world, however, the hunt for Nazi war criminals remains a headline-grabbing mystery—one that is about to unfold.

⚡⚡

On May 31, 1985, police in Günzburg, Germany, acting on an anonymous tip, raid the home of Hans Sedlmaier. The former manager at Karl Mengele and Sons is in his seventies now, and retired from the farm machinery company. While on vacation recently, he was overheard bragging that he once sent money to Josef Mengele.

The police visit takes Sedlmaier by surprise. As investigators enter his home, the Mengele confidant dashes into a closet and reaches for a specific jacket. The authorities wrench the coat away from him. Inside, they find a date book with addresses and phone numbers written in code.

Intrigued, they press their search. In a study used only by Sedlmaier's wife, the police find photocopies of letters from Josef Mengele.

"How could you do that?" an outraged Hans Sedlmaier asks his wife. The former Nazi has been meticulous in destroying all missives from the Angel of Death.

Because of Josef Mengele's drowning six years ago, Sedlmaier no longer sends regular mail to or receives it from South America or needs to visit the special post office box set up for Mengele. In fact, while Sedlmaier was complicit in Mengele's escape and life as a fugitive, the German statute of limitations for a crime is just five years. Thus, Hans Sedlmaier cannot be prosecuted.

But these discoveries are sensational. Police demand that Sedlmaier and his wife take a seat, then immediately begin combing through the date book in an attempt to decode its contents. Within hours, they have their answers. A call is made to police officials in Brazil.

The crimes instantly begin to unravel. A list of addresses in Brazil contained in the book leads directly to Gitta Stammer and her husband, who are identified as conspirators to hide Mengele in the 1960s and '70s. Wolfram and Lisolette Bossert are also implicated in covering up his death. In a sign that the global community is working together to hunt down Nazis, this information is relayed to Brazilian authorities, who immediately take action.

The Bosserts are questioned and threatened with prison. In less than an hour they admit everything. The couple lead authorities to the small hillside cemetery of Nossa Senhora do Rosario and grave 321. On the morning of June 6, 1985, the forty-first anniversary of the D-day invasion, a lone grave digger pokes his shovel into the ground and begins digging down to the coffin. He is surrounded on all sides by television crews, reporters, Brazilian police, and West German officials. Lisolette Bossert is crying.

It takes an hour to reach the white coffin. Opening the lid, officials are confronted by a skeleton wearing clothing. The bones are handed up to a pathologist, one at a time. The dentures are passed along first. Then the skull. Each of these is placed inside a second coffin. Later, they will be tested in a laboratory to confirm that these are the remains of Dr. Josef Mengele.

On June 21, a team of scientists from the United States, Brazil, and West Germany hold a press conference to announce that these bones are, in fact, those of the Angel of Death. When asked whether he has any doubts about the findings, American pathologist Dr. Lowell J. Levine remarks, "Absolutely none."

A spokesman for Simon Wiesenthal says he is only "99 percent" convinced the bones are those of Mengele. "We would be less than candid if we said we were not disappointed he was found dead," states Rabbi Marvin Hier, an associate of Wiesenthal's.

"Josef Mengele is a dark page in the history of medicine," declares Brazilian pathologist Dr. Roberto Teixeira. "He was an antiphysician, not a scientist. We must turn the page and close this book."

Yet there are many pages left to be written. Simon Wiesenthal believes that Martin Bormann is still alive, and other vicious members of the SS remain at large, including some lesser-known war criminals—the women of the SS.

24

S<small>EPTEMBER</small> 21, 1989
S<small>AN</small> F<small>RANCISCO</small>, C<small>ALIFORNIA</small>
A<small>FTERNOON</small>

In the lower Nob Hill section of the city, on the top floor of a run-down five-story apartment building with a communal bathroom, Elfriede Huth is celebrating the thirtieth anniversary of her arrival in the United States. It is a quiet commemoration, known only to Elfriede, for she likes to keep her past a secret.

At age sixty-seven, the plump German-born woman with dyed red hair is happily married to a singing waiter named Fred Rinkel. The two met at a dance held at the local German club. He is Jewish, she is not, though there have been times over the course of their twenty-six-year marriage when she has attended synagogue: something that would seem unfathomable in her youth.

The truth is that Elfriede Huth was once a concentration camp guard. Huth was a member of a group known as the *weiblichen SS-Gefolge*s—"female civilian employees of the SS." At the Ravensbrück concentration camp in Northern Germany, this brutal group terrified and ultimately executed women and babies. So evil was this group, they were given a special name: the Raven's Women.

⚡⚡

Located fifty miles north of Berlin, on the shores of Schwedt Lake, with its clear blue water, the Ravensbrück camp was built before the war began. The entire six-acre facility is surrounded by a sixteen-foot-high gray wall. The air smells of pine from the local forests. There are no guard towers or gun emplacements, but a high-voltage fence rings the perimeter. The *Lagerstrasse*—main street—running through the center of the camp features a canteen for the SS guards that includes an extensive kitchen. The street is lined with a dozen barracks where the prisoners sleep on three-tiered bunks. Each incarcerated woman is allowed a mattress filled with wood shavings, a simple sheet, and a blue-and-white blanket. The camp is surprisingly bucolic, with chicken coops, rabbit hutches, orchards, and vegetable gardens—all there in an attempt to keep Ravensbrück as self-sufficient as possible. Red salvia flowers and linden trees are interspersed among the barracks. The centerpiece of the camp is the *Appellplatz*, a broad dirt area the size of a soccer pitch where prisoners stand each morning for roll call.

Between its opening in May 1939 and forced closing in 1945, tens of thousands of lesbians, Gypsies (also known as Roma), political prisoners, prostitutes, Jews, and gentile women known as "race defilers"—Aryans who had sex with Jews—populate the camp. Also among the prisoners are nuns, captured Allied spies, women who had abortions, and assorted other enemies of the Third Reich. All the inmates are women, sentenced to slave labor.

SS men essentially run the camp, but the day-to-day supervision of the prisoners falls to SS women. Almost all are under thirty years old. They rise along with the prisoners at 4:00 a.m. for roll call and supervise the camp routine, which begins with a breakfast of watery turnip soup. After that, the inmates are marched off to perform labor while singing German patriotic songs.

A select group of women guards known as *Hundeführerin* are armed with lethal weapons, not guns but dogs.

Elfriede Huth is among those armed.

Heinrich Himmler, himself, personally orders that Ravensbrück's female guards not carry firearms. To the female populace, Himmler believes, a ferocious dog is far more terrifying than a gun. These German shepherds are not intended just to snarl and bark. In Himmler's own words, the animals should be "trained to savage to death anyone except their handler."

The first sound women prisoners hear upon their arrival at Ravensbrück station is the barking of vicious dogs, straining at their handlers' leashes. Guards cry out "Achtung, achtung"—"Attention, attention"—to inspire fear, then shout insults such as "whore" and "slut." The prisoners are made to stand at attention, then marched into the camp, where they are stripped and deloused before being handed their striped inmate dresses and caps. Should any prisoner fall down or faint while disembarking from the cattle trucks, the dogs are set free to attack. Any prisoner attempting to help the fallen is also targeted. Likewise, if a prisoner is too ill or weak to stand during the morning head count, guards set the dogs upon them. Well trained, the animals circle the stricken prisoner in small packs, awaiting the signal to attack.

Elfriede Huth is not forced to become a *Hundeführerin*—she volunteers. Ravensbrück offers female guards fine compensation, spacious living accommodations in villas just outside the main camp, and higher status in the Nazi Party. Twenty-one-year-old Elfriede has spent most of the war working in a munitions factory in her hometown of Leipzig, overseeing slave laborers. It was early in 1944 when she received a letter from the camp commandant, SS-Hauptsturmführer Fritz Suhren, informing her that she had been chosen to work as a guard. An elated Elfriede reports to work on June 15.

The first day of training is simple: a line of prisoners stands before Elfriede and her new group of guards. At the command of Deputy Chief Wardress Dorothea Binz, each trainee must select a prisoner and then beat her. This is a test. Most new guards do as they are told immediately, Elfriede Huth among them. Those few who ask why the inmate should be beaten are dismissed. Those recruits brave enough to refuse to strike a prisoner are themselves taken into custody.

Soon, Elfriede takes possession of the German shepherd that will remain at her side daily. The dog's name is Albert. He has black ears and tan markings on his snout. In photographs, he sits in docile fashion at Elfriede's feet as she gazes toward the camera in her guard uniform and peaked cap.

Elfriede's indoctrination takes place at a time when Ravensbrück is home to two of the most sadistic women in wartime history. Dorothea Binz is a young blonde personally responsible for the training of new guards. Just nineteen when she began her SS career in 1939, Binz openly cavorts with her lover, an SS officer named Edmund Bräuning, who is employed at the camp. One of her favorite pastimes is strolling arm in arm with Bräuning through Ravensbrück, giggling as she stops to watch prisoners whipped and beaten. Binz herself is good with the bullwhip and is fond of letting her own German shepherd off leash to attack inmates.

Ravensbrück is a slave labor camp. Its primary focus is not extermination, although the harsh living conditions mean that more than twenty thousand women will die here. Guards periodically undertake "selections," in which the camp population is thinned by randomly choosing prisoners for death. These unfortunates will either be taken out to the woods and shot, or loaded onto trucks the prisoners call *Himmelfahrt*—"heaven bound"—for transportation to a gas chamber. The prisoners never know when the "selections" will take place, but the presence of Binz on the *Appellplatz* is a sure sign. Prisoners hold their breath in fear as she strolls through their ranks with her Alsatian and coiled whip. Binz is always immaculately coiffed, her blond bob tucked perfectly under her cap. Her uniform blouse and blazer are creased and starched. Even at 4:00 a.m., she looks wide-awake and focused.

The Raven's Women all seek to emulate her appearance. Even some prisoners will remark about the beauty of their guards and the pride they take in their daily hygiene. A special hair salon for female guards ensures a coiffure just as smart as that of Binz.

Despite the rigors of their job, the dog handlers revel in the stylish cut of their culotte skirts, knee-high leather boots, and gray blazers. Some are fond of wearing pink underwear.

There is nothing specific in the choices Binz makes—the prisoner might be ill, or showing defiance by looking at the guards the wrong way, or simply the victim of bad luck. And not all are killed immediately. Some are sent to the infirmary, where they become "rabbits"—the subjects of gruesome medical experiments conducted by female doctors.

Ravensbrück prisoners are also killed by typhus, dysentery, or exposure to the cold during winter mornings of roll call that can last for hours. But when the camp constructs a gas chamber of its own late in 1944, the number of "selections" increases from a few dozen weekly to several hundred, then into the thousands. Between January and April 1945, 6,993 women and children are murdered. If a baby is born while in the camp, it is immediately taken from its mother and placed in a crib with five or six other infants—packed in so tight that many die from suffocation. As Germany suffers setbacks in the war, Ravensbrück crematoriums burn around the clock, clearly visible through the curtains in the guards' quarters.

In a recorded observation, Dorothea Binz leaves the camp on a bicycle to monitor a group of prisoners working in the forest. When it appears that one woman is not putting forth the proper effort, Binz leans her bicycle against a tree and beats the woman with a pickax until her mutilated body is unrecognizable. Then Binz shines her bloody boots with the dead woman's skirt.

On another occasion, a truckload of prisoners is being driven out of the camp to be murdered. Binz runs after the truck, yelling, "Wait for me. I want to watch."

⚡⚡

Dorothea Binz has a soul mate at Ravensbrück who is, perhaps, even more terrifying. Irma Grese spends her days in a constant pursuit of human suffering. She kicks inmates with her boots until they are unconscious, forces prisoners to kneel for hours at a time while holding a rock above their heads, and is particularly fond of whipping well-endowed women across their bare breasts. She is one of the few guards who carries a pistol. To ensure that her dog maintains a strong appetite for female flesh, she is in the habit of not feeding him before reporting for duty.

Grese is an insatiable nymphomaniac, forcing herself on prisoners and fellow camp guards—men and women alike. To Irma Grese, whom the prisoners nickname "the Beautiful Beast," this punishment is more than cruelty or perversion—it is a hobby. One prisoner, a Romanian gynecologist named Gisella Perl, will testify that she believes Grese becomes "sexually aroused just watching the women suffering."

Among the many lovers Irma Grese takes during World War II is Dr. Josef Mengele.*

As the Soviet army closes in on Berlin in 1945, many SS guards flee, terrified of abuse at the hands of Russian soldiers. Elfriede Huth is one of them. In April, she walks the 120 miles to Leipzig, a city reduced to rubble and now under Soviet jurisdiction. There she returns to her home at Holzhauser Strasse 36 and her previous life as a seamstress, sewing fur coats. It is as if nothing has happened. When asked to name all of her previous residences on her United States visa application in 1959, Elfriede will carefully omit any mention of her wartime service.

Of the more than thirty-five hundred German women who serve as SS camp guards, most will succeed in hiding their evil doings. Fewer than two hundred will be imprisoned. The actual number of convictions is unknown, for the German court system does not keep a running tally of female camp guards arrested for war crimes. Those few who are caught generally serve very short sentences.

This is not the case for Dorothea Binz and Irma Grese. Taking the advice of her lover, SS officer Edmund Bräuning, Binz flees on her bicycle in April 1945 as the Allies race for Berlin. Bräuning also goes on the run, quite successfully. He is never heard from again.

---

* Grese met Mengele at Auschwitz, where she was employed for a period of time.

But Dorothea Binz does not get far. She is captured by British troops in May and held for a short time in a former concentration camp, before transfer to Hamelin Prison outside Hamburg. She is among sixteen Ravensbrück staff members put on trial. Seven of these are women, of whom three are former inmates who conspired with the SS against their fellow captives. Binz is convicted and hanged on May 2, 1947. The famed British executioner, Albert Pierrepoint, is her hangman. Just before the hood is placed over her head, Dorothea Binz removes her necklace and hands it to Pierrepoint. "I hope you won't think we were all evil people," she says as her last words.

A moment later, the trapdoor swings open and she drops to her death.

⚡⚡

In March 1945, Irma Grese is transferred to the Bergen-Belsen concentration camp and chooses not to flee as the British army closes in. Along with other camp administrators, she is forced by the British to bury the many bodies covering the grounds. Grese stands trial in late 1945. Throughout the war, she had dreamed of becoming a movie star once the fighting was over. But the Belsen Trial, as the legal proceedings are known, ensure that she will never set foot outside a prison again. A long line of victims testify to her brutality. And while more than half of the forty-five SS officials and Nazi collaborators on trial receive lengthy prison terms, Grese is the only woman condemned to die.

Her hangman is again Albert Pierrepoint.* Grese's last word to the executioner is "Schnell"—"Quickly."

Pierrepoint complies.

---

* Albert Pierrepoint is thought to have hanged more than four hundred criminals during his career. Great Britain does not have an official executioner, but for many years Pierrepoint held that unofficial title. Two hundred of the hangings over which he presided were of Nazi war criminals.

ϟϟ

Almost fourteen years later, on September 21, 1959, TWA Flight 771 lands in San Francisco. The United States' borders are amazingly porous. With the Cold War intensifying, people fleeing from countries such as East Germany and other satellite nations of the Soviet Union are given quick approval to migrate to America. In this way, an estimated ten thousand former Nazis successfully relocate to the United States and now live under assumed identities.

Elfriede Huth is the latest to arrive. She could have chosen any port of entry into the United States but picked San Francisco because her brother Kurt, a former Wehrmacht soldier, settled in nearby Berkeley after the war and has offered to take her in. Though Elfriede has managed to avoid arrest since the war, the East German secret police have recently begun a vigorous prosecution of Nazi war criminals in an effort to embarrass West Germany. The time for her to run has come.

There is no documented evidence of atrocities committed personally by Elfriede Huth, but there is no doubt she was brutal. Dog handlers who showed lenience toward prisoners, or who held back when it came time to set their animal loose to attack inmates, were relieved of their duties. Their ruthless actions were considered a part of their obligation to protect the German homeland from all enemies. The barbarities of all concentration camp guards have been well documented.

Nonetheless, Elfriede believes she can conceal her past.

However, unbeknownst to her, a random but grave mistake was made in the waning days of the war: Elfriede's Ravensbrück camp identity card was not among those destroyed by the SS, giving potential investigators a clear starting point to discover her postwar location.

ϟϟ

Thirty years after coming to America, Elfriede Huth still takes precautions. Because she lied on that long-ago visa application, she will never apply for U.S. citizenship for fear of an investigation into her SS past.

Her husband, Fred, known as "Fritz" in his native Berlin, found asylum in China during the war. Now, the couple are fond of being together, to the point of being standoffish to others. They never socialize. Elfriede doesn't allow Fred to talk on the phone with most friends or relatives.

It is common among San Francisco's Jewish immigrant population to play a game of one-upmanship: who left Germany earliest before the war, who left latest, who survived the death camps. Elfriede refuses to socialize in these circles, knowing that too many questions may be asked.

Otherwise, life in America is satisfying. Fred is dashing and

Elfriede Huth, Ravensbrück concentration camp guard

flamboyant. He is punctual and sings opera, sometimes on the Powell Street trolley car. The couple often spends nights ballroom dancing in their fifth-floor flat. Fred usually sings along to the music in his polished tenor. The two of them always dress well and are fond of strolling arm in arm throughout the city. Neighbors call Fred "Einstein," for his bushy gray mustache and strong resemblance to the scientist. Elfriede, meanwhile, is often referred to as "a sweet lady."

Elfriede is just happy to be in the United States. Not once has anyone shown suspicion about her Nazi past.

Not even her husband.

Fred openly acknowledges to Elfriede that he lost both his parents in Nazi death camps. But Elfriede never speaks about the war—and Fred never asks.

Thus, after almost three decades of marriage, Fred Rinkel has no idea that his wife once terrorized innocent Jewish women and children in the Ravensbrück concentration camp.

But someone knows. And that someone is coming.

25

March 17, 1992
Buenos Aires, Argentina
2:42 p.m.

The Ford F-100 panel van is on the move. After an hour and a half of summoning his courage in a nearby parking lot, a young man starts the engine and proceeds down Arroyo Street. The rear of the vehicle is weighed down with 220 pounds of metal shards packed into high explosives. There is great patience in the driver's approach to his target in this tranquil neighborhood. He takes almost three minutes to drive just two blocks to a pedestrian walkway.

Suddenly, the van swerves up off the street onto the sidewalk, whereupon the driver detonates his cargo, instantly killing himself and twenty-nine other people. Shrapnel flies through the air, and buildings erupt in a fountain of dust and stone. Bodies are crushed in the debris. The nearby Mater Admirabilis Catholic Church is also partially destroyed, and the parish priest is among the dead. But neither Father Juan Carlos Brumana nor the local sanctuary in which he once celebrated Mass is the primary target of the suicide bomber.

Instead, the Israeli embassy, on the corner of Arroyo and Suipacha

Streets is no more. The five-story building where Mossad agent Zvi Aharoni once planned the abduction of Adolf Eichmann has been completely destroyed. In addition to the dead, 242 men, women, and children lie wounded, many of them trapped in the extensive rubble. Body parts are strewn up and down the street.

On the surface, it appears that the Nazis have finally had their revenge.

※

Mossad agents quickly fly from Tel Aviv into Buenos Aires to track down the killers. The many threats by local Fascist organizations over the years, as well as numerous plots against the embassy by anti-Jewish organizations, instantly place suspicion on Nazi terror groups.

For newly installed Argentinean president Carlos Saúl Menem, the attack could not come at a worse time. He has openly been seeking a dialogue with Israel to heal the fractured relationship between the government of Argentina and its Jewish population. On February 3, just six weeks before the bombing, Menem signed an executive decree making Argentina's secret government files on Nazi war criminals available to the public. It is not a popular decision—supporters of the former Argentinean president Juan Perón claimed this was an attempt coordinated by the "Jews" to "tarnish the memory of General Perón."

But Menem stood firm.

"We are taking this step to make this country and its affairs as open as possible. Argentina has been hiding a truth for forty years that the whole world wants to see. This is a debt Argentina is paying to the world."

The files are housed in forty cardboard containers. Much of the evidence has been "cleansed" over the decades to remove details that could be embarrassing to Argentina. For this reason, these records will not prove any collaboration with the Third Reich.

But many pieces of information are remarkable. Among the files are documented chronicles of Nazi travel in and out of Argentina, as well as banking records revealing the flow of gold and other securities to war criminals. The records also prove that the Catholic Church and the Red Cross have long been complicit in the smuggling of Nazis into Argentina and other South American nations. Most damaging of all, the new evidence proves that Argentinean officials were fully aware that Dr. Josef Mengele once lived in their country.

But to Simon Wiesenthal's international army of investigators, the file they most want to see is the one with information about Martin Bormann. In the wake of Mengele's death, Wiesenthal has toned down his rhetoric. He is eighty-four now, and in semiretirement, but no less determined to find Nazi war criminals like Bormann than he was forty-five years ago. Wiesenthal is still haunted by the many deaths he witnessed during the war, and the memory of relatives who died. To carry on his legacy, he now loans his name to a group in Los Angeles calling itself the Simon Wiesenthal Center. The longtime Nazi hunter is paid a stipend for the use of his brand.

As an indication of the ongoing power of the Nazi movement in Argentina, a representative of the Simon Wiesenthal Center sent to Buenos Aires to view the new evidence has already received death threats. Shimon Samuels has received several harassing phone calls to his hotel room, condemning his ongoing pursuit of Nazis. However, one call, allegedly from a policeman, is different. The caller offers to sell Samuels photographs of Martin Bormann taken after the war.

This is the sort of hard evidence Simon Wiesenthal wants to see. Bormann would be ninety-two this year. Wiesenthal was not convinced by the German discovery of Bormann's skull twenty years ago and does not believe that Hitler's personal secretary died in Berlin. Any tangible proof that Bormann might have entered Argentina would be dramatic.

Simon Wiesenthal is initially disappointed when President Menem goes on the record stating that Argentina has no official files relating to Bormann. Then, as if by magic, Menem locates two thick

Martin Bormann, whose disappearance at the end of World War II remained a mystery for decades, shown in 1942

files pertaining to Bormann. The files contain hearsay stating that the Nazi was living in Bolivia, Colombia, and the backcountry of Argentina. The Argentinean president makes no assertion of validity, but the information is widely dispersed.

⚡⚡

Martin Bormann was always the subject of mystery.

Unlike other Nazi chieftains, Himmler, Göring, and the Führer himself, Bormann did not want any publicity. He even objected to having his picture taken. But his power was well known throughout the Reich. In May 1941, Martin Bormann became Adolf Hitler's top aide, and he remained so until the Nazi surrender in May 1945.

Bormann wielded authority in the Nazi regime surpassed only by Hitler himself. One German writer stated shortly after the war ended that Bormann was "Germany's secret ruler." Bormann remained at the Führer's side almost around the clock, so complicit in the evil perpetrated by the Third Reich that some Nazi insiders called him "Hitler's Mephistopheles." Bormann oversaw Adolf Hitler's personal finances and carried out orders the Führer often made in an irrational frenzy. SS chief Reinhard Heydrich, who would be assassinated by Czech partisans in 1942, marveled at Bormann's ambition, referring to him as "a real master of intrigue and deceit."

Walter Schellenberg, SS foreign intelligence chief, described Bormann as "a thickset man, with square shoulders and a bull neck. His eyes were like those of a boxer advancing on his opponent. . . . Those who were rivals and even enemies always underestimated his abilities."

Bormann was zealous in his determination to see the Jewish extermination to its ultimate end. "The permanent elimination of the Jews from the territories of Greater Germany can no longer be realized through emigration but by the use of implacable force in the camps in the East," Bormann decreed.

On September 30, 1944, as the Allies were making advances toward Berlin, it was Bormann who decided that prisoners of war were no longer subject to military justice. Instead, those enemy soldiers and pilots in Nazi captivity would be treated no differently than the Jews. Prisoner of war camps would be under the domain of Heinrich Himmler and the SS.

Unlike Adolf Hitler, who frequently inserted himself into formulating battle strategy, Bormann had no interest in the actual fighting of the war. On October 1, 1946, when the Nuremberg Trials convicted him in absentia for his war crimes, Bormann was acquitted of the first count against him, that of concerted planning or conspiracy in a wartime effort. Instead, he was convicted solely of war crimes and crimes against humanity. By empowering the SS to run extermination camps and pursue a policy of genocide against the Jewish people, Martin Bormann enabled every atrocity that occurred: from the evil experiments of Dr. Josef Mengele at Auschwitz, to Klaus Barbie's torture sessions in Lyon, to the snarling German shepherds at Ravensbrück.

And without the decisions and decrees of Martin Bormann, Simon Wiesenthal might never have been sent to the death camp at Mauthausen.

Even though he's an old man, not a day goes by that Simon Wiesenthal doesn't think of the horrors he endured. This is why, from his home office in Vienna, the Nazi hunter eagerly awaits news that may finally lead to the capture of Martin Bormann.

⚡⚡

But Wiesenthal is once again disappointed. Shimon Samuels of the Los Angeles Wiesenthal Center reports that he is convinced there are still a number of Nazis living in Argentina, but he finds nothing in the files to prove that Martin Bormann is there. "We don't really think Bormann lived here, but it is a tantalizing story," Samuels tells the *New York Times*. And that story remains firm for four years.

Until the discovery of Martin Bormann's passport.

26

September 25, 1991
Lyon, France
8:30 p.m.

There is no mystery about the location of Klaus Barbie.
 The Butcher of Lyon has just thirty minutes to live. The Nazi lies unconscious in a prison wing at the Hôpital Jules-Courmont. Intravenous feeding tubes drape from his arms. A respirator mask covers his nose and mouth, making it possible for him to breathe, and a powerful drip bag of painkilling drugs dulls the agony of cancer. The Nazi war criminal was brought here from his cell at St. Joseph's penitentiary three weeks ago, terminal leukemia coursing through his bloodstream. Barbie is seventy-seven and weighs just 104 pounds.

 In the terminology of Nazi hunters, Klaus Barbie is about to "age out," meaning he is dying of natural causes, having enjoyed the long and full life denied to his many victims—raising a family, running a business, traveling the world. Though tried and convicted by a French court for his wartime legacy of torture and murder in 1987, Barbie was not executed, as many would have wished. France abolished the death penalty in 1981. So instead of facing a French firing squad, as was once the custom, Barbie was sentenced to a life term in prison. Amazingly, he is up for parole in 2002.

Barbie's trial reopened old wounds from World War II, forcing France to confront a quiet history of many citizens collaborating with Nazis during the occupation. So many Frenchmen and -women were marked for life by Barbie's personal brutality that his trial was delayed four years as authorities gathered testimony from his victims.

Finally in court, Barbie did not flinch, never once backing down from his beliefs or expressing remorse for his barbaric actions.

"In times of war there are no goods and no bads," Barbie told Agence France-Presse in a 1985 interview, conducted in the wake of the Bitburg controversy. "I am a convinced Nazi. I admire the Nazi discipline. I am proud of having commanded one of the best corps of the Third Reich. If I should be born one thousand times I would be one thousand times what I have been.

"I am not a fanatic.

"I am an idealist."

At 9:00 p.m., the "idealist" breathes his last.

The Butcher of Lyon has departed the earth.

27

June 17, 1996
Bariloche, Argentina
Day

The middle-aged man of German descent steps into the offices of his local newspaper. "I want the story of Bormann's death to be written as it really was," he announces in a thick accent to the small team of journalists. Before the staff at *La Mañana del Sur* (Southern Morning) can dismiss him as a crackpot, the gentleman—who refuses to give his name—produces a most dramatic piece of evidence: the alleged passport of the heinous Nazi Martin Bormann.

The shocked journalists have more than a passing awareness of SS war criminals. The resort town of Bariloche has a reputation as a Nazi haven. Its steep mountains and thick forests are reminiscent of Bavaria. The local architecture features the lacquered wooden beams and mottled brick of alpine chalets. The local cafés serve the same plump sausage, green olive pizza, and thick black beer more common to Europe than South America. Located a thousand miles from Buenos Aires, in a region not easily accessible to the outside world before the age of commercial air travel, Bariloche was an ideal place for former SS officers to remain hidden after World War II. It has long been rumored to be the site of clandestine Nazi social gatherings.

Just last year, Nazi Gestapo chief Erich Priebke was captured here and then extradited to Italy to stand trial for the 1944 murders of 335 Roman citizens.* The deaths were retribution for a bomb blast that killed thirty-three German soldiers. Adolf Hitler personally ordered that ten Italians be shot for each Wehrmacht death. Priebke rounded up men and boys, ordered that their hands be tied behind their backs, then took them to the Ardeatine Caves outside Rome. Over a twenty-four-hour period the victims were led inside the cave five at a time, then shot in the back of the head by candlelight.

For good measure, Priebke killed five more citizens than the Führer demanded.

Like many of his SS brethren, Priebke was rounded up and imprisoned after the war, only to escape and make his way to South America via the Italian ratlines. He lived under his own name in Bariloche, where he ran a local deli and was active in the German-Argentinean cultural association. In 1996, Priebke is tried in Italy, where he pleads not guilty.†

The staff at *La Mañana del Sur* are well acquainted with the Priebke case, which has attracted worldwide press coverage. Now the Bormann passport presents the paper with another chance to create a media stir. The document certainly looks authentic. It is in almost perfect condition, bearing the number 9892. It was issued on January 3, 1946, in Genoa, Italy, by the Uruguayan embassy. The photograph of a balding man in a dark jacket bears a strong resem-

---

* Incredibly, Priebke was tracked down in Bariloche by American journalist Sam Donaldson. After ABC News ran the story, the Bariloche police had no choice but to arrest the Nazi.

† The court will rule in Priebke's favor, causing Shimon Samuels of the Simon Wiesenthal Center to declare that Italy itself is guilty of war crimes. Prosecutors appealed the verdict, and this time Priebke was convicted. Priebke died while under house arrest in 2013. Argentina refused to allow that his body be returned to Bariloche so that he might be buried next to his wife.

blance to Martin Bormann. The name "Ricardo Bauer," to whom the passport was issued, is a known alias of Bormann.

The passport fell into the hands of the unnamed German visitor to the offices of *La Mañana del Sur* several years ago, when he purchased property from "a man I suspected was a Nazi in exile." The passport was left behind on the premises, but when the German buyer tried to return it, the man he thought to be Bormann turned him down, stating that he was moving away for good and would not be needing it anymore. The German then departed, leaving the passport behind.

In June 1996, *La Mañana del Sur* publishes the story, which flashes around the world. In Buenos Aires, a representative of the Simon Wiesenthal Center states for the record, "We do not discount it, nor do we endorse it."

The Israeli embassy in Buenos Aires does doubt the story. That sentiment is echoed by the CIA. "Many are heavily discounting that the passport, issued in Genoa in 1946, actually belonged to Bormann," reads an internal CIA memo, written just days later.

That document continues: "The ongoing trial of Priebke undoubtedly is making the newspapers, particularly small, regional papers like the one that 'broke' this story on Bormann, eager to cash in on public interest in Nazi hunting. We also side with the skeptics in this sensationalist story, and wait to be convinced by better evidence than the fuzzy picture resembling Bormann on the Uruguayan passport."

A few years later, "better evidence" finally turns up.

ᛋᛋ

It is mid-August 1999. The Baltic Sea is calm as the small boat motors away from the German coast into open water. A small urn carrying the cremated remains of Martin Bormann is the vessel's most prized cargo. In response to a recent British book by Christopher Creighton titled *Op JB*—short for Operation James Bond—that claims that Winston Churchill had Bormann spirited out of Germany in the final days of the war and taken to Britain, German authorities have had enough of the entire Bormann matter. They decide to put it to rest, once and for all.

So it is that in May 1998, almost fifty-three years to the day after the Nazi is thought to have died in Berlin, DNA testing is performed on the skull discovered in a German rail yard in 1972. An eighty-three-year-old relative of Martin Bormann provides a specimen of the family's DNA to be compared with that of the alleged Bormann skull.

The samples match.

But there are still questions. The German man in Bariloche claims that Martin Bormann died from liver cancer on Argentinean soil. Other investigators who agree with that scenario suggest that Bormann's body was then smuggled back to Berlin to be reburied in the rail yard. That would explain how Bormann's skull contained dental work from the 1950s and how his bones were coated in a dark red soil found only in South America. But most people dispute that scenario.

The German government doesn't care. It only wants to prevent neo-Nazi groups from making a shrine of Bormann's grave. Thus, authorities have ordered that his ashes be committed to the Baltic Sea.

Without ceremony, the captain brings the boat to a halt. The urn is dumped into the water. It bobs on the surface for an instant, then sinks below the waves.

⚡⚡

Six years later, Simon Wiesenthal is retired from full-time Nazi hunting, though he still keeps himself apprised of ongoing investigations. He is well aware that most Nazis have already died of old age, and those who remain will not be far behind. Even before the 1998 DNA findings about Martin Bormann, Wiesenthal had come to believe that the Nazi was already dead. The CIA even used Wiesenthal's reputation to buttress their own findings about Bormann when the alleged passport was unearthed in Bariloche: "Famed Nazi hunter Simon Wiesenthal has reportedly reaffirmed his complete belief that Bormann died in Germany in 1945," the report stated.*

Strangely, even after the discovery of Dr. Josef Mengele's body in 1985, Simon Wiesenthal could not accept that the Angel of Death had truly been located. At first he believed official reports but then changed his mind. "I see the whole matter of Mengele in absolutely another light," Wiesenthal stated in 1989. "It was too perfect."

The remark is so controversial that even Rabbi Marvin Hier, international chairman of the Simon Wiesenthal Center, backpedals. "Simon is very much his own man," Hier tells the *Los Angeles Times*. "He's been that way for forty-five years."

It is only in 1992, when DNA testing on Mengele's bones confirm his identity, that Wiesenthal reluctantly lets go of his favorite conspiracy theory. However, he remains a "relentless Nazi hunter," as described by the *New York Times*.

To Simon Wiesenthal, it was not just about hunting Nazis but the historical implications: "When history looks back I want people to know the Nazis weren't able to kill millions of people and get away with it," Wiesenthal once stated.

On the morning of September 20, 2005, at the age of ninety-six, Simon Wiesenthal dies peacefully in his sleep. The relentless Nazi hunter was fulfilled. The world will never forget the gross atrocities committed by the Third Reich.

---

* This was the opposite of what Wiesenthal believed. Though unsure of Bormann's true fate, Wiesenthal long continued to have suspicions about the West German discoveries and DNA issues with the alleged Bormann skeleton. The confidential nature of the CIA report allowed them to internally state otherwise.

28

October 4, 2004
San Francisco, California
Morning

Investigator Eli Rosenbaum climbs the five flights of stairs to the top floor of the shabby apartment building. As always, the forty-nine-year-old graduate of Harvard Law School is nattily dressed in a dark suit and tie, looking very much like the federal agent he is. Rosenbaum did not have to make this trip from his office in Washington, D.C., but he likes to be on the scene when a Nazi is confronted. In his twenty-five years seeking out war criminals as head of the Department of Justice Office of Special Investigations (OSI), Rosenbaum has unmasked 132 Nazi murderers.

He is about to confront the 133rd.

Rosenbaum knocks on the door. Elfriede Huth Rinkel answers. "She did not seem terribly surprised I had found her," Rosenbaum will later tell reporters. Elfriede is eighty-two now. She leans on a cane and invites Rosenbaum to come inside. She is still plump and still wears her hair dyed red. Her husband, Fred, succumbed to a massive heart attack this past January, which devastated her, leading to a deep, lingering depression. Fred is buried in a Jewish cemetery

Eli M. Rosenbaum, the Nazi hunter who brought Elfriede Huth to justice more than five decades after she went into hiding

south of San Francisco and she hopes to lie next to him one day in their double plot. Now, Elfriede gets by on Social Security—an investigation will reveal she has been paid more than $120,000 by the U.S. government since her retirement—in fact, her monthly stipend has just been increased to include widow benefits.*

Elfriede offers Rosenbaum a place to sit. He has found her through a meticulous cross-referencing of U.S. immigration records and lists of known concentration camp guards. Rosenbaum's staff at OSI includes lawyers and historians dedicated to unearthing such documents.

The investigator has also obtained Elfriede's official Ravensbrück record card that SS officials mistakenly failed to destroy in the camp's

---

* In June 2015, a report by the inspector general of the Social Security Administration will reveal that between February 1962 and June 2015, the United States paid $20.2 million in Social Security benefits to suspected Nazi war criminals.

final days. Rosenbaum confronts Elfriede about her time at Ravensbrück, nine months that included the greatest number of murders and atrocities in the camp's six-year history.

"I did nothing wrong," Elfriede insists, adding that she had no choice but to work in the slave labor camp. She admits that she is the same Elfriede Huth who once handled vicious dogs, and also admits to lying on her visa application in 1959 by omitting her service at Ravensbrück.

But Elfriede Huth insists to Rosenbaum that she did not witness any atrocities.

Rosenbaum is offended by her lack of remorse. He personally knows the horror of Nazi violence, having lost several relatives to the Holocaust. He might not even be alive if his grandparents had not fled Germany after the *Kristallnacht* pogroms in 1938. So he makes it his business to be relentless in tracking down Nazis. The investigator has a low profile, keeping to a strict regimen of hard work. He is constantly aware that time is against him. As is clear by one look at Elfriede, many former Nazis will die of old age before they can be brought to justice. Rosenbaum personally avoids publicity and believes the term *Nazi hunter* is too swashbuckling for his life's work. "It's not a sport, it's not a game—it is something that has to be done by professionals," he tells a journalist.

Now, as Rosenbaum sits in Elfriede's dilapidated apartment, she shows him a picture of her husband's gravestone with its prominent Star of David. In her own mind, the former persecutor of Jews has been living a life of atonement. She married a Jewish man and gives to Jewish charities. That should be enough to absolve her.

"Have you converted to Judaism?" Rosenbaum asks.

"No," she admits, adding that despite not being a Jew, it is her wish to be buried next to her husband. She points again to the photograph, and her name and date of birth are already chiseled into the headstone.

Rosenbaum believes this will be impossible. Even though he cannot actually arrest Elfriede for war crimes, she can be deported to Germany for lying on her visa application.

"If I am deported, I would like to request that my coffin be brought back to the U.S. for burial," Elfriede says. She has already told Rosenbaum she will not fight the deportation process, preferring to maintain her privacy rather than engage in an expensive public legal battle.

It is an absurd request. Rosenbaum is powerless over what happens to Elfriede after death, but once the news gets out about her Nazi past, the likelihood of a Jewish cemetery allowing a Ravensbrück camp guard to be buried in one of its plots is nonexistent.

Rosenbaum leaves Elfriede's apartment, off to begin the deportation process.

Soon after, the elderly woman returns to the cemetery and sells her burial plot. She also purchases a new headstone, showing only her husband's name beneath a Star of David.

ᛋᛋ

Back in 1946, as Elfriede's peer, the notorious Dorothea Binz, stood trial for war crimes, observers were struck by how ordinary she appeared—as if she "might have stepped out of a bread queue in any German city," wrote one journalist covering the trial.

The same is true for Elfriede Huth Rinkel. She is so outwardly normal that no one suspects her Nazi past. Since she is legally still a German citizen, the Department of Justice is forbidden from making the charges against her public. Throughout the deportation process, she does not tell anyone what is happening, not even her aging brother, Kurt.

In the summer of 2006, Elfriede moves out of her apartment so that it might be renovated. When a neighbor asks how soon she will be returning, Elfriede tells him that she's decided to return to her homeland. Tired of the United States, and free to go home after Fred's death, she longs to live out her final days in Germany.

Kurt drives Elfriede to San Francisco Airport on September 1, 2006. After more than sixty years of silence and secrecy, the habit is hard to break, and it will not be until Kurt reads the astounding news in the *San Francisco Chronicle* that he will know his sister's vile past and her real reasons for fleeing the country.

Eli Rosenbaum sees to it that all documents related to Elfriede's past be sent to German officials in Cologne. Only upon her departure from America does the investigator make an official statement.

"Thousands of innocent women were brutalized and murdered at Ravensbrück through the active participation of Elfriede Rinkel and other guards," Rosenbaum announces to the press. "Her presence in the United States was an affront to surviving Holocaust victims who have made new homes in this country."

Shock runs through San Francisco's Jewish community. "She was so small and quiet—you would never imagine she could have done things like that," remarks one elderly woman.

A neighbor, Alice Fung, is stunned. "She was a sweet lady. She cared about other people. But she was a very private person."

Another of Elfriede's neighbors, Gunvant Shah, who lived across the hall for thirty years, is saddened. "I feel deeply hurt. She is like a grandmother," Shah tells reporters, then adds: "She is eighty-four years old. She felt remorse. She felt the burning in her heart. Where is the humanity?"

⚡⚡

Eli Rosenbaum is a realist. He carries on the work first begun by Nazi hunter Benny Ferencz in the years immediately following the war. Decades ago it was the jurist Ferencz who once noted how fruitless the job could be: "I had 3,000 *Einsatzgruppen* members who every day went out and shot as many Jews as they could and Gypsies as well. I tried twenty-two, I convicted twenty-two, thirteen were sentenced to death, four of them were actually executed, the rest of them got out after a few years," Ferencz famously opined.

"The other 3,000—nothing ever happened to them."

That is the daily struggle for Eli Rosenbaum: finding those members of the SS who have not been brought to justice. He knows he will never locate them all. But as the deportation of Elfriede shows, there are days when justice is served by finding just one.

⚡⚡

Incredibly, Elfriede Huth Rinkel is set free in Germany. Officials there examine the evidence against her, then choose not to file charges, stating that they can find no proof that she committed a crime.

In 2007, a reporter tracks Elfriede down to an exclusive senior citizens' home just outside Düsseldorf. "Elfriede Rinkel" is emblazoned on a plaque outside her room. No longer a "sweet old lady," a bitter Elfriede has become so rude that residents at Senioren Residenz on Linsellesstrasse admit to being stunned by her brusque behavior. The home's administrators shield Elfriede from visitors. Her lush accommodations are funded by the monthly Social Security checks she still receives from the U.S. government. With no law in place to stop these payments, there is nothing anyone can do about it.*

"Forget it," Elfriede Huth Rinkel snarls when journalists finally get her to answer the phone. "There is nothing to say."

As of the writing of this book, Elfriede Rinkel remains alive at age ninety-five.

---

* These Social Security payments to Elfriede and other suspected Nazi war criminals will continue until January 2015, when a new law called No Social Security Benefits for Nazis ends this practice.

29

March 27, 2016
New York, New York
Morning

Hitler's favorite SS commando has been dead since 1975, his coffin draped in the Nazi colors three decades after his service to the Third Reich came to an end. The funeral of Otto Skorzeny was attended by dozens of former Schutzstaffel comrades who relived old times singing the Führer's favorite songs and offering the one-armed Fascist salute on the chapel steps.*

Sitting quietly among them, a Mossad agent surveyed the church, a Jew surrounded on all sides by Nazis. Yet he was there not to spy but to say good-bye to the SS officer.

In his Nazi heyday, the tall, garrulous Skorzeny was recognizable by the dueling scar running the width of his left cheek. During the Second World War, the Austrian native was dubbed "the most dangerous man in Europe" by the United States and its allies because

---

* Skorzeny's funeral service was held in Madrid at Cementerio de Nuestra Señora de La Almudena, one of Europe's largest cemeteries. His body was later cremated and the ashes buried in the Skorzeny family plot in Vienna.

of his ruthlessness and feats of military daring that bordered on the impossible.

Now, forty-one years after the funeral of Otto Skorzeny, on this warm spring Saturday, the journalistic writing team of Dan Raviv and Yossi Melman are revealing shocking new details about the life of this staunch Nazi who once worked to implement Hitler's Final Solution against the Jews.

Raviv, a clean-shaven American who once worked for CBS News, and Melman, a bearded Israeli columnist in his midsixties, are specialists on the Mossad and Israel's extensive spy network. Raviv and Melman bring to life ghosts from the world of Nazi hunting such as Isser Harel, Peter Malkin, and Simon Wiesenthal. The reporters published a story just today in the *Forward*, one of the world's leading Jewish newspapers.

Relying on conversations with former Mossad agents, some of them still so deeply undercover that their names cannot be revealed, the writers spin a tale of murder, betrayal, and intrigue unlike any other in the seventy-year search for Nazi war criminals.

SS-Obersturmführer Otto Skorzeny, the journalists claim, had a second career after World War II ended: he worked for the State of Israel.

⚡⚡

The year is 1962. Mossad director Isser Harel still basks in the glory of the kidnapping of Adolf Eichmann two years ago and is eager to continue hunting down Nazis. The infamous SS commando Otto Skorzeny is an obvious target. The Nazi, now fifty-four and much heavier than he was during the war, is known to live in Spain with his forty-two-year-old wife, Ilse. Though Simon Wiesenthal has placed Skorzeny high on his list of Nazi war criminals deserving prosecution, the former SS man makes no effort to hide his identity or whereabouts, for he lives under the protection of the nation's Fascist dictator, Generalissimo Francisco Franco. Skorzeny's sense of security is so complete that in 1957 he publishes a memoir of his commando exploits during World War II.

For this reason, the Mossad team investigating Skorzeny is well aware that kidnapping the commando and bringing him to trial in the manner of Eichmann is unrealistic. Diplomatic relations between Spain and Israel are poor, due to Franco's support of Hitler during the war and Franco's subsequent announcement that Jews were conspiring with Freemasons to take over the world. An attempt to extract Skorzeny from his lavish Madrid villa would prompt an enormous international incident.

So, the Mossad decides it would be much easier to simply kill him.

Meanwhile, the nation of Israel faces a more immediate Nazi threat. Teams of German scientists who once labored in Adolf Hitler's rocket program, designing the V-1 and V-2 weapons that were fired most effectively at Great Britain, are at this time being employed by Egypt at a site known as Factory 333 outside Cairo. The Egyptian government is trying to produce a new generation of rockets capable of annihilating Israel.*

To the Mossad, Skorzeny's World War II transgressions demand his assassination, but that can wait. Stopping these proposed rocket attacks is far more urgent. "These are people who are marked to die," is Harel's explanation for the reign of terror he plans to level against the Nazi scientists working for Egypt.

In what will become known as Operation Damocles, Harel will use intimidation, letter bombs, and threats against the families of any rocket expert working with the Egyptians. Anonymous phone calls will be placed in the dead of night, warning the scientists that

---

* The Nazi World War II rocket program was based in Peenemünde, on the Baltic Sea. The men involved were among the top intellects in the world on the subject of rocket propulsion. After the war, their talents were in great demand. The space programs of the United States and the Soviet Union were greatly advanced by the presence of these former Nazis. Dr. Wernher von Braun, who led the team at Peenemünde, was vital to the NASA (National Aeronautics and Space Administration) lunar landings and lived out his life in the United States. In the 1950s, von Braun teamed up with animator Walt Disney, where he served as technical adviser and host of television shows about space travel.

their lives are in jeopardy should they continue their research. In the mind of Isser Harel, former Nazis making rockets for Egypt is a continuation of the Holocaust.

With his usual meticulous attention to detail, Harel orders his agents to compile a dossier on each of the scientists. One individual of note is Dr. Heinz Krug, a forty-nine-year-old former Peenemünde researcher. Krug now runs a corporation known as Antra, based in Munich, but is secretly involved in making Egyptian missiles. It is common for him to commute to Cairo for work. But as Harel's agents begin a barrage of midnight calls, Krug knows his safety is compromised. He imagines that the Mossad will do to him precisely what they did to Adolf Eichmann.

In desperation, Krug contacts a former Nazi, someone he can trust, a man with the experience and cunning to protect him from the Israeli threat. He calls Otto Skorzeny.

Unfortunately for Heinz Krug, Isser Harel has called Skorzeny first.

ᛋᛋ

Rumors about the former SS commando are legend. He is thought to be the leader of Die Spinne network of former Nazis.* Gossip has him seducing Eva Perón. Skorzeny is even thought to have a fortune in looted Nazi wealth so vast that some compare him with King Solomon.

But facts may trump rumors. A soldier since the age of twenty-three, Skorzeny distinguished himself in the early days of World War II, fighting throughout Poland and Russia. As a member of the Waffen SS, Skorzeny was familiar with plans for Jewish geno-

---

* Even though the clandestine Nazi organization called ODESSA achieved fame in Hollywood, it was the group Die Spinne that allegedly aided most of the war criminals who escaped. Though details on all of the postwar Nazi networks are shrouded in deception and innuendo, it is widely believed that Die Spinne was the work of Skorzeny and Reinhard Gehlen. The assistance of Gen. Francisco Franco made it possible for Die Spinne to use Madrid as its home base. The ODESSA organization has never been confirmed as a source in aiding war criminals.

cide, as the firing squads and mobile gas vans for murdering Jews were common along the Eastern Front. The depth of his participation in the genocide is unclear.

Then came September 1943. Adolf Hitler himself ordered Skorzeny to rescue embattled Italian dictator Benito Mussolini from members of the Italian government who had taken him hostage. "Il Duce" was being held at the Campo Imperatore Hotel, high atop a ski resort in central Italy's Gran Sasso massif. Rather than fighting their way up the mountain, Skorzeny and his band of paratroopers land by glider.

The Italians selected the Campo Imperatore for its remote location and commanding views, allowing them advance warning of any attack. Mussolini is heavily guarded, as he begins his third week as a prisoner of the Italian state.* The hotel is empty of guests, its only residents being Il Duce and the two hundred military police known as carabinieri standing by to repel would-be rescuers.

Otto Skorzeny has the forethought to take custody of an Italian prisoner named Gen. Fernando Soleti, who collaborated in the coup against Mussolini before falling into German hands. Having no choice but to assist the Nazis, Soleti is among the German troops landing atop the mountain in gliders. As the SS surrounds the Campo Imperatore Hotel, Soleti cries out to the Italian carabinieri inside, ordering them not to shoot lest they be shot themselves for treason.

No one fires.

Skorzeny rushes into the hotel, where he destroys the radio room, making it impossible for the Italian guards to send a belated cry for help. Then he finds Mussolini.

"Duce," Skorzeny tells the Italian Fascist. "The Führer has sent me to set you free."

---

* On July 25, 1943, the Grand Council of Fascism, Italy's governing body, requested that King Victor Emmanuel III be returned to the throne. This effectively ended the reign of Benito Mussolini. The dictator was taken into custody, where he remained until his rescue by the Nazis.

"I knew that my friend Adolf would not forsake me," replies Mussolini.

Time is of the essence. A lightweight German Storch aircraft lands on the rocky plateau. Mussolini is placed on board the two-man plane. The German paratroopers will flee the mountaintop on foot, fighting their way through the Italian partisans, if necessary.

However, Otto Skorzeny insists on flying out with his prize. The pilot revs the engines to their maximum before attempting a takeoff. Skorzeny's weight makes that impossible. The Storch arrives at the edge of a steep plateau without gaining altitude. As the horrified SS troops look on, the getaway plane drops straight down. But Otto Skorzeny's legend is only enhanced by what happens next: the pilot uses this new airspeed to gain control. He levels the Storch long before it can hit the valley floor. The pilot soon lands just outside Rome, where Mussolini and Skorzeny then board another plane for the flight to Vienna.

The mission would be the making of Skorzeny. Two days later, Hitler himself awards his fellow Austrian the Third Reich's most valuable prize: the Iron Cross.

⚡⚡

Skorzeny would continue to dazzle the Führer with his courage, conducting missions behind Allied lines, kidnapping politicians disloyal to the Third Reich, and even attempting the assassination of Allied leaders Winston Churchill, Joseph Stalin, and Franklin Roosevelt at the Tehran Conference. Operation Long Jump, as the plan was known, was called off when Soviet spies uncovered the mission.

The Nazi publicity machine made much of Skorzeny, so it was no surprise that he was arrested by Allied authorities following the war. During the Dachau Trials of 1947, he was charged with ordering his men to wear U.S. Army uniforms and for stealing Red Cross parcels from prisoners of war. Skorzeny was acquitted but then held in prison pending further charges.

On July 27, 1948, three former SS officers wearing stolen U.S. military police uniforms walked Skorzeny out of the penitentiary gates in a brazen prison break. Shortly afterward, Skorzeny allegedly began the smuggling of more than six hundred Nazis to South America through his Die Spinne network. He remained a fugitive from justice until 1952, when a West German court declared him officially denazified, allowing him to travel freely without fear of arrest. It was shortly thereafter that Skorzeny made his way to Buenos Aires as a guest of the dictator Juan Perón. While acting as Perón's adviser, he is thought to have consorted secretly with Eva Perón in the guise of serving as her bodyguard.

This blend of fact and innuendo follows Skorzeny. But there is no doubt about what transpired the night of September 11, 1962, in a dark woods outside Munich.

ϟϟ

The operation begins with Otto Skorzeny sitting at a Madrid bar with his wife, Ilse. She is a middle-aged beauty with glamour that seems at odds with Skorzeny's bloated appearance. The SS man has been deeply unsettled by the Mossad's kidnapping of Adolf Eichmann and, like many former Nazis in exile, believes it is only a matter of time before the Israelis come for him, too. He is also well aware that Simon Wiesenthal has placed him on a list of known war criminals. So Skorzeny treats all strangers with suspicion.

At the end of the bar, Skorzeny notices a couple sitting down. The woman is just shy of thirty, flirtatious and chatty. Her partner is more subdued. The barman, hearing them speak German, introduces the pair to Skorzeny and his wife. As they strike up a conversation, the couple explain that they are tourists who have just been victimized—robbed on the streets of Madrid. All of their possessions, including luggage and passports, are missing. In an act of kindness, Ilse offers to let them spend the night at the Skorzeny home.

The moment is a setup. The German tourists are, in fact, Mossad. Another team of agents has been following Otto Skorzeny for several weeks, tracking his patterns of behavior. Mossad boss Isser

Harel has decided that Otto Skorzeny is the perfect man to break the inner circle of scientists. They will trust him, as no member of the SS will have more credibility than Skorzeny. Thus, incredibly, Harel wants to recruit the commando to work for Israel and help eliminate the German scientists.

The two couples have a few more drinks before traveling to the Skorzeny home. Upon entering the villa, there is a bit of tension in the air, which is increased when Otto Skorzeny suddenly levels a gun at the Mossad agents.

"I know who you are, and I know why you're here. You are Mossad, and you've come to kill me," Skorzeny says.

"You are half right," the Israeli man coolly replies. "We are from Mossad. But if we had come to kill you, you would have been dead weeks ago."

"Maybe, I would just rather kill *you*," replies Skorzeny.

"If you kill us, the ones who come next won't bother to have a drink with you," comes the response. It is the woman this time. "You won't even see their faces before they blow out your brains. Our offer to you is just for you to help us."

Otto Skorzeny is stunned. "You need something done?"

The Mossad agents nod in agreement and explain the mission Isser Harel has in mind.

Then the Nazi names his price. It is not money. It is a moment that shows the incredible power that Nazi hunters now hold over SS war criminals.

"I need for Simon Wiesenthal to remove my name from his list," Skorzeny tells the Mossad.

"That will be done," says the male Mossad agent.

The deal has been made: SS-Obersturmbannführer Otto Skorzeny now secretly works for Israel.

Within days, he is on a flight to Tel Aviv.*

⚡⚡

---

* Simon Wiesenthal refused to cooperate. To convince Skorzeny that his name had been removed from the list, the Mossad forged a letter stating it had occurred.

Much of Otto Skorzeny's career as a Mossad agent is still confidential. Among his handlers was Rafi Eitan, one of the agents who tackled Adolf Eichmann on Garibaldi Street and later witnessed his hanging. Fifty years after it transpired, "Mr. Kidnap" will only admit to "running" Skorzeny and will give few other details of their work together.

But it is known that on the night of September 11, 1962, three Mossad agents are in a car closely following a white Mercedes sedan. They wear gloves still dirty from digging a small grave that afternoon. Their location is a highway just north of Munich. The sun is going down.

Inside the white Mercedes are Otto Skorzeny and Heinz Krug, the embattled Nazi rocket scientist who is meeting with Skorzeny about securing protection from the Mossad. The SS man is calm and reassuring, informing Krug that the car behind him carries three bodyguards whom he will introduce in a nearby wooded location.

If Krug is suspicious, he does not show it. As Isser Harel predicted, no Nazi could be more trustworthy to another Nazi than the great Otto Skorzeny.

The two cars pull off the highway into a forest. The trees blot out the setting sun. Heinz Krug turns off the engine and steps out from behind the wheel. He turns to look at the second vehicle, curious about his new bodyguards. Krug is a heavyset man who wears his hair combed straight back. His neck is thick, shoulders broad.

Otto Skorzeny walks behind Krug and suddenly fires the first bullet into the back of Krug's skull. Skorzeny likes to kill, and does so without hesitation. The second shot is fired as Krug lies dead on the ground.

Working quickly, Skorzeny and the Mossad agents douse the corpse with acid so that it cannot be identified, then they kick the body into the grave dug earlier in the afternoon. In order that tracking dogs will never find the body, the agents cover it with lime. One of the Mossad agents is Yitzhak Shamir, destined to become prime minister of Israel. Another is Peter Malkin, a former member of the Eichmann kidnap squad.

The final member of the Mossad team is named Joe Raanan. It is Raanan, a fellow Austrian, who works most closely with Skorzeny during his time with Mossad, training the former Nazi in the ways of a spy. Raanan keeps Skorzeny very busy. In November 1962, five Egyptian workers at Factory 333 are killed as a result of a letter bomb posted in Egypt by Skorzeny. In the end, the hiring of the SS commando proves to be a successful move by Mossad; German scientists start refusing to work in Egypt. By 1964, the rocket program ceases to exist.

In the interim, the Mossad's covert attacks produce another victim. Isser Harel is asked to step down as Mossad director, charged with inept handling of the situation with Egypt. His replacement, Meir Amit, will then send out an order prohibiting Mossad agents from hunting Nazis, demanding that the spy agency totally "stop chasing ghosts from our past."

Thus, when Otto Skorzeny dies of cancer in July 1975, Joe Raanan is the lone Jew among dozens of former Nazis who travel to Madrid to pay their respects.

The word *atonement* is not on Joe Raanan's mind as he watches the funeral, for Otto Skorzeny never mentioned such a thing. But it is remarkable that the Führer's favorite SS commando would one day play a key role in defending the Jewish homeland.

⚡⚡

Back in New York City, the chroniclers of the Skorzeny-Mossad story, Dan Raviv and Yossi Melman, are besieged with reactions to their article in the *Forward*. "Newspapers and websites all over the world were quoting our article—and that was a surprise," Raviv will write. "The sensational interest in how the Israelis recruited Skorzeny—and how he was so cold-blooded that he volunteered to commit a murder to impress them—shows that there's an undying fascination with Nazis. They are mankind at its worst; and the facts we revealed—that one evil man could be manipulated to act against other evil Nazis in Egypt—show yet again how astounding Israel's spy agency can be."

Dan Raviv is correct. It was indeed "tiny Israel" and its supporters who finally brought down the heinous SS executioners.

With Nazi money and ruthless power available even after World War II, killing the SS was no easy task. But it had to be done.

And it was.

Postscript

Heinrich Himmler's body remains buried in an unmarked grave, somewhere in a German forest. Allied trucks were driven over the grave immediately after his self-inflicted death to obscure the location. The reason he chose to commit suicide after initially attempting to make contact with the Allies is still unclear. Upon his capture by the British, Himmler seemed to believe the Allies might protect him to some extent. But in his short captivity his fears got the better of him. The consensus is that Himmler panicked during the second body search, leading him to bite down on his cyanide vial.

ᛋᛋ

As for the remaining members of Himmler's travel group, **SS Col. Werner Grothmann**, Himmler's personal bodyguard **Josef Kiermaier**, and **Maj. Heinz Macher** escaped prosecution and lived well into old age. **Drs. Rudolf Brandt** and **Karl Gebhardt** were not so fortunate. Both were among the worst SS war criminals. Both men conducted gruesome experiments on human beings in concentration camps. Brandt was not even a medical doctor at all, having earned his doctorate in law. This did not prevent him from murdering and then beheading Jews in order to remove the flesh from their bones and study their skeletons for racial characteristics. Rudolf Brandt and

Karl Gebhardt were hanged for war crimes on June 2, 1948. Intelligence officer **SS-Gen. Otto Ohlendorf** was convicted of war crimes and hanged on June 7, 1951. While later generations of SS war criminals would be cremated to avoid neo-Nazi groups from making shrines of their graves, Brandt, Gebhardt, and Ohlendorf were all buried in traditional cemeteries. Ohlendorf's grave is the simplest of these. He is buried beneath a headstone shaped like a crucifix in the Heger Friedhof Cemetery in Osnabrück, Germany.

⚡⚡

At the time of this writing, **Benjamin Ferencz**, the original Nazi hunter, is ninety-seven and living in Florida with his wife of seventy years, Gertrude. Ferencz has been widely honored for his pivotal role in the Ohlendorf trial and is an outspoken advocate for compassion and tolerance and the use of judicial means to bring war criminals to trial. Ferencz was particularly incensed by the execution of Osama bin Laden in 2011, arguing in a letter to the *New York Times* that the "illegal and unwarranted execution—even of suspected mass murderers—undermines democracy." To maintain his vitality, Ferencz swims and does one hundred push-ups each day. He was the subject of a May 2017 Lesley Stahl story on *60 Minutes*.

⚡⚡

Evita Perón was not immediately laid to rest after her state funeral in August 1952. The subsequent journey of Evita's corpse is bizarre. She was embalmed through a process utilizing glycerin, giving her body a lifelike appearance. Instead of being buried immediately, Evita's corpse was placed on public display in her former office. It remained there for two years, awaiting the construction of a permanent monument the size of the Statue of Liberty in which she would be entombed. In 1955, a military coup ousted Juan Perón from the Argentinean presidency. He fled the country, leaving Evita's body behind. The corpse disappeared for sixteen years, before it was finally discovered in an Italian crypt. The body was missing one fingertip and appeared to have been beaten with blunt objects. Damage to the legs suggested that it had been stored in a standing position. Evita's body was returned to Juan Perón, now remarried and living in Spain with his new wife. Perón placed the corpse on display in his dining room, where it remained for two more years until his return to power in Argentina in 1973. Evita Perón was finally laid to rest on October 22, 1976, in Buenos Aires's La Recoleta Cemetery. The tomb is said to be strong enough to withstand a nuclear attack in order that no one will ever steal her body again.

⚡⚡

Juan Perón remained in exile until June 20, 1973, when he returned to Argentina and served a third term as president. An estimated three million supporters awaited his plane at Buenos Aires's Ezeiza Airport. A scene of bedlam ensued, and snipers supporting the opposition party opened fire on the crowd, killing thirteen. Perón died suddenly one year later, on July 1, 1974. His body is entombed in the La Chacarita Cemetery in Buenos Aires.

⚡⚡

West German prosecutor **Fritz Bauer** was found dead in the bathtub of his Frankfurt home on July 1, 1968. Bauer's corpse was discovered one day after he drowned. There were a large number of sleeping pills in his system and a glass of red wine next to the tub. German officials will speculate that he committed suicide due to stress. Bauer was long known to struggle with societal pressure, hiding both his true religion and sexual orientation.

After years of secrecy, Bauer had recently disclosed publicly that he was the German administrator responsible for helping the Mossad pinpoint the exact location and false identity of Adolf Eichmann. Zealous about eradicating former Nazis from positions of authority in the West German government, Bauer had accumulated a long list of enemies and received numerous death threats.

But to those who know Bauer, suicide made little sense.

Bauer was eulogized by one former member of the U.S. Nuremberg Trials prosecution team as "the greatest ambassador the [German] Federal Republic ever had"—a man with "clear vision of what needed to be done to help Germany." Bauer long argued that any soldier working in a death camp was complicit in the murder of prisoners. Almost fifty years after his death, as a series of books and films on Bauer showed his heroism, the German legal system finally adopted this point of view in dealing with its Nazi past.

⚡⚡

Petra Kelly, the outspoken German environmental activist and politician who claimed that Josef Mengele had returned home to Günzburg for his father's funeral, was brutally murdered in her Bonn apartment by her lover in October 1992.

⚡⚡

Vera Eichmann returned to live in the house on Garibaldi Street shortly after her husband's execution, where she dedicated her life to reading the Bible. Three years later, she moved back to Germany with her youngest son, Ricardo, where she died in 1993 at the age of eighty-four. The three other Eichmann boys—Nick, Dieter, and Horst—all remained in Buenos Aires.

Ricardo Eichmann served for a short time in the German air force. He then returned to school, earning a postgraduate degree in archaeology. He currently lives in Berlin and works at the German Archaeological Institute, where he serves as head of the Orient department. Ricardo has no recollections of his father and turns down all requests for interviews. However, in the summer of 1995, he traveled to London to meet face-to-face with Zvi Aharoni, the man responsible for his father's kidnapping. During a three-hour lunch of sandwiches and whiskey, the two men discussed the incident. "In a way, my father has come back to me," Ricardo Eichmann said afterward. "Now I have to push him away."

⚡⚡

Rolf Mengele admitted his part in the cover-up of his father's location and returning to Brazil once more after his father's remains were located. Since 1985, Rolf has led a quiet life as a German attorney. At the time of this writing he is still alive in Freiburg, Germany. The public uproar over the discovery of Dr. Josef Mengele's corpse made worldwide headlines, but the Angel of Death's bones never made it back to the Fatherland for reburial. Nor were they burned and scattered at sea. Instead, medical students in São Paulo study them regularly as part of their forensic pathology curriculum.

⚡⚡

Zvi Aharoni retired from the Mossad in 1970. After the Eichmann kidnapping, he successfully ran the Mossad's Nazi hunting division, which was based in Paris. Unable to capture Josef Mengele or Martin Bormann, the group was shut down in 1964. Aharoni worked for a Hong Kong bank after leaving the spy agency. His first wife died in 1973 and he remarried shortly thereafter to a British woman he met in Hong Kong. The couple eventually moved to England, where Aharoni published his memoirs and worked in security for a London hotel. Eager to set aside the horrors of his previous career, Aharoni preferred to go by the name of Hermann Arndt in the last years of his life. He died on May 26, 2012, in the village of Devon, having told few of his neighbors about his role in the Eichmann kidnapping.

⚡⚡

In May 2010, a ceremony was held in Israel by El Al to celebrate the fiftieth anniversary of the Adolf Eichmann kidnapping. Among the attendees was the flight's navigator, **Shaul Shaul**, who courageously met with Buenos Aires airport controllers when the flight was halted just before takeoff. Not in attendance was **Zvi Tohar**, the cool and collected El Al pilot who defied Isser Harel's order to take off from Buenos Aires. He died of a heart attack in 1970 at the age of fifty-five.

⚡⚡

Isser Harel entered the world of politics after resigning from the Mossad on March 25, 1963. He served one term in the Israeli Knesset before leaving office. Subsequently, he continued to spar publicly with Simon Wiesenthal about the Eichmann kidnapping, having published his own version of events in 1975, when the restriction on Mossad silence was lifted. His book, *The House on Garibaldi Street*, was subsequently made into a television movie in 1979. Harel lived out his remaining years in the Tel Aviv suburb of Zahala, where he enjoyed writing and reading biographies. Isser Harel died on February 18, 2003.

⚡⚡

Rafi Eitan, who directed the Eichmann operation and personally helped subdue the Nazi during the kidnapping, enjoyed a long career with the Mossad. This included his work with Otto Skorzeny in the 1960s. After Eichmann and Skorzeny, Eitan later led the successful assassination operation against Ali Hassan Salameh, the man who coordinated the murder of Israeli athletes at the 1972 Olympic Games. Eitan's spy career came to an end when it was disclosed that he had worked with American Jonathan Pollard as a handler. Pollard served twenty-nine years in American federal prisons for stealing military secrets from the United States. At the time of this writing, Eitan is in his nineties, living in Israel.

⚡⚡

Elfriede Huth is ninety-five years old at the time of this writing. Her location is currently unknown, but she is believed to still reside in Germany, just a few hours' drive from the Ravensbrück Memorial. The site is built on that of the former extermination camp, fifty miles north of Berlin.

⚡⚡

Simon Wiesenthal resisted a move to Israel during his lifetime, believing that his hunt for Nazi fugitives could better be pursued from his office in Vienna. However, in death Wiesenthal had no such qualms. He was laid to rest in the seaside Herzliya Cemetery in Tel Aviv in September 24, 2005.

※

Eli M. Rosenbaum continues hunting Nazis and other war criminals to this day. In 2010, the Office of Special Investigation merged with the Human Rights and Special Prosecutions Section of the U.S. Department of Justice. This expanded jurisdiction now allows Rosenbaum to search for not just former Nazis but perpetrators of genocide and modern-day war crimes around the world.

※

Though his body was identified by its DNA, cremated, and the ashes dropped into the Baltic Sea, there are some who believe that the corpse of **Martin Bormann** was a fake. Pointing to the method of DNA testing in 1996 as compared with more modern methods, these doubters continue to propel various conspiracy theories about the actual fate of Hitler's top assistant. However, at this writing, if Bormann were still alive, he would be a remarkable 118 years old.

※

Of course, there are also those who believe that **Adolf Hitler** survived the war. Despite eyewitness evidence that he shot himself, some insist that he escaped to South America in a Nazi submarine. A declassified 1955 CIA report showed a photograph of a man bearing a strong likeness to the Führer in the Venezuelan city of Maracaibo in that same year. The accuracy of the photograph was never confirmed.

Sources

As always, the Killing books are researched through a comprehensive examination of books, newspapers, magazines, archives, and personal travel. However, the web of myth, secrecy, and inconsistencies surrounding this subject matter required a more in-depth sort of research. For example, the existence of groups such as ODESSA and Die Spinne is still widely debated, more than seven decades after World War II ended. This is just one of the many mysteries that continue to confound Nazi hunters. We have presented the facts both for and against any such speculative issues, letting readers draw their own conclusions.

What is known for certain is that millions were murdered in the Holocaust. The eyewitness testimony to Nazi atrocities delivered at the Nuremberg Trials and other postwar tribunals is brutal and detailed. In many cases we have abridged these sworn statements, removing long or repetitive passages, but no words have been changed in any way.

This also holds for the testimony of Adolf Eichmann and his accusers. Readers wishing to read the entire testimony of the Eichmann or Nuremberg trials will find them available online.

Many of the conversations recorded in this book come directly from books by figures such as Benjamin Ferencz, Zvi Aharoni, and

Isser Harel, who played such pivotal roles in bringing Nazi war criminals to trial. Harel's *The House on Garibaldi Street* and Aharoni's *Operation Eichmann* (with Wilhelm Dietl) are particularly specific about conversations and events leading up to the Eichmann kidnapping. It's worth noting that Ferencz has placed his memoirs, in their entirety, on his website for easy reading: www.benferencz.org. There is no charge.

From a research point of view, the years immediately following World War II were best discovered through the eyewitness memoir of Ferencz and transcripts of the postwar tribunals. This testimony was essential to early portions of the book. Information about Eichmann was gleaned from the numerous first-person accounts published subsequent to his execution. Newspapers and magazines began following the world of Nazi hunting more closely after the Eichmann trial and continue to do so to this day, as the many accounts of Elfriede Huth's saga illustrate. In addition, a number of authors have stepped forth to investigate the murky world of postwar Nazi flight and the existence of the ratlines that made these escapes possible. We are indebted to reporting in the *New York Times*, *Los Angeles Times*, *Time* magazine, *Der Spiegel*, and a host of other print sources for their insight.

The authors consulted a small library of works about the Nazi world in order to better understand the Holocaust and the methods utilized by SS murderers to evade justice for their crimes. However, all works of history lean on a smaller bank of key resources as a gateway into the research: *The Nazi Hunters* and *Hunting Eichmann* by Neal Bascomb; *The Nazi Hunters* by Andrew Nagorski; *Hunting Evil* by Guy Walters; *Simon Wiesenthal: The Life and Legends* by Tom Segev; *Nazi Hunter: The Wiesenthal File* by Alan Levy; *Nazis on the Run: How Hitler's Henchmen Fled Justice* by Gerald Steinacher; *The Nazis Next Door: How America Became a Safe Haven for Hitler's Men* by Eric Lichtblau; the seminal *Eichmann in Jerusalem: A Report on the Banality of Evil* by Hannah Arendt; and the equally spectacular *Eichmann Before Jerusalem: The Unexamined Life of a Mass Murderer* by Bettina Stangneth. The best research we came across concerning the validity of claims about the existence of an ODESSA group can be found in *The Real Odessa: How Peron Brought the Nazi War Criminals to Argentina* by Uki Goni.

It is worth taking a moment to discuss Paul Manning's *Martin Bormann: Nazi in Exile*. Manning was a respected journalist with a lifetime of impeccable credentials. There is no reason to believe he would somehow revert to a more sensational standard to document the search for Bormann. The many specific details contained within the book are compelling, presenting a plausible case for Bormann's successful escape from Berlin in 1945—although in many cases Manning does not provide sources. Readers are encouraged to draw their own conclusions. If nothing else, the claims made by Manning and the later scientific evidence about Bormann's demise make for a striking contrast. The search for Martin Bormann remains one of history's great detective stories, and Manning's book clearly shows why Bormann's last days still remain a mystery to many.

Finally, there is no substitute for visiting in person the exact locations of Nazi horrors in order to attempt to comprehend what happened there. A considerable amount of our research time was spent in Germany, Austria, and the Czech Republic, where there are many powerful memorials to the Holocaust. The Memorial to the Murdered Jews of Europe, located in Berlin, is not easily forgotten—nor is the location of Adolf Hitler's former Führerbunker, located just a few hundred yards away. But it is the camps such as Auschwitz, Ravensbrück, and Dachau that serve as the most haunting reminder of the past. Setting foot inside them is fundamental to understanding what transpired—and why Nazi hunters are still relentless in their search.

Illustration Credits

Maps by Gene Thorp
Page 4: akg-images
Page 26: PhotoQuest/Getty Images
Page 34: PJF Military Collection/Alamy Stock Photo
Page 50: AP Photo
Page 57: akg-images/Fototeca Gilardi
Page 66: akg-images/picture-alliance/dpa
Page 96: akg-images/Interfoto
Page 122: akg-images/WHA/World History Archive
Page 152: Courtesy El Al
Page 156: Image in the public domain via Wikimedia Commons
Page 218: akg-images/picture-alliance/dpa
Page 228: akg-images/picture-alliance/dpa
Page 247: U.S. Dept. of Justice
Page 252: akg-images
Page 264: Chuck Kennedy/KRT/Newscom

Index

Page numbers in *italics* refer to illustrations.

ABC News, 258n
ABC Restaurant and Bar, 62, 62n, 108, 113
abortion, 240
Aharoni, Zvi, 101–9, 250, 285
   background of, 105–7
   capture of Eichmann, 121–54, 180
   interrogation of Eichmann, 136–38, 146, 160
   search for Eichmann, 101–19
   search for Mengele, 179–84, 210
   transport of Eichmann to Tel Aviv, 141–54
Alps, 8, 10, 41
American Chemical Foundation, 9
Amit, Meir, 278
Andrus, Burton C., 28
anti-Semitism, 3, 53, 99, 219
   in Argentina, 52–54, 62, 101–2, 140, 180–82, 182n, 249–51
   in Brazil, 213–15
   global rise of, 101–2, 157–58
   postwar, 8–10, 17, 83, 93–99, 101–2, 104, 180–82, 190, 200, 213–15, 260
Antra, 272
Arab League of Buenos Aires, 140

Argentina, 10, 47, 48, 49–54, 61–62, 86, 90, 179, 196, 250, 252, 275
   Eichmann in, 61–62, 65–84, 101–19, 121–54
   Jews in, 180–81, 250
   May Revolution, 126–27
   Mengele in, 48, 62, 83, 96–97, 132, 145, 148–49, 158, 179–82, 206
   Nazism in, 51n, 52–54, 60–62, 65–84, 86, 101–19, 121–54, 179–82, 182n, 249–51, 254, 257–58
   Perón presidency, 52–54
   ratlines to, 43, *44*, 45, 60–61
Argentinisches Tageblatt, 72
Aronheim, Eugenie, 106
Aronheim, Heinrich, 105, 106, 107
Aronheim, Hermann. *See* Aharoni, Zvi
Associated Press, 35n
Asunción, 98, 196, 234
Atlantic Monthly, 157
Auschwitz, 7, 16, 46, 48, 58, 60, 96, 97, 107, 163–66, 177, 189–90, 210, 211, 217, 229
   medical experiments, 16, 42, 43, 95, 211, 253
   tattoo, 189

Austria, 3, 16, 59, 60n, 80, 108, 182, 193–96, 207–9, 215, 216
  Jews, 3, 16, 107, 142, 160, 196, 196n
  postwar, 41
Avengers, 68, 68n
Axmann, Artur, 87

Bach, Gabriel, 164–66
Baltic Sea, 259, 260, 271n
Barbie, Klaus, 16, 22, 45–47, 215–23, 235, 255–56
  aided by Americans, 45, 47, 216
  arrest of, 228–29
  in Bolivia, 215–23, 228
  as Butcher of Lyon, 16, 216, 217, 221, 255
  convicted in absentia, 217, 217n
  death of, 255–56
  escape of, 16, 45, 216
  interrogation techniques of, 220–23
  Izieu roundup of Jewish children, 45–47, 229
  search for, 45–47, 215–23
  trial of, 228, 228, 229, 256
  war crimes of, 16, 45–47, 216, 218–23, 253, 255–56
Bariloche, 196, 257–58, 258n, 260
Barrett, Soledad, 182n
bathtub torture, 223
Battle of the Bulge, 19
Bauer, Fritz, 65–66, 66, 67–77, 283–84
  in concentration camp, 67, 67n, 103–4, 104n
  search for Eichmann, 65–82, 103–5, 108, 113
Bavaria, 30, 95
Beer Hall Putsch, 94, 94n
Belgium, 53, 54
  Jews, 58
Belsen, 59
Belsen Trial, 245
Ben-Ari, Mordechai, 127
Ben-Gurion, David, 102, 193
Ben-Zvi, Yitzhak, 185

Bergen-Belsen, 7, 77n, 196n, 231–32, 245
Berlin, 12, 16, 31, 32, 33, 58, 106, 108n, 161, 196, 199, 247, 251
  fall of, 1, 84–88, 199–202
  postwar division of, 199–200, 200n
  Soviet occupation of, 84–88, 199, 244
Berlin Wall, 199–200, 200n
Bertioga, 210, 225
Besymenski, L., 88
Binz, Dorothea, 241–45, 266
Bitburg, 231–32, 256
Blaschke, Hugo, 202
Blobel, Paul, 39
Bolivia, 109, 252
  Barbie in, 215–23, 228
  Nazi community, 216–23
Bonn, 200
Bormann, Martin, 16, 84–91, 196, 199–203, 209, 217n, 251–52, 252, 253–54, 287
  alleged skeleton of, 200–203, 260, 261n
  as Brown Eminence, 85, 85n
  buried at sea, 259–60
  dental history, 202–3, 203n, 260
  DNA findings on, 260
  escape of, 16, 84–91
  in Hitler's bunker, 84–87
  as Hitler's confidant, 85–86, 252–53
  passport of, 254, 257–61
  physical appearance of, 253
  role in Holocaust, 253
  search for, 84–91, 196, 196n, 197, 199–201, 201n, 202–3, 203n, 251–54, 257–61, 261n
Bossert, Liselotte, 225–27, 237
Bossert, Wolfram, 225–27, 237
Brandt, Rudolf, 8, 281, 282
Brandt, Willy, 200
Bräuning, Edmund, 242, 244
Brazil, 141, 148, 191–98, 205–12
  Jews in, 213–15
  Mengele in, 182–84, 205–12, 225–27, 233
  Nazi community, 182–84, 205–15

Bremervörde, 12
Brixen, 42
Brumana, Juan Carlos, 249
Brunsbüttel, 10
Budapest, 77n
Buenos Aires, 48–54, 80, 86, 97, 101, 179, 249–51
   Eichmann in, 61–62, 65–84, 101–19, 121–54
   Ezeiza Airport, 101, 140, 142, 145–54, 180
   May Revolution, 126–27

Cairo, 271, 272
Canada, 47
CAPRI, 61, 108
Castro, Fidel, 156n
Catholic Church, 3, 31–32, 140, 249
   Nazism and, 38–39, 39n, 45, 61, 140, 216, 251
CBS News, 88, 201n, 270
Central Intelligence Agency (CIA), 22n, 45, 68, 69n, 137, 196n, 216, 217n, 259, 260, 261n
children
   in concentration camps, 163, 169, 229, 239, 243
   Izieu roundup of, 45–47, 229
   medical experiments on, 16, 42, 43, 95, 163, 211, 243, 253
Chile, 197, 233
Christianity, 93, 187
Churchill, Winston, 259, 274
Clay, Lucius D., 39, 39n
Cohen, Haim, 103, 104, 105
Cold War, 246
Cologne, 93–95, 99, 218, 235
Communism, 45, 140, 199, 214, 217, 217n
concentration camps, 3–5, 7, 20–22, 46, 56–59, 67, 67n, 70, 77n, 95, 104, 104n, 107, 192–95, 231–32, 235, 238–48, 272–73
   conditions, 20–21, 162–76, 194–95, 239–43
   female guards and prisoners, 239–48
   gas chambers, 3–4, 37, 42, 46, 58, 163, 166–77, 189, 243, 273
   liberation of, 5–6, 20–21
   map of, 7
   medical experiments, 16, 42, 43, 95, 163, 211, 243, 253
   record keeping, 21
   survivors' testimony against Eichmann, 160–76
   see also specific camps
Coronel Suárez, 71, 72
Creighton, Christopher, *Op JB*, 259
Cuba, 156n, 217n
cyanide, 8, 14, 15, 29, 85n, 137, 157n, 200
Czechoslovakia, 3

Dachau, 7, 70, 162–63
   medical experiments, 163
   war crimes trials, 39n, 274
Dakar, 148
D-day, 14, 19
Death's Head Units, 3
de Gaulle, Charles, 51n, 220
Denmark, 53, 67, 104
Devil's Island, 219, 219n
Diamant, Manus, 60, 60n
Diem Bien Phu, Battle of, 83n
Die Spinne, 60, 60n, 209, 209n, 213, 272, 272n, 275
disease, 20, 243
Donaldson, Sam, 258n
Doron safe house, 123, 130
Dreyfus, Alfred, 219
Dulles, Allen, 22, 22n, 216
Düsseldorf, 198, 268
Dutch Jews, 194, 231
dwarfs, medical experiments on, 42, 43

East Germany, 113, 199–200, 200n, 234, 246
Eban, Abba, 141
Ebensee, 21
Egypt, 66, 68, 184, 271–72, 278

Eichmann, Adolf, 16, 29–30, 55–57, *57*, 58–84, 97, 179, 184, 191, 216, 250, 270–72, 275, 277, 278
   in Argentina, 61–62, 65–84, 101–19, 121–54
   capture of, 117, *118*, 119, 121–54
   celebrity of, 60, 83
   escape of, 16, 30, 56, 59–63, 65
   Garibaldi Street house of, 113–15, 117, *118*, 119, 123
   hanging of, 185–90
   Holocaust survivors' testimony against, 160–76
   imprisonment in Israel, 155–56, *156*, 158, 185–90
   interrogation of, 136–38, 146, 160
   Klement alias of, 61–62, 103, 108, 112, 115, 137
   Mossad's role in capture of, 75–84, 101–19, 121–54, 270
   physical appearance of, 55–56, 73, 119
   reunion with family, 62
   role in Holocaust, 55–59, 77n, 107–9, 115, 138, 159–76
   search for, 55–84, 101–19, 193
   sentenced to death, 176–77
   transport to Israel, 124–27, 131, 136, 140, 141–54
   trial of, 155–77, 180
Eichmann, Dieter, 73, 111–16, 129, 138–40, 149, 284
Eichmann, Klaus, 149
Eichmann, Nick, 70–75, 80, 82, 113, 129, 138–40, 284
Eichmann, Ricardo, 140, 284
Eichmann, Vera, 59, 61–62, 73, 117, 122, 129, 139, 284
   capture of her husband and, 139–40, 153
   final visit with her husband, 187
   immigration to Argentina, 61–62, 80
Eilat, 124
Einsatzgruppen, 8, 22, 33–40, 267
   files, 33, 35
   trials, 33–34, *34*, 35–39, 39n, 40

Eisenhower, Dwight D., 2, 24
Eitan, Rafi, 123, 130, 132–34, 150, 187–88, 277, 286
El Al, 125, 125n, 126–27
   Britannia aircraft, 125–26, 141–54
   transport of Eichmann to Israel, 125–27, 131, 136, 140–54
Elbe River, 10, 13
Enabling Act of 1933, 69n
Escobar, Pablo, 217
Espejo, José, 49–51
Estonia, 46
Ethiopian Jews, 125n
eye for an eye, 63, 63n

Fascism, 51n, 52, 140, 273
Federal Bureau of Investigation (FBI), 90, 196, 196n
   Bormann case and, 90–91
Feldblum, Léa, 46
Ferencz, Benjamin, 19–22, 31–34, *34*, 35–40, 267, 282
   Einsatzgruppen trial and, 33–40, 40n
   Ohlendorf case and, 32–35, 35n, 36–40
Ferencz, Gertrude, 31, 32, 38
Final Solution, 4–5, 29n, 34–37, 55–59, 106, 163, 270
Fischhorn Castle, 24
Flying Circus, 25, 25n
Forward, 270, 278
Fourth Reich, 8, 108, 108n, 200
France, 1–2, 8–10, 16, 41, 45, 54, 85n, 158n, 255–56
   fall of, 25, 219–20
   Indochina, 83, 83n
   Izieu roundup of Jewish children, 45–47
   Jews, 16, 58, 164–66, 217, 235
   postwar, 216, 217
   Resistance, 219–22
   World War II, 19, 25, 45, 164, 216, 218–22, 256
Franco, Francisco, 51n, 270, 271, 272n

Frank, Anne, 196, 196n, 231
The Diary of Anne Frank, 196n
Frankfurt, 31, 65, 68, 72, 202
French Foreign Legion, 83, 83n
French Guiana, 219n, 229
Freude, Rodolfo, 53
Friedman, Yehudith, 130
Fritzsche, Hans, 27n
Fuldner, Carlos, 138–39

Gagarin, Yuri, 160
gas chambers, 3–4, 37, 42, 46, 58, 163, 166–77, 189, 243, 273
Gebhardt, Karl, 8, 281, 282
Gehlen, Reinhard, 60n, 272n
Gellhorn, Martha, 157, 157n
General Confederation of Labor of the Argentine Republic (CGT), 49–50
Genoa, 43, 48, 60, 62, 75, 216, 258–59
genocide (term), 33, 33n
George VI, king of England, 51n
Gerhard, Wolfgang, 182–83, 207, 227n
  Mengele uses name of, 207, 226–27
German Club, 216, 217
German Reich Party, 104
German shepherds, 213, 215, 240–44, 246, *247*, 253, 265
Germany, 1–2, 65, 79, 198, 215, 231–34, 268
  air force, 24–25, 25n, 28
  anti-Semitic policies, 3–5, 20, 57–59, 69, 69n, 83, 93–99
  army, 13, 71, 159, 215, 218, 219
  attitudes about war criminals, 76
  end of war, 1–2, 5–6, 8–10, 84–88
  Final Solution, 4–5, 29n, 34–37, 55–59, 106, 163, 270
  industry, 8–10, 32–33, 86
  invasion of Soviet Union, 8, 84, 220
  Jews, 3–5, 20, 58, 69, 69n, 93–99, 105–7, 160
  Kristallnacht, 70, 94, 95, 99, 106, 107, 265
  postwar, 5–10, 16, 23–29, 41–42, 60, 69, 69n, 76, 83, 86, 93–99, 113, 196, 199–201, 201n
  postwar Nazism, 8–10, 17, 83, 93–99, 101–4, 190, 200
  racial purity and laws, 3, 69, 69n, 94–95
  refugees, 5–6
  rocket program, 271, 271n, 272, 278
  surrender of, 1–2, 10, 13, 94
  World War I, 25, 25n, 94, 95
  World War II, 1–2, 5, 8, 53n, 57, 84–88, 94, 218–22, 244, 253, 271–74
Gestapo, 33, 70, 85, 88, 161, 216, 220–22, 235, 258
ghettos, 56–57, 57n, 166
Giovanna C, SS, 61
Glawe, Ernesto, 208
Globke, Hans, 69, 69n
gold, 77, 86, 108, 108n, 112, 171, 251
Goldenes Kreuz Inn, 42, 42n
Goldman-Gilad, Michael, 189
Göring, Hermann, 24–26, *26*, 27–29, 161, 252
  arrest of, 24
  suicide of, 28–29
  trial of, 24–29
Great Britain, 1, 12, 22, 41, 51n, 68, 68n, 158n
  army, 12–16
  intelligence, 2, 84
  rule over Palestine, 68n, 186
  World War II, 12–16, 103, 184, 245, 245n, 259, 271
Greece, 55, 93, 197
  Jews, 55
Green, Horacio Enrique, 181–82
Grese, Irma, 243–44, 244n, 245
Grodno, 170, 172
Grothmann, Werner, 8, 11, 14, 281
Grüber, Heinrich, 160–64
Guevara, Che, 217, 217n
Günzburg, 42, 95–99, 99n, 205, 236
Gypsies, 3, 40, 170, 240, 267

Haifa, 124, 158, 190
Hamelin Prison, 245
Hammurabi, 63n
Harel, Isser, 75–77, 97, 99, *122*, 193, 194, 270, 286
   Mengele case, 97, 132, 148–49, 184
   role in Eichmann's capture, 75–84, 103–5, 109, 121–54
   Skorzeny case and, 270–79
   transport of Eichmann to Israel, 141–54
Hausner, Gideon, 168–72, 174–75
Haussmann, Emil, 40n
Havel, Herbert, 197
Havel, Renate, 197
Heath, James, 35–37
Hemingway, Ernest, 157n
Hermann, Lothar, 70–74, 81–82, 102, 103, 109, 158
Hermann, Sylvia, 70–75, 80, 81, 102, 115, 138
Heuberg, 67, 67n, 104n
Heydrich, Reinhard, 253
Hier, Marvin, 238, 261
Himmler, Heinrich, 3–4, *4*, 5, 22, 27, 43, 58, 222, 252, 253, 281
   escape and capture of, 2, 6–10, *11*, 12–16
   plot against Hitler, 12–13
   role in Holocaust, 3–5, 58, 194, 241
   suicide of, 15–16, 28
Hitler, Adolf, 1–5, 8, 16, 25–26, 52, 53n, 60, 84, 93, 98, 104, 125, 140, 142, 194, 196, 199, 202, 214, 217, 252–53, 258, 269, 271–74, 287
   Beer Hall Putsch, 94, 94n
   Himmler's plot against, 12–13
   last will and testament, 86, 86n
   Mein Kampf, 38, 94
   papacy and, 45
   rise of, 3, 25, 69n
   suicide of, 1, 13, 16, 84–85
   underground bunker, 84–87, 200, 201
Hitler Youth, 87, 182, 207, 227n

Hitzinger, Heinrich, 6
Hollman, Fritz. *See* Mengele, Josef
Holocaust, 4–5, 29n, 34–37, 42, 46, 55–59, 63, 79, 93, 106, 113, 155, 193–95, 232, 253, 265, 270, 272
   deniers, 104, 196n
   Eichmann's role in, 55–59, 77n, 107–9, 115, 138, 159–76
   female guards and prisoners, 239–48, 264–67
   Himmler's role in, 3–5, 58, 194
   survivors, 76, 156, 160–76, 193–95, 267
   survivors' testimony in Eichmann trial, 160–76
   see also concentration camps
homosexuals, 3, 67, 104, 104n
Hoover, J. Edgar, 90
Hull, Cordell, 9
Hull, William, 187
Hundeführerin, 240–46
Hungary, 55, 76
   Jews, 55, 58, 76–77, 77n, 82
Huth, Elfriede. *See* Rinkel, Elfriede Huth
Huth, Kurt, 246, 266–67

immigration, 5, 45
   of Jews to Israel, 67, 106, 124, 125, 125n
   of Nazis to Argentina, 52–54, 61–62, 65–84, 101–19
Indochina, 83, 83n
industry, 8–10, 32–33, 86
Interpol, 81
Iraqi Jews, 125
Israel, 63, 63n, 65–70, 75, 79–80, 215, 232, 250, 270, 271, 279
   air travel, 125–26, 126n, 127
   -Arab conflict, 67, 125, 140, 184
   attitudes about Nazi war criminals, 76–77
   birth of, 66
   capture of Eichmann in Argentina, 117, *118*, 119, 121–54
   cargo shipping, 124–25

Eichmann case and, 75–84, 101–19, 121–54, 193
Eichmann transported to, 124–27, 121, 136, 140–54
Eichmann trial, 155–77, 180
hanging of Eichmann, 185–90
Jewish immigration to, 67, 106, 124, 125, 125n
Knesset, 75
law, 186
Mengele case and, 97–99, 132, 148–49, 179–84, 196, 197, 205–12, 227, 234
Mossad. *See* Mossad
Skorzeny as agent for, 270–79
Israel Defense Forces, 79
Italy, 31–32, 45, 48, 60, 216, 258, 258n, 273, 273n, 274
Mafia, 33
postwar, 41–43, 47, 48, 48n
refugees, 48
Izieu roundup of Jewish children, 45–47, 229

Jackson, Robert H., 4, 23–24, 90–91
Jerusalem, 102–4, 155, 185
Eichmann trial, 155–77, 180
Jewish Brigade, 68n
Jewish Documentation Center, 208, 232, 236
Jews, 3, 20, 25, 265
culture, 106
death rates, 5
deportation and transport, 4, 16, 36, 55, 58, 107, 163, 165–74, 229, 235
displaced persons, 6, 6n
Eichmann and, 55–59, 77n, 107–9, 115, 138, 159–76
executed by Einsatzgruppe D, 35–37
extermination of, 3–5, 29n, 34–37, 42, 46, 55–59, 93, 106, 133, 160–76, 189, 192–95, 195n, 238–48, 253, 270–73
ghettos, 56–57, 57n, 60n, 166
immigration to Israel, 67, 106, 124, 125, 125n
Izieu roundup, 45–47, 229
medical experiments on, 16, 42, 43, 95, 163, 211, 243, 253
Nazi persecution of, 3–5, 20, 34–37, 55–59, 93–95, 160–76, 192
postwar anti-Semitism, 8–10, 17, 83, 93–99, 101–4, 190, 200, 213–15, 260
sayanim, 111, 116, 119
synagogue vandalism, 93–94, 99
testimony in Eichmann trial, 160–76
wealthy, 76–77, 77n, 82, 94, 171
Jodl, Alfred, 1, 2

Kaltenbrunner, Ernst, 29, 29n
Kamaradenwerk, 213–15
Karen, Zeev, 130, 132, 134
Kastner, Rudolf, 76–77, 77n
Kastner train, 77, 77n, 82
Kelly, Petra, 99n, 284
Kennedy, Robert F., 198
KGB, 88
Kiermaier, Josef, 8, 12, 13, 281
Kiesinger, Kurt Georg, 234
Kiev, 35
Kirya, 79
Klarsfeld, Beate and Serge, 217–18, *218*, 222–23, 228, 234–36
Kohl, Helmut, 232, 233
Kolmeshöhe Cemetery, 231–32
Kreisky, Bruno, 208–9
Kristallnacht, 70, 94, 95, 99, 106, 107, 265
Krug, Heinz, 272, 277
Krumnow, Albert, 202
Krupp, 9
Krupp, Gustav, 27n
Kuwait, 79, 83

Lago Nahuel Huapi, 84
Landau, Moshe, 159, 160, 161–63, 165, 166–68, 173–74 176–77
Landsberg Prison, 38, 94
La Paz, 215–23
last meals of death row inmates, 186, 186n

le Carré, John, 69n
Leipzig, 241, 244
Lemkin, Raphael, 33, 33n
lesbians, 240
Less, Avner, 160
Levine, Lowell J., 238
Lindwasser, Avraham, 173–76
Linz, 16, 59, 195, 196n
Lischka, Kurt, 235
London, 99, 166, 184, 220
Los Angeles Times, 261
Luftwaffe, 24–25, 26, 28
Lüneberg, 14–16, 22
Lyon, 16, 45, 46, 216, 217, 221, 253, 255

Macher, Heinz, 8, 11, 14, 281
Madrid, 271, 272, 275, 278
Majdanek, 163
Malkin, Peter Zvi, 130–34, 134n, 270, 278
Manning, Gerry, 89, 89n
Manning, Paul, 88–89, 89n, 201, 201n
 Martin Bormann: Nazi in Exile, 88, 89n
Mauthausen, 194–95, 253
McCloy, John, 39n
medical experiments, 16, 42, 43, 95, 163, 211, 243, 253
 Mengele and, 16, 42, 43, 95, 211, 253
Mediterranean Sea, 41, 48, 124, 190
Melman, Yossi, 270, 278
Menem, Carlos Saúl, 250–52
Mengele, Josef, 16, 84, 95, 96, *96*, 97–99, 113, 145, 158, 179–84, 205–12, 216, 244, 244n, 251
 aliases of, 41–48, 207
 as Angel of Death, 16, 48, 96, 211, 227
 in Argentina, 48, 62, 83, 96–97, 132, 145, 148–49, 158, 179–82, 206
 in Brazil, 182–84, 205–12, 225–27, 233
 death and remains of, 225–27, 237–38, 251, 261
 DNA testing on, 261
 escape of, 16, 41–43, *43*, 47–48, 60, 61

 medical experiments on prisoners, 16, 42, 43, 95, 211, 253
 in Paraguay, 97–99, 113, 184, 206, 209, 233–36
 physical appearance of, 97, 183
 residences in South America, *206*
 search for, 48, 62, 96–99, 132, 145, 148–49, 179–84, 196, 197, 205–12, 227, 232–38, 261
 stroke of, 208, 210, 226
Mengele, Karl, 96–99, 99n
Mengele, Karl-Heinz, 97
Mengele, Martha, 96–97, 197, 207
Mengele, Rolf, 98, 208, 209–12, 285
Mercedes-Benz, 10, 114, 115, 191
MI5, 84
Milan, 32, 184
Montgomery, Bernard Law, 13, 14
Mösenbacher, Maria, 60n
Moses, 63n, 66
Mossad, 67, 67n, 68–69, 69n, 99, 192–94, 214, 250, 270
 Eichmann case, 75–84, 101–19, 121–54, 155–77, 185–90, 193
 Mengele case, 97–99, 132, 148–49, 179–84, 184n, 196, 197, 205–12, 227
 Operation Eichmann. *See* Operation Eichmann
 Skorzeny as agent for, 270–79
Moulin, Jean, 218–22, 222n, 228, 229
Munich, 25, 70, 94n, 272, 275, 277
Murphy, Michael, 15
Murrow, Edward R., 88
Mussolini, Benito, 32, 52, 53n, 273, 273n, 274

Nagar, Shalom, 188–89
NASA, 271n
Naumann, Erich, 39
Nazi hunters, 17, 60
 Zvi Aharoni, 101–19, 121–54, 179–84
 Avengers, 68, 68n
 Fritz Bauer, 65–66, *66*, 67–82, 103–5, 108, 113

Benjamin Ferencz, 19–22, 31–34, *34*, 35–40, 267
Isser Harel, 75–84, 97, 103–5, 109, 121–54, 193, 194, 270
Beate and Serge Klarsfeld, 217–18, *218*, 222–23, 228, 234–36
Mossad, 75–84, 97–99, 101–19, 121–54, 179–84, 192–94, 250, 270
Eli Rosenbaum, 263–68
terminology, 265
Simon Wiesenthal, 193–98, 201–3, 208–10, 227, 232–34, 236, 251–54, 260–61
see also Nazi war criminals; *specific cases*
Nazi Party, 3, 138, 138n
anthems, 214, 269
in Argentina, 51n, 52–54, 60–62, 65–84, 86, 101–19, 121–54, 179–82, 182n, 249–51, 254, 257–58
Beer Hall Putsch, 94, 94n
in Bolivia, 216–23
in Brazil, 182–84, 205–15
Catholic Church and, 38–39, 39n, 45, 140, 251
industrial crimes, 8–10, 32–33, 86
Kristallnacht, 70, 94, 95, 99, 106, 107, 265
loyalty oath, 67, 103, 104n
medical experiments, 16, 42, 43, 95, 163, 211, 243, 253
persecution of Jews, 3–5, 20, 34–37, 55–59, 93–95, 160–76, 192
postwar, 8–10, 17, 83, 93–99, 101–4, 190, 200, 213–15, 260
record keeping, 21, 24, 201n
rise of, 3, 25, 67
rocket program, 271, 271n, 272, 278
salute, 217, 269
stolen wealth, 77, 86, 108, 108n, 112–13, 201*n*, 251, 272
swastika, 83, 93, 98, 181, 182n, 214
women in, 239–48, 263–68
Nazi War Crimes Disclosure Act (1999), 196n

Nazi war criminals, 2, 4, 6, 10, 10n, 16–17, 39n
in Argentina, 51n, 52–54, 60–62, 65–84, 86, 101–19, 121–54, 179–82, 182n, 249–51, 254, 257–58
Avengers and, 68, 68n
Barbie case, 16, 45–47, 215–23, 228, *228*, 229, 255–56
in Bolivia, 216–23
Bormann case, 16, 84–91, 196, 196n, 199–201, 201n, 202–3, 203n, 251–54, 257–61
in Brazil, 182–84, 205–15
Eichmann case, 16, 30, 55–84, 101–19, 121–54, 155–77, 180, 185–90, 193
Einsatzgruppen trial, 33–40, 40n
female SS guards, 239–48, 263–68
Himmler's escape and capture, 6–10, *11*, 12–16
Mengele case, 16, 41–48, 60, 61, 96–99, 132, 145, 148–49, 179–84, 196, 197, 205–12, 227, 232–38, 261
as Mossad agents, 270–79
Nuremberg Trials, 4, 21, 23–29, 33–40, 42, 53, 55, 69n, 76, 90, 158, 195, 217n, 253
Ohlendorf case, 32–40
Operation Eichmann. *See* Operation Eichmann
Priebke case, 258, 258n, 259
ratlines to South America, 43, *44*, 45, 60–61, 216
Skorzeny case, 269–79
Stangl case, 191–93, 197–98
New York City, 19, 99, 198, 269, 278
New York Times, 201n, 233, 254, 261
Nir, Arye, 185, 186, 189
Nokmim, 68
North King, 47–48
Nuremberg Trials, 4, 21, 23–29, 31, 32, 33–40, 42, 53, 55, 69n, 76, 90, 158, 195, 217n, 253
Einsatzgruppen trial, 33–40, 40n
Göring and, 24–29

Nuremberg Trials (*cont'd*)
   photographs, 24
   verdicts and hangings, 27, 27n, 28–29, 37–38, 38n, 39, 39n, 40

Oberdachstetten, 56
ODESSA, 10n, 60n, 203, 209, 213, 235, 272n
Office of Special Investigations (OSI), 263, 264
Office of Strategic Services (OSS), 22
Ohlendorf, Otto, 8, 12, 13, 22, 32–40, 45, 282
   hanging of, 38–39, 39n, 40
   trial of, 35–38
Operation Damocles, 271–72
Operation Eichmann, 121–54
   forged passports and documents, 143–44, 151–53
   as illegal operation, 119, 121, 131, 149–54, 157–58, 158n
   interrogation of Eichmann, 136–38, 146
   kidnapping of Eichmann, 117, *118*, 119, 123, 129–44
   Plan Number One, 146
   search for Eichmann, 101–19
   snatch team, 132–34
   Tira safe house, 123, 129–32, 135–47
   transport to Israel, 124–27, 131, 136, 140, 141–54
Operation Ezra and Nehemiah, 125
Operation Long Jump, 274
Operation Magic Carper, 125
Operation Paperclip, 91
Operation Solomon, 125n
Operation Tierra Del Fuego, 86

Palestine, 68n, 75, 106, 107
   British rule, 68n, 186
   Jewish immigration to, 67, 106, 106n, 124, 125, 125n
Panzerfaust, 87

Paraguay, 97, 196, 209, 209n
   Mengele in, 97–99, 113, 184, 206, 209, 233–36
Paris, 31, 107, 144, 164, 184, 218, 222, 222n, 235
Patton, George S., 19, 108n
Perl, Gisella, 244
Perón, Eva, 49–50, *50*, 51, 51n, 52–53, 53n, 54, 272, 275, 282–83
   death of, 54, 62
Perón, Juan, 49–50, *50*, 51, 51n, 52–53, 53n, 54, 150, 275, 282–83
   as Nazi sympathizer, 52–54, 60
Peru, 197
Pierrepoint, Albert, 245, 245n
Piotrków Trybunalski, 57
Pius XII, Pope, 31–32, 38, 45, 51n, 140
Poland, 5, 16, 107, 158n, 166, 173, 215, 272
   ghettos, 57, 60n, 166
   Jews, 57, 60n, 166–73
Portugal, 10
Posadas, 84
POW camps, 56, 56n, 60n, 65, 220, 253
press, 1–2, 261
   anti-Nazi, 72
   Austrian, 108
   on Eichmann, 60, 60n, 79, 108, 113, 146, 157, 164, 188
   Israeli, 79, 83
   Jewish American, 270, 278
   Nazi, 62
   Paraguayan, 236
   see also specific publications
Priebke, Erich, 258, 258n, 259

Raanan, Joe, 278
race defilers, 240
Ramleh Prison, Israel, 185–90
Rasch, Otto, 34–35, 40n
Rath, Ernst vom, 107
ratlines, 43, 60–61, 216
   to South America, 43, *44*, 45, 60–61, 216
Ravensbrück, 7, 239–48, 253, 264–67
   female guards, 239–48

Raven's Women, 238–48
Raviv, Dan, 270, 278, 279
Reagan, Nancy, 231
Reagan, Ronald, 231–32
Recife, 141, 148
Red Cross, 43, 47n, 60, 168, 216, 251, 274
   identity papers, 43, 43n, 48
Red House Report, 9
Red Sea, 124
refugees, 5–6, 6n, 43, 43n, 48
Reich Citizenship Law, 69n
Reims, 1–2
Rhine River, 94
Richthofen, Manfred von, 25n
Rinkel, Elfriede Huth, 239–47, *247*, 248, 263–68, 286
   deportation of, 263–68
   as Ravensbrück guard, 239–48, 264–67
   in United States, 246–48, 263–67
Rinkel, Fred, 239, 247–48, 263–66
Rodan, Bobby, 101
Rodriguez, Felix, 217n
Romania, 20
Rome, 31–32, 45, 93, 141, 184, 258, 274
Rommel, Erwin, 85n
Roonstrasse Synagogue, 93–95, 99
Roosevelt, Franklin D., 89, 274
Rosenbaum, Eli, 263–64, *264*, 265–68, 287
Royal Air Force, 152
Royal Army Medical Corps, 15

SA (Sturmabteilung), 25
Sachsenhausen, 162, 163, 201
Salto, SS, 62
Samuels, Shimon, 251, 254, 258n
San Francisco, 239, 246, 263, 266–67
São Paulo, 182–84, 191–93, 205–12, 226
sayanim, 111, 116, 119
Schacht, Hjalmar, 27n
Schellenberg, Walter, 253
Schmidt, Francisco, 81, 82
Schule, Erwin, 79

Schumacher, Kurt, 104n
Scottish Black Watch, 13–14
SD (Sicherheitsdienst), 33
Secret Field Police, 10
Sedlmeier, Hans, 43, 205, 207, 227, 236–37
Selvester, Tom, 13–15
Senegal, 148
Servatius, Robert, 159–60
Shamir, Yitzhak, 277–78
Shaul, Shaul, 141, 153, 285
Shin Bet, 101, 179
Shinnar, Felix, 65, 68–70, 75
Silberbauer, Karl, 196, 196n
Sillitoe, Percy, 84
Sirota, Graciela Narcisa, 181–82, 182n
Skorzeny, Ilse, 270, 275
Skorzeny, Otto, 60, 60n, 269–79
   death of, 269, 269n, 270, 278
   as Mossad agent, 270–79
   Mussolini rescued by, 273–74
Slovakian Jews, 55
Smith, Bedell, 2
Sobel, Henry, 213–14
Sobibór, 192, 214
Social Security benefits for Nazi war criminals, 264, 264n, 268, 268n
Soggnaes, Reidar, 203n
Soleti, Fernando, 273
South Africa, 10, 99
South America, 10, 60n, 68, 86, 88, 96, 97, 101, 108, 112, 121, 141, 179, 183, 191, 216, 257, 275
   ratlines to, 43, *44*, 45, 60–61, 216
   see also specific countries
Soviet Union, 1, 6, 12, 35, 41, 45, 67, 91, 113, 158n, 182n
   army, 6, 16, 199
   Communism, 45
   German invasion of, 8, 84, 220
   ghettos, 57
   Jews, 8, 57
   occupation of Berlin, 84–88, 199, 244
   postwar, 6, 22, 88, 246

Soviet Union (cont'd)
  POWs, 5, 8, 13, 220
  space program, 160, 271n
  spies, 67, 274
  U-2 spy plane incident, 156n
  World War II, 8, 12, 13, 57, 84–88, 220, 272, 274
space travel, 160, 271, 271n, 272, 278
Spain, 10, 43, 126, 270, 271
  Fascist, 51n, 60n
Speer, Albert, 26
SS (Schutzstaffel), 2–5, 29, 83, 83n, 85, 94, 95, 140, 169, 194, 196, 201, 232, 267
  Barbie, 16, 45–47, 215–23, 228, *228*, 229, 255–56
  blood type tattoo, 43, 68, 137
  Bormann, 16, 84–91, 196, 196n, 199–201, 201n, 202–3, 203n, 251–54, 257–61
  Death's Head Units, 3
  Eichmann, 16, 30, 55–84, 101–19, 121–54, 155–77, 180, 185–90, 193
  Einsatzgruppen, 8, 22, 33–40, 267
  Himmler, 2–4, *4*, 5, 6–10, *11*, 12–16
  Mengele, 16, 41–43, *43*, 47–48, 60, 61, 96, *96*, 97–99, 132, 145, 148–49, 179–84, 196, 197, 205–12, 227, 232–38, 261
  motto, 55
  oath, 59–60
  Ohlendorf, 32–40
  ratlines to South America, 43, *44*, 45, 60–61, 216
  Skorzeny, 269–79
  skull insignia, 3
  Stangl, 191–93, 197–98
  Waffen, 3, 87, 88, 272
  women in, 239–48, 263–68
Stalin, Joseph, 274
Stammer, Geza, 207, 237
Stammer, Gitta, 207, 237
Stangl, Franz, 191–93, 214
  capture of, 191–93, 197–98
Stangl, Isolde, 191, 192
Stangl, Theresa, 191, 192, 193

Star of David, 146, 235, 265, 266
Stasi, 234
Stivers, Herbert Lee, 29
Strasbourg meeting (1944), 8–10
Strickner, Jakob, 41
Stroessner, Alfredo, 209, 233
Stumpfegger, Ludwig, 87, 201, 202
Subsequent Nuremberg Trials, 33–34, *34*, 35–40
Sudanese troops, 219–20
Suhren, Fritz, 241
swastika, 83, 93, 98, 181, 182n, 214
Sweden, 53, 67
Switzerland, 10, 22, 43, 553, 60, 76, 77, 77n, 98, 184

Tacuara, 140, 149, 181, 182n
Tallinn death camp, 46
Talmor, Emanuel, 80–81
tattoos, 43
  Auschwitz, 189
  SS blood type, 43, 68, 137
Taylor, Telford, 31, 33
Tehran Conference, 274
Teigman, Kalman, 166–73, 192
Teixeira, Roberto, 238
Tel Aviv, 76, 79–80, 104, 106, 117, 119, 126, 136, 141, 250, 276
Third Reich, 3, 16, 93, 125, 221, 250, 252, 261, 269, 274
Thomas, W. H., 203n
Time magazine, 51, 208, 209
Tira safe house, 123, 129–32, 135–47
Tohar, Zvi, 152, *152*, 153, 285
Torah, 63, 63n, 176
Transylvania, 20
Treblinka, 166–76, 192, 197
  survivors' testimony about, 166–76
Truman, Harry S., 23–24, 89–91
  policy on Nazi war criminals, 90–91, 196
Tucumán, 61
twins, medical experiments on, 42, 43, 211

United States Security Council, 157–58, 158n
United States, 1, 2, 9, 22, 23, 32, 41, 47, 90–91, 158n, 216, 231–32
  anti-Semitism in, 94
  Barbie aided by, 45, 47, 216
  Jews, 20, 40, 94, 247–48, 267
  policy on Nazi war criminals, 90–91, 196, 231–33, 263–68
  POW camps, 56, 56n, 60n, 65
  space program, 271n
  spies against Soviet Union, 22
  World War II, 19, 56, 89
U.S. Army, 19, 28, 108, 274, 275
  Counterintelligence Corps, 45
  Seventh Army, 24
  Third Army, 19, 108n
  War Crimes Unit, 19–22, 56
U.S. Freedom of Information Act, 233
U.S. Supreme Court, 90
Uruguay, 196, 258

Vatican, 31–32
  Nazism and, 38–39, 39n, 45, 61, 140, 216, 251
Venetian Jews, 57n
Victor Emmanuel III, king of Italy, 273n
Vienna, 99, 107, 142, 195, 197, 208, 236, 254, 274
von Braun, Wernher, 271n

Waffen SS, 3, 87, 88, 272
Wagner, Gustav Franz, 214–15
Wannsee, 58
Warsaw, 170, 173, 174
  ghetto, 57, 60n, 166

Washington, D.C., 90, 91
Weg, Der, 62
Wehrmacht, 3, 71, 159, 215, 218, 219
Wellers, Georges, 164–66
Wells, C. J., 15, 16
Whitaker, Norman, 15
Wiesenthal, Cyla, 195, 195n
Wiesenthal, Simon, 99n, 193–98, 200, 279, 275, 276, 276n, 286–87
  Bormann case and, 196, 197, 201–3, 209, 251–54, 260–61, 261n
  in concentration camp, 194–95, 253–54
  death of, 261
  I Chased Eichmann: A True Story, 193
  Mengele case and, 196, 197, 205, 208–10, 212, 227, 232–38, 261
  as Nazi hunter, 193–98, 201–3, 208–10, 227, 232–36, 251–54, 260–61
Wiesenthal Center, Los Angeles, 251, 254, 258n, 259, 261
Wisliceny, Dieter, 55–56
Wolff, Karl, 22, 22n
women, SS, 239–48, 263–68
Woods, John C., 27, 28
World War I, 25, 25n, 94, 95, 105
World War II, 1–3, 19, 38, 53n, 79, 84–89, 218–22, 269, 272
  D-day, 14, 19
  end of, 1–2, 8–10, 132

Yemenite Jews, 125, 188

Zlatin, Miron, 46
Zlatin, Sabina, 45–46
Zurich, 22, 187

About the Authors

Bill O'Reilly is a trailblazing TV journalist who has experienced unprecedented success on cable news and in writing nineteen national number-one bestselling nonfiction books. There are more than nineteen million books in the Killing series in print. He lives on Long Island.

Martin Dugard is the *New York Times* bestselling author of several books of history, among them the Killing series, *Into Africa*, *Taking Paris*, *Taking Berlin*, and *Taking London*. He and his wife live in Southern California.

READ ALL OF BILL O'REILLY'S KILLING SERIES!

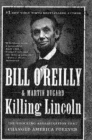
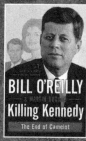

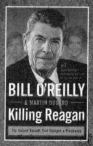
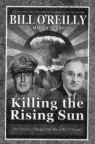
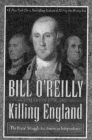

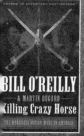

THE KILLING SERIES
ON AUDIO

Read by **Bill O'Reilly**
and Audie Award–winning narrator **Robert Petkoff**

"[O'Reilly's] deep, powerful voice, timing, emphasis, and tone create tangible tension throughout.... [His] narration proves a great boon to this historical account, which will thoroughly engage listeners."
—**PUBLISHERS WEEKLY** ON *KILLING KENNEDY*

Visit MacmillanAudio.com for audio samples and more!
Follow us on Facebook, Instagram, TikTok, and X.

macmillan audio